A BURNS HANDBOOK

A BURNS HANDBOOK

By

JOHN D. ROSS, LL.D., F.S.A. (Scot.)

ENEAS MACKAY
STIRLING

First published 1931

Printed in Scotland
at the Observer Press, Stirling

INSCRIBED

To Mr. J. TAYLOR GIBB, F.S.A. (Scot.),

a native and life-long resident of
Mauchline; author of " Mauchline
Town and District," etc.; a distinguished Burns Scholar, Critic
and Lecturer, and for many years
a Vice-President of the Burns
Federation.

PREFATORY

For many years past it has been my privilege to respond to numerous inquiries regarding certain features in the life and writings of our National Poet, and from suggestions made by many of my more recent inquiring friends for " A Book of General Information on Matters associated with Robert Burns," I undertook the congenial task of compiling the present work.

Many of my correspondents were endowed with a wonderful spirit of hero-worship, others were profuse in assurances that the Universal Brotherhood of Man was gradually but surely coming to the front in many of the busy centres of the world; while still others, after paying tribute to the genius of the Poet, added a few words of respect to the memory of Bonnie Jean.

Other Burns letter, (so I termed them), but of a somewhat different character, reached me from time to time, and on several occasions I have been requested to name the best short biography, poem and essay available for general reading on the subject of Burns. As a rule I had only one reply for communications of this kind : " From the many standard biographical sketches of the Poet now to be had, it is impossible to single out, or to recommend, any one in particular as being superior to the others. They are all good for reading or for study, besides being valuable on account of the different viewpoints from which they are

written. The best short poem on the subject is
the one entitled ' To a Rose,' brought from near
Alloway Kirk, in Ayrshire, in the Autumn of
1822, by Fitz-Green Halleck, and the best short
essay is universally conceded to be the work of
Thomas Carlyle.

The present work, however, is in no sense one
of criticism—though many crisp pieces of criticism
are embodied in its pages—rather it is essentially
a guide, or a help to a knowledge of the origin of
the more popular poems and songs of the Poet,
as well as to incidents and events past and present,
directly or indirectly connected with his life, his
name and fame.   There are also included
numerous bibliographical and other literary
references, all useful and interesting in themselves,
and in some instances not readily obtainable
elsewhere. And while the work, along with its
companion volume " Who's Who In Burns," must
prove invaluable to the writer or to the speaker
on the subject of Robert Burns, it is specially
adapted for furnishing information to such readers
as may desire a fuller knowledge concerning many
matters appertaining to the Poet, than they can
obtain from a casual or random consultation of
his life and writings.

It would have afforded me considerable satisfaction had the scope of the work permitted my
including in it several of my favourite excerpts
—especially a few drawn from foreign sources—
on the Poet. Unable to accomplish this, I am
tempted to solace myself by inserting here the
following from the noted French scholar, Auguste

Augellier : "Weigh his defects, his faults, as heavily as you like, the scale where the pure gold is, easily turns the balance. Admiration increases as we examine his qualities. When one thinks of his sincerity, his uprightness, his kindness towards people and animals, his contempt for anything base, his hatred of any trickery—which in itself would be an honour—his disinterestedness, the many beautiful impulses that form his heart, the high inspirations of his mind, the intensity, the idealism which was necessary to him to keep his soul above his fate ; when one thinks that he felt all these generous feelings so intensely that they formed part of his intellectual life, that they came from him as jewels, so keenly did he feel them, so like was his soul to a furnace where precious metals were molten, that it might be said he was one of Nature's noblemen, and of great goodness. When it is remembered how much he suffered, how much he overcame, and how much he accomplished, with what misery his genius had to fight to be born and to live, the perseverance of his years of apprenticeship, his intellectual exploits, and, after all, his glory; one says to oneself that what he did not succeed in, or what he did not undertake, was as nothing compared to what he achieved, and that he was a man who accomplished much. And what remains to be said except that the clay of which he was made was full of diamonds, and that his life was one of the most valiant and the proudest that any poet ever lived." To this I would add the testimony of the distinguished American orator, Robert G. Ingersoll :

" The name of Robert Burns can never die. He is enrolled among the immortals and will live for ever. This man left a legacy of riches untold, not only to Scotland, but to the whole world. He enriched our language, and among succeeding generations he has scattered the gems of thought. His heart blossomed in a thousand songs, songs of all times, all seasons, suited to every experience of the heart and to ever phase of thought, songs for the dawn of life, songs of the cradle, songs for growing boys and girlhood, songs for the hours of courtship, and for the sweet and sacred relationship of man and wife ; songs for the cheerless and friendless, songs of joy for the joyless, songs for the vanished days ; and songs that were filled with light and hope for days to come ; songs for the sunshine and for the storm ; songs that set the pulse throbbing and stir the heart of man."

The information contained in the work has been gleaned from authoritative sources, and due credit has been accorded wherever possible.

J. D. R.

A BURNS HANDBOOK

A

ABERDEEN.

"Bon-Accord," stands at the mouth of the river Dee and ranks as a Royal and Parliamentary Burgh. It was created a royal burgh by William the Lion in 1179. Burns in the Journal of his Highland Tour (1787) makes the following reference to the city : "Come to Aberdeen—meet with Mr. Chalmers, printer, a facetious fellow—Mr. Ross, a fine fellow, like Professor Tytler—Mr. Marshall, one of the *poetae minores*—Mr Sheriffs, author of ' Jamie and Bess,' a little, decrepid body with some abilities—Bishop Skinner, a Non-juror, son of the author of 'Tullochgorum,' a man whose mild, venerable manner is the most marked of any in so young a man—Professor Gordon, a good-natured, jolly-looking professor."

ABERDEEN BURNS CLUB.

The Aberdeen Burns Club has been in existence since 1871, although it is credited on the Federation Roll (No. 40—1889) with being organized in 1887. It has a membership of one hundred and fifty. Twelve or more meetings for addresses, etc., are held each year. This includes the "25th" which, needless to say, is celebrated with all the honours. In 1928 the Burns Federation held its Annual Conference in the city.

ABERDEEN ALMANAC, REFERENCE TO.

" For my own affairs, I am in a fair way of becoming as eminent as Thomas à Kempis or John Bunyan ; and you may expect henceforth to see my birth-day inserted among the wonderful events, in the Poor Robin's and Aberdeen Almanacks, along with the Black Monday, and the battle of Bothwell Bridge." Letter to Gavin Hamilton, 7th December, 1786.

ABERDEEN STATUE.

Unveiled by Professor Masson of Edinburgh, 15th September, 1892. Mr. Henry Bain Smith of Aberdeen, was the sculptor. The statue is of bronze, nearly ten feet high, and the pedestal on which it stands is Kemnay granite. The cost was defrayed by public subscription. On the pedestal is the word " Burns." At the unveiling, the statue was draped with the Union Jack, attached by cords to a flagstaff behind, to aid the operation of unveiling. To the end of the unveiling cord was affixed a tassel of chaste design. The tassel, which was of solid silver, was— almost fitting emblem for such a ceremony— in the shape of a Scottish thistle. On one side was engraved the Bon-Accord Arms, while the other bore the following inscription :—" To Professor Masson of Edinburgh, as a souvenir of his unveiling The Burns Statue at Aberdeen, on 15th September, 1892."

"It is a statue of which the city will always be proud," said Lord Provost Stewart at the ceremony of unveiling, "and if we have been proud of ' Robbie ' in the past, we will be still prouder that we have set up a monument like that to his memory."

ABERFELDY. See under Falls of Moness.

ADAMHILL.

A farm in the parish of Craigie, near Lochlea, occupied at one time by John Rankine, the poet's friend—

> "O rough, rude, ready-witted Rankine
> The wale o' cocks for fun an' drinking ! "

Rankine's daughter, Anna, claimed the honour of being the one who saw the poet through the barley on a Lammas night when corn rigs were bonnie.

ADDRESS TO THE DEIL.

Gilbert Burns says :—" It was, I think, in the winter of 1784, as we were going with carts for coals to the family fire, (and I could yet point out the particular spot), that Robert first repeated to me the ' Address to the Deil.' The curious idea of such an address was suggested to him by running over in his mind the many ludicrous accounts and representations we have from various quarters of this august personage."

The most cursory study of Burns's

"Address," and the numerous allusions to the Evil One scattered throughout the poetical and prose works of Burns, is sufficient to demonstrate that the popular conception of his fantastic majesty must have been an unfailing source of amusement to the poet in his jovial moods, and a most fascinating subject on which to exercise his mind in his creative moments. We say the popular conception, because Burns's Deil is essentially the vulgar black Deil of Scottish superstition, modified to meet the exigencies of eighteenth-century Scots Calvinism ; and although the poem is not, perhaps, of the highest value as a work of art, charged with genuine poetry, as a rhymed exposition of the satanical elements of Scottish ecclesiasticism it has no equal, and the closing verse is sufficient in itself to have secured immortality to any production.—Peter Ross.

ADELAIDE, SOUTH AUSTRALIA, STATUE.

The Adelaide statue, of which W. J. Maxwell was the sculptor, owes its existence to a brilliant oration delivered in the town-hall on January 25th, 1893, by the Hon. J. H. Gordon, M.L.C., in the course of which he mentioned that he had lately seen the statue of the poet erected in the city of Ballarat, and thought Adelaide ought to have a similar memorial. The statue was unveiled on Saturday, 5th May, 1894, by the Hon. John Darling,

M.L.C., who delivered an impressive speech. The chair was occupied by His Excellency the Lieutenant-Governor, the Hon. S. J. Way, and there was a large and enthusiastic gathering of the various Scottish Societies and of the general public.

The statue is of Angaston marble, is full life-size and stands on a pedestal of Monaro granite. On the die is the inscription " Robert Burns 1759-1796 " and on the base —" Presented to the City of Adelaide by the Caledonain Society, and unveiled by the Chief, Hon. John Darling, M.L.C., 5th May, 1894."

AFTON MSS.

This consisted of a parcel of manuscripts presented by Burns to Mrs. Alexander Stewart, who resided at the time at Stair. She afterwards built a home on the Enterkin estate and called it " Afton Lodge."

The Manuscripts comprised the following twelve pieces:—" A Mother's Lament for the loss of her only son," " Verses written in the Hermitage at Friar's Carse," " Election Ballad addressed to Robert Graham of Fintry," " The Five Carlins," " On seeing a wounded hare limp by me," " Elegy and Epitaph on Captain Matthew Henderson," " Tam o' Shanter," " Lament of Mary Queen of Scots," " Craigieburn Wood," " Sweet Afton," " Poem on Sensibility," and " A

Fragment" which was meant for the beginning of an "Elegy on the late Miss Burnet of Monboddo."

These manuscripts, contained in a small volume of sixty-eight pages, enclosed in a morocco case, are now in the Cottage Museum at Alloway. They were gifted to the Cottage, 22nd September, 1880, by William Allison Cunninghame, grandson of Mrs. Stewart.

AFTON WATER SONG.

The identity of the heroine of this song has yet to be discovered. Gilbert Burns said she was the poet's Highland Mary, but later editors connected her with Mrs. Stewart of Stair. Burns himself gives us no clue, simply saying " the song was written as a compliment to the small river Afton that flows into the Nith, near New Cumnock, which has some charming wild romantic scenery on its banks."

AILSA CRAIG.

A rocky island, conical in shape, near the mouth of the Firth of Clyde, and ten miles W. by N. of Girvan. Its circumference is about two miles and its height eleven hundred and twenty-nine feet. On the N.W. side the perpendicular cliffs are from two hundred to three hundred feet high. A lighthouse was erected in 1883. Only a few persons inhabit the island. Burns makes mention of Ailsa Craig in " Duncan Gray cam' here to woo."

AIRS, attached to Burns's Songs, The. **See under Dick, James C.**

ALBANY, N.Y., STATUE.

Unveiled 30th August, 1888. Cost about thirty thousand dollars. The sculptor was Mr. Charles Calvery and the donor was Miss Mary M'Pherson, a native of Scotland. The Address at the unveiling was delivered by Rev. Dr. Collyer. The four panels on the pedestal have representations of " The Cottar's Saturday Night," " Auld Lang Syne," " Tam o' Shanter," and the poet with a daisy in his hand. To Mr. Peter Kinnear credit was due for carrying out successfully all details in connection with the erection of the statue. In 1889 Mr. Kinnear issued A Historical Sketch of the Burns Statue, the M'Pherson Legacy to the City of Albany, erected in Washington Park, September 20, 1888, Albany, U.S.A.

In an article published in *The Knickerbocker Press*, Albany, on the fortieth anniversary of the unveiling, Mr. David M. Kinnear says : " The history of this monument makes a very interesting story. The money for it was given by an old Scottish lady, a resident of Albany, named Mary M'Pherson, who provided for it in her will. The correct title of it is " The M'Pherson legacy to the City of Albany " and it is the property of the city. The man who carried it forward from the

B

start to finish was Peter Kinnear, my father,
who was executor of the Mary M'Pherson
estate. . . . . Many people have pronounced
it the finest Burns monument, not only in the
United States, but in the world. At the present
time, in various cities and towns in Europe,
America and Australia, there are about 140
Burns monuments and not one of them is any
more beautiful, more artistic and more true
to life than the one in Albany."

ALLAN, THE.

A small stream in the shires of Perth and
Stirling. It enters the Forth, after running
a course of about twenty miles, at the Bridge
of Allan, near Stirling. One of the poet's best
songs is entitled " By Allan Stream."

ALLAN PORTRAIT OF BURNS, THE.   See under Portraits of Burns.

ALLOWAY KIRK AND KIRKYARD.

Historians tell us that the old church is
supposed to have been erected about the year
1516, and its appearance to-day will certainly
not lead to doubts as to its age. It had thus
been in use for two hundred and forty years,
when its gates were finally closed in 1756.
Even in Burns's time it was all but a roofless ruin, and since then nearly every bit of
wood about it has been carried off, no doubt
to be turned into " relics " and sent to the

remotest corners of the earth. The old bell in the tiny belfry adds not a little to the romantic look of the ruin; and it has its history too. When the parishes of Alloway and Ayr were joined, an attempt was made by the Ayr authorities to carry off the bell, but the Alloway crofters manfully rose and successfully resisted the removal of the interesting relic. If there were as many open windows in the old ruins a hundred years ago as there are now there would assuredly be ample opportunity for Tam o' Shanter getting a good view of the uncanny dancing party on that memorable night. Alloway Kirkyard is a lowly resting place, one of the lowliest in Scotland, but the grave of the sainted father is kept green. Around it crumble many grand monuments, and the ashes of some " landed gentry " are carefully conserved in a mixture of memorial stones, nettles, rank weeds and noxious grasses. But no weed ever grows on the grave of this honest, typical Scots farmer, and the path around it, worn by the feet of pilgrims from many lands, is a higher, sweeter, more enduring tribute to his virtues, than though the spot had been covered by a memorial that rivalled in beauty Agra's famous Taj Mahal.

ALLOWAY MONUMENT.

This great and imposing cenotaph is situated on the banks of the river Doon, in the immediate neighbourhood of the " Auld Clay Biggin," the " Auld Brig o' Doon," and " Alloway's Auld Haunted Kirk." The designer of the Memorial was Thomas Hamilton, a noted Edinburgh architect. The foundation stone was laid on the 25th January, 1820, by Mr. (afterwards Sir) Alexander Boswell with full Masonic honours and the building was completed and opened to the public on the 4th July, 1823. The cost up to day of opening was three thousand two hundred and forty-seven pounds, made up from funds supplied by subscriptions from Burns lovers in nearly all parts of the world. A well-written " Description of the Monument " appears in the little hand-book entitled " Burns Monument—Short History and Catalogue of Relics," published by the trustees 1925 : " It is an ornate structure," says the History referred to, " in striking contrast to the Gothic plainness of the remains of the 'Auld Kirk,' and the ' Auld Brig.' From foundation to apex it is suggestive of building as designed by the ancients. Generally speaking it consists of a three-sided basement storey supporting a Greek peristyle. The structure, as a whole, may be described as classical, and as regards the upper portion, pure Grecian. It is, however, impossible to doubt that for the substructure the architect took as his model the type of building characteristic of the Egyptians ; for the walls sloping

inward from the perpendicular, the high
straight doorway opening and other openings,
and the triangular plan, are very suggestive
of the architecture of that highly civilised
people. It is true that primarily the three-
sided arrangement of the base had nothing to
do with any order of architecture. That
peculiarity was determined by the desire to
make the under structure correspond to the
three divisions of the County of Ayr—Cunningham, Kyle, Carrick; but it is probable that the
pyramidal form suggested to the architect
that the Egyptian style would be appropriate
to the substructure, and he accordingly
adopted that style to build on the triangular
foundation. . . . The substructure to a height
of about 15 feet is built of rough-hewn coarse-
grained Ayrshire sandstone of a warm tint,
and at each of the three angles there is a blunt
projecting corner. . . . The whole of the basal
part is very massive masonry, which
appears likely to last for ages. The stone-
work of the superstructure is of a different and
finer quality, and was, no doubt, chosen as
lending itself to fine sculpture. It is a grey-
hued stone of a texture combining the ingred-
ients of fine sandstone and Caithness flag. . . . .
Several of the stone courses of the superstructure are coincident with the triangular base.
Above these courses, and directly over the
doorway and its two corresponding apertures,
and resting on large blocks of stone with

scroll ornaments in straight lines, are projecting ascending ornaments, which have in the centre representations of the daisy, the

' Wee modest crimson tipped flower,'

of the Poet's inimitable lyric, and its modesty is typified by its inconspicuousness in the centre of the surrounding sculpture. Each of the three representations is an exact reproduction of the other two. The architect adopted the Grecian monument as his model, but he deviated from it to the extent of increasing the number of columns, and of modelling their design on those in the temple of Jupiter Stator in Rome. The tripod is of copper, and it was gilt when first put up, but the gilt had disappeared, and it is now of the neutral colour of the temple. . . . The total height of the monument is stated to be about 70 feet. The sides of the triangular building at the ground level, including the projecting corners, which act as buttresses, are each about 38 feet long. The whole is a beautiful example of the classical form of monument that was almost universal at the time it was put up. It is surrounded by a hexagonal iron railing about 17 feet from the walls. The railing is supported at the six angles by massive cylindrical stone pedestals, each carrying a metal tripod which is a fanciful reproduction of the finial of the monument. . ."

On a terrace on the southern part of the

monument stands a marble bust of the Poet, presented to the trustees by the sculptor, Mr. Patric Park of London, in 1847.

This great shrine is visited by fifty thousand persons annually—pilgrims from near and far—all of whom carry away with them pleasant memories of the Memorial and its beautiful surroundings.

ALONZA AND CORA. With Other Poems, etc. By Elizabeth Scot, of Edinburgh. (London, 1801).

This is a small volume of poetry by Mrs. Scot, " the guidwife of Wauchope House," who sent the poet a Rhyming Epistle, while he was in Edinburgh. His well-known reply appears in the above mentioned volume. A brief sketch of Mrs. Scot will be found in " Who's Who in Burns."

" It is a thin volume, published in London and edited by some one (evidently a Scot) who preferred to remain anonymous. Most of the verse in the volume is the usual eighteenth century romantic stuff, differing little from thousands of other like effusions. The piece which gives title to the volume is taken from Marmontel's ' Incas of Peru.' The three Scots poems, including the Address to Burns, are the best in the volume, and one cannot but regret that the authoress did not make greater use of her native Doric in her poetical compositions.–George F. Black, Ph.D.

A MAN'S A MAN FOR A' THAT.

One of the greatest songs ever composed in any language. Beranger, the French poet, declared : " This song is not a song for an age, but for an eternity." It has frequently been called the World's Anthem, and had Burns written nothing else this one song would have immortalized his name. It is known, and has been sung and recited in every part of the civilized world.

Burns when sending the song to Thomson said : " A great critic, Aikin, on songs says that Love and Wine are the exclusive themes for song-writing. The following is on neither subject, and consequently is no song ; but will be allowed, I think, to be two or three pretty good prose thoughts inverted into rhyme."

ANECDOTES. Interesting and Characteristic Anecdotes of Burns. (Edited by John Ingram. Glasgow : Thomas D. Morison, 1893).

" Oft and again, in my public capacity I have been asked where such and such a fact or anecdote relating to Burns would be found, after many volumes had been searched through, and much time and temper wasted on the part of the despairing reader. Some of these stories or anecdotes are contained in one work, some in another, some are dis-interred from the pages of long dead and forgotten periodicals, while only a small pro-portion of them are common to a few of the best biographies of the Poet. Thus, by gathering them all into a single collection, ready reference can be made to one volume, instead of, as hitherto, to many."—Preface.

ANNUAL BURNS CHRONICLE AND CLUB DIRECTORY.

Instituted 4th September, 1891. Published by The Federation. No. 1 (1892), edited by John Muir, F.S.A. (Scot). Nos. 2 to 34 (1893 to 1925) edited by D. M'Naught, LL.D. Second series, volume 1 (1926) to date, edited by J. C. Ewing, Glasgow. For index to Nos. 1-30, see under Douglas, Albert. With the new series the title underwent a slight change. The title page now reads—" Burns Chronicle and Club Directory. Instituted 1891. Published annually."

A RED, RED ROSE. See under " O, My Love is like a Red, Red Rose."

ATLANTA, GEORGIA, U.S.A., BURNS CLUB OF.

Federated 1914. No. 238. Membership about one hundred. Was organized at an annual dinner held on the 26th January, 1896 at the Aragon Hotel, Atlanta. Among those present were Dr. Joseph Jacobs, Judge William L. Calhoun, Donald M. Bain, Hamilton Douglas, Dr. Amos Fox, James M'Whirter,

A. A. Myer, Piromis H. Bell, Dr. John Roach Straton, Alexander W. Bealer, and Harry Silverman. Mr. Hamilton Douglas was elected President, Mr. Donald M. Bain, Vice-President, and Dr. Jacobs, Secretary. In 1897 at the suggestion of Mr. Eugene Overdorfer, the Club purchased fourteen acres of land nearly four miles from the City. Here it was proposed that the Club erect a copy of the Auld Clay Biggin, and under the superintendence of Mr. R. M. M'Whirter, the proposition was quickly and carefully followed out.

" The Cottage," writes Dr. Jacobs, " built of granite, is tastefully furnished, and has a large and well-selected library with many appropriate pictures and paintings relating to the poet. Since the building of the Cottage meetings have been held regularly each month in it, and at these many well-known scholars of the United States, including governors and judges of the Supreme Courts and a number of distinguished foreigners, have been entertained."

The special features of the Club are : Social and Literary meetings all the year round ; Annual Celebrations of the Poet's birthday ; Dogwood Day Barbecue in the Spring when the dogwood is in bloom ; and sundry entertainments throughout the year.

AUCHINCRUIVE.

An estate in the parish of St. Quivox, Ayrshire. It was purchased about 1750 by Richard Oswald, who occupied it until his death in 1784. He was the husband of Mrs. Oswald, on whom Burns composed the well-known " Ode, Sacred to the Memory of Mrs. Oswald of Auchincruive."

AULD BRIG OF AYR. See also under "Brigs of Ayr, The."

Tradition is uncertain concerning the exact date of the " Auld Brig." Some authorities place its origin about 1232, basing their opinion on a legend that it was erected by two maiden ladies named Love after the sweetheart of one of them had been drowned in crossing the ford at the spot during a flood, while others make it younger by a century and a half. Six centuries at least look out upon the visitor from its mediæval arches. To Burns, however, the romance associated with the " Brig " is due.

" The Brigs of Ayr "—the poem which has immortalized the " Auld Brig "—was composed in 1786. The poet had spent a night in Ayr and dreamed himself into the fantasy of the poem, probably after returning from a midnight ramble by the river, and in sight of the contrast between the " Auld Brig " and the coming new one. In fancy he sees " two dusky forms dart through the midnight air," and alight opposite each other—the one on the " Auld Brig," the other on the " rising piers " of its rival to be. These " Sprites " derived their features from the architecture of the bridges, " Auld Brig appear'd of ancient Pictish race, the vera wrinkles Gothic in his face ; " whereas " New Brig was buskit in a braw new coat, that he, at Lon'on, frae ane Adams got." Thereupon the " Sprites " of the two bridges engage in a duel in verse, which in point of tone and manner is reminiscent somewhat of the " flyting " of old days between such Scottish vernacular poets as Dunbar and Kennedy. It is modernity pitted against antiquity in a tourney of wit ; the embryonic commercialism of Scotland in the last quarter of the eighteenth century against the old, slow-sure soporific methods of the then departing ages ; the pride of years against the conceit of youth. In course of the " flyting," the " Auld Brig " dares to utter the famous prophecy :—" I'll be a brig when ye're a shapeless cairn," which came true in 1877, when Provost Ballantyne's new bridge of 1785-88, then ninety years old, fell to pieces and was superseded by the existing structure.

Some years ago the " Auld Brig " began to show the effects of Time, and it became apparent that it would either have to be demolished or completely over-hauled and preserved. Public sentiment favoured the latter course and through the efforts of Lord Rosebery, Mr. R. A. Oswald of Auchincruive and Mr. James A. Morris, architect, a sufficient sum was raised for its preservation. The work was successfully completed in 1910, and we are now assured that the " Auld Brig " will hold together for hundreds of years to come.

According to Mr. Morris " the Brig proper consists of four beautifully shaped segmental arches, each from fifty-two to fifty-three feet span, three massive piers of fifteen feet in thickness with irregular cutwaters and heavy land abutments on either bank. It rises twenty-seven feet above high water mark, and the tidal flow is about eight feet. The width of the ' Brig ' footways averages twelve feet between the parapets, and the steeply sloping roadways at the south end and between houses gives the ' Brig ' and approaches an approximate length of over five hundred feet ; but the ' Brig ' proper between the abutments is two hundred and fifty-five feet long."

AULD BRIG O' DOON.

Like its famous counterpart, the " Auld Brig o' Ayr," its age is enshrined in the mists of antiquity ; although judging from its style of architecture and its massive and solid style of masonry it was evidently built about the beginning of the fifteenth century. For many generations it served as the only

"Brig," dividing the districts of Kyle and Carrick.

In 1815 the highway line was changed and the new bridge built, which practically left the "Auld Brig" useless for passenger and other traffic, consequently it was neglected and uncared for.

But gradually the fame of Burns and the prominent part assigned by him to the "Auld Brig" in his immortal poem of "Tam o' Shanter," worked a change and about 1832 a number of gentlemen subscribed a sufficient sum to put it in proper repair and since then it has been well cared for.

"AULD CLAY BIGGIN, THE." See under "Burns's Cottage."

"AULD KILLIE." See Kilmarnock.

AULD LANG SYNE.

"Auld Lang Syne" is a happy phrase. It is one of the Scottish idioms that you cannot express in English. The nearest we can get to it in English is "Old Long Since," and such a translation is ludicrous.

The inventor of the phrase is unknown. Probably the earliest record we now have of its being adopted to song is when Sir Robert Ayton made use of the words. Ayton flourished in the reign of James VI. An elegant courtier, possessing a gift of rhyming, Ayton nevertheless left nothing of outstanding excellence to posterity. His version of the song consists of ten verses of eight lines each, beginning :—

> " Should old acquaintance be forgot,
>   And never thought upon,
> The flames of love extinguished,
>   And freely past and gone ?
> Is thy kind heart now grown so cold
>   In that loving breast of thine,
> That thou can'st never once reflect
>   On old long Syne ? "

Allan Ramsay also turned out a set of very mediocre verses on this subject :—

> " O'er moor and dale, with your gay friend,
>   You may pursue the chase,
> And, after a blythe bottle, end
>   All cares in my embrace ;
> And in a vacant rainy day,
>   You shall be wholly mine ;
> We'll make the hours run smooth away,
>   And I laugh at lang syne."

Under the title of " The Auld Minister's Sang," the Rev. John Skinner, author of " Tullochgorum," sings of " Auld Lang Syne." But the worthy clergyman could hardly expect his verses to achieve fame, for he catches but a glimpse of the spirit of his theme and its possibilities as a subject :—

> " Should auld acquaintance be forgot
>   Or friendship e'er grow cauld ?
> Should we nae tighter draw the knot,
>   Aye as we're growing auld ?
> How comes it then, my worthy friend,
>   Who used to be so kin',
> We dinna for each other speir,
>   As we did lang syne ?"

Next comes Lady Nairne, the sweet Jacobite songstress ; but, although the author of many charming songs that enrich Scottish literature, she does not score a success with her " Auld Lang Syne " which only consists of sixteen lines :—

" What guid the present day can give,
    May that be yours and mine ;
But beams of fancy sweetest rest,
    On auld lang syne.

" On auld lang syne, my dear,
    On auld lang syne,
The bluid is cauld that winna warm
    At thochts o' lang syne.

" We twa hae seen the simmer sun,
    And thought it aye would shine,
But mony a cloud has come between
    Since auld lang syne.

" But still my heart beats warm to thee
    And sae to me does thine ;
Blest be the power that still has left
    The friends o' lang syne."

Then came Robert Burns, who with master hand composed his immortal song. The versions we have alluded to, make no impression on us. But Burns's words go straight to the heart, for he grasped the idea that every human being has an Auld Lang Syne, and that it is human nature to look back lovingly to the days that are gone. That Burns struck a universal chord in the song is proved by the fact that his "Auld Lang Syne" has been translated into many languages; and a Scottish paper some time ago chronicled the fact that two zealous Scots in Paris singing the words, were joined in the chorus by some Frenchmen singing in their native tongue.

Note that word 'paidled'—what a fine, pithy one it is. The line would have been shorn of much of its strength had the poet made it read, 'We twa hae waded in the burn.'

Can it be explained why Burns, when sending the song to Mrs. Dunlop, tried to convey the idea that the words were not entirely his? In the letter he says: "Is not the Scots phrase, Auld Lang Syne, exceedingly expressive? There is an old song and tune which has often thrilled through my soul. You know I am an enthusiast in old Scots songs. I shall give you the verses." And then followed the song that has delighted and cheered not only Scots, but has become universal, and will be sung by generations yet unborn.

Auld Lang Syne! Magic words, that can carry us across leagues of space and back over years of time; that make the grey-haired grandfather in a far-off land more a bonneted boy on a Scottish braeside, spending a careless summer day with school friends, all unthinking of the weary path of life in the years to come.

C

AULD LICHTS, THE.

From the days of John Calvin, the members of the Scottish Church had been divided among themselves in their interpretation of certain parts of their Faith, and in Burns's time the contending parties through-out Ayrshire were locally known as the " Auld Lichts " and the " New Lichts." The New Lichts were liberal and rational in the observance of their religious duties, while the Auld Lichts clung tenaciously to the strict Calvinistic doctrine, and were cold in their friendship towards any one opposed to the belief they held regarding Predestination, Original Sin, a fire and brimstone Hell, etc. Burns's common sense made him throw in his lot with those of the New Licht party.

AULD NANCE TINNOCK'S.   See Nance Tinnock's Inn.

AULD REEKIE.

A name at one time applied to the old part of Edinburgh from the cloud of smoke that usually hung over it, especially in the mornings and evenings. Burns makes use of the name on one or two occasions.

" As to the origin of the familiar and not inappropriate appellation of ' Auld Reekie ' for Edinburgh, which is as old as the reign of Charles II, history and tradition alike are dumb. Of course, we have all heard the story of the old gentleman in Fife who regulated the time of his evening worship in summer by the appearance of the thickening smoke over the City in the late twilight, and who would call in the family, saying, ' it's time noo bairns, to tak' the beuks an gang to our beds, for yonder's Auld Reekie, I see, putting on her night-cap,' but we hesitate to believe that the sobriquet was employed there for the first time ; hesitate no less, either, although convinced that it was the prevailing smoke that suggested the word ' Reekie.' "— Robert Ford.

AUMOUS DISH, THE.

A plate or dish in which alms were received. It usually consisted of a wooden vessel, half platter, half bowl and was carried by every professional mendicant. Burns makes a slight reference to it in the opening stanza of " The Jolly Beggars."

AUTOBIOGRAPHY.

The original manuscript of this important and valuable document, in the form of a letter addressed to Dr. John Moore, 2nd August, 1787, by the poet, is now preserved for all time in the British Museum. " Bib. Eg. 1660." It was purchased at Mr P. Cunningham's sale (Sotheby's) 26th February, 1855. Lot 145. This autobiographical letter has formed the basis of all the poet's numerous biographies.

AYR.

Situated at the mouth of the river from which it derived its name. It is the capital of the Burns Country and the " Auld Toon " as well as the surrounding district for many miles is reminiscent of the poet, his friends and his time. It is nearby to the " Auld Clay Biggin," in which he was born and it is more or less associated with the early years of his life. The town is one of the most ancient in Scotland. To quote from an article entitled " Ayr and its Story " in the Official Guide to Auld Ayr, by the late William Robertson, J.P. :—

" If Ayr were not older than the period during which it has been a Royal Burgh, these more than seven hundred years would amply suffice to testify to a very respectable antiquity. But the fact that it was elevated to the dignity of a Royal Burgh in 1202 demonstrates that by that period it had attained to a very considerable eminence. And antiquarian research proves that it had. In fields adjacent to the town evidences have been forthcoming that in the Christian centuries stern conflicts had been waged between the Romans and the people of the district— Roman weapons of war, camp utensils, and pottery, mingled with Celtic remains of the same period. And after the Romans had ceased from their occupation of Scotland, having been withdrawn to defend their own citadel on the Tiber and their own waning power, it is on substantial record that the roving tribes, Picts, Scots, and Britons, had followed the way of the time—and unfortunately the way of all time since then—and had joined in frequent conflict ere yet Scotland had become one single unit and so girded itself for the long struggle that was to follow with its formidable adversary adjacent in the South.

" Since then, history has been generally and sufficiently reliable. Just landward of Ayr itself is the Carrick district, where Robert the Bruce, the hero of Bannockburn and an early holder of the title of the Earl of Carrick, was born. The titular designation that pertained to Bruce is now one of the sub-titles of the Prince of Wales, the Colonel-in-Chief of the Territorial Regiment, the Royal Scots Fusiliers. A few miles north of Ayr are the ruins of the ancient castle of Dundonald, whence sprang, by an Ayrshire wife, the Stewart race of Sovereigns, long identified with Scotland, and later, with the Union of the Crowns, with the United Kingdom. To these notabilities, necessarily of the first interest in relation to the Crown, falls to be added Sir William Wallace, the first of the two great heroes in Scotland's War of Independence, and nationally recognized as the greater of the two, who, though he was born in the neighbouring shire of Renfrew, was of pure Ayrshire descent, on both sides. It was in Ayr that Wallace began his campaign for the freedom of his country; it was on his own castle of Turnberry that Robert the Bruce struck his first decisive blow in the long and bloody struggle that ended at Bannockburn.

" In those days Ayr and the county of which it is the capital were in the main stream of Scottish history. Wallace wrought wonderously on the streets of the old town, and burned the Barns that were the headquarters of the English garrison that occupied the town — burning the garrison in addition. Later Bruce stormed the Castle of Ayr, and drove the English out ; and there were many weary months during which he was a fugitive in the county, pursued by hostile Scots as well as by English forces. After the battle of Bannockburn it was in Ayr that the Scots Parliament met in the ancient Parish Church of St. John the Baptist, Ayr's Patron Saint to this day, and bestowed the succession to the Crown in Robert the Bruce and his heirs for ever. And it was from Ayr that the fleet sailed that carried the King's gallant brother to Ireland to win a kingdom for himself in subduing the country of which he was the nominal Monarch.

" During the next three hundred years it was only when the nobles of the shire and the other great landowners were fighting in

the wars with England that they were at
peace with one another. These were the
long years of the blood feud. No savage
warrings between the Highland Clans, no
vendettas that ever were waged, could have
been pursued more relentlessly than were the
struggles for ascendency between the rival
families. It was the way of the times in
Ayrshire to kill off-hand a hereditary enemy.
Many castles were burned, large expanses of
the country areas were laid waste ; the cattle
were slaughtered in the fields, the sheep on
the braes, the peasants in their homes ; one
Earl was murdered just after he had
negotiated a ford in a river in North Ayrshire,
another Earl was hacked to pieces not far
from Ayr, and many leading men of lesser
degree shared the same fate. Desperate
battles, too, were fought. And even after the
Reformation in 1560, when John Welsh, the
son-in-law of John Knox, came to Ayr as the
parish minister, he found the town in such a
state of endless tumult and violence that it
was not safe for any citizen to walk
the streets. . . . . . . After the union of the
Scottish and English Parliaments, Scotland
experienced nearly half-a-century of depression. The renaissance set in towards the
middle of the eighteenth century, and the progress has been unabated in every direction.
Of all the immediately personal influences
that Ayrshire has given to Scotland and to

English-speaking world at large none can compare with that of Robert Burns. He came upon the scene when Scotland was throbbing with a new life, and when industry was in the dawn of a new era. It was he that voiced for his fellow-countrymen the dignity of labour and the independence of man. Of these he was the prophet ; of these he was the poet. Long before him, Ayrshire had given her sons to the War of Independence. She had stood for the right of all men to think for themselves in matters of the faith.

" Burns followed in an honourable sequence. He sang for his fellow man in his day and he is singing for him still. Beyond that, he too, like Wallace before him, wrought wonderously : so wonderously that the humble cottage of his birth has become, in its own way, a Mecca for pilgrims from all parts of the English-speaking world."

There is much to be seen in Ayr that is of intense interest to the Burns student and lover. There is the Auld Brig—The Wallace Tower—The Burns Statue, by Sir Thomas Brick, R.A. (q.v.)—The Tam o' Shanter Inn (q.v.)—The Auld Kirk with its Kirkyard and the Martyrs Monument—The Old Tolbooth—The site of the old Market Cross—The Kirk Port—and various other places each of them well worthy of a visit.

> " Auld Ayr, wham ne'er a town surpasses,
> For honest men and bonnie lasses."

So sung the poet a hundred and fifty years ago, and while the men of the town to-day are just as honest, and the lasses just as bonnie as of yore, these truths in themselves make no direct appeal to us. Rather, it is the knowledge that the poet once trod the streets, sometimes in joy and sometimes in sorrow, that he associated with the people and that through his own personality and genius he made the town famous the world over; these are the things that attract us to the place and make us love to linger along its byways and through its lanes, and for the moment makes us almost imagine that we are one of its own people.

AYR, THE RIVER.

Rises in the eastern border of the country and flows about thirty-three miles westward to Ayr Bay. Burns termed it, " Just one long lengthened tumbling sea." It is closely associated with many of his poems and songs. The Rev. Hamilton Paul says : " The scenery of Ayr, from Sorn to the ancient burgh at its mouth though it may be equalled in grandeur, is scarcely anywhere surpassed in beauty. To trace its meanders, to wander amid its green woods, to lean over its precipitous and rocky banks, to explore its caves, to survey its Gothic towers, and to admire its modern edifices, is not only highly delightful, but truly inspiring. If the poet, in his excursions along the banks of the river, or in penetrating into the deepest recesses of the grove, be accompanied by his favourite fair one, whose admiration of rural and sylvan beauty is akin to his own, however hazardous the experiment the bliss is ecstatic."

AYR STATUE.

Unveiled 11th July, 1891, by Sir Archibald Campbell (Lord Blythswood), after various models were exhibited, and on the recommendation of Mr. Hamo Thornycroft, R.A., it was decided to select the model submitted by Mr. G. A. Lawson, F.R.S.A., London. The public unanimously endorsed the decision, and the sculptor was instructed to proceed with the work.

It was a difficult matter for the committee to fix on a suitable central site, says an early report. Various places were suggested, and it was not till after careful consideration that the vacant ground opposite the old Cattle Market was fixed upon. Fortunately, the committee had little trouble in getting the Town Council to agree, seeing that the horse fairs which used to be held there had been removed to the new Cattle Market. The situation is central, being immediately opposite the main entrance to the railway passenger station, so that visitors to the town will have no trouble in finding it. The ground is laid off in flower plots, and enclosed by an artistic iron railing supplied by Sir William Arrol.

In connection with the pedestal, the committee were also very fortunate. Sir John M'Dowall, a native of Ayr, but who has been for a long time engaged in business in Greece, while paying a visit to his old friends, generously offered to send from Greece a block of marble for the pedestal ; but on learning that the sculptor was afraid that stone would suffer from the climate, he kindly consented to give the equivalent in money. The pedestal, which was designed by Messrs Morris & Hunter, architects, London and Ayr, is a selected rock from Kemnay Quarries, Aberdeenshire. It stands 12ft. 3in. in height, the spread of the base being 12ft. The stone forming the die weighs about five tons, the amount of granite used in the erection of the pedestal being 25 tons. The lower part of the die has a space on each side for a bronze bas-relief, and already one for the front panel has been promised. Between the die and the main cornice there is a sculptured granite frieze, worked from models prepared by Mr. David M'Gill, gold medallist, South Kensington, who is a native of Kilmarnock. The architects have taken a new line in regard to the arrangement of the frieze, a ribbon scroll upon it showing the names and dates of the Poet's various residences, beginning at Alloway, 1759, then Mount Oliphant, Lochlea, Kirkoswald, Irvine, Mossgiel, Edinburgh, Ellisland, and finally Dumfries.

The statue, which is placed with the face looking towards the poet's birthplace and the "banks and braes o' bonnie Doon," is undoubtedly a credit to Mr. Lawson, and is sure to add to his reputation. To a close observer it will at once be seen that the sculptor's principal object has been to get as near as possible to the real man. He has taken the Poet as a son of the soil, but still a man of independence, the crossed arms and the slightly clenched right hand clearly bearing out that characteristic. The costume is of the simplest kind, and there is no tendency to overdressing.

B

BACHELORS' CLUB, THE.

This was a debating and social society founded at Tarbolton, 11th November, 1780, by Burns, his brother Gilbert, and five others, viz., Hugh Reid, Alexander Brown, Thomas Wright, William M'Gavin, and Walter Mitchell, all of the parish of Tarbolton. These young men had met previously and resolved, " For our mutual entertainment, to unite ourselves into a club or society, under such rules and regulations that, while we should forget our cares and labours in mirth and diversion, we might not transgress the bounds of innocence and decorum." At the first regular meeting of the Club Robert Burns was unanimously elected President. One of the rules and regulations was " Every man, proper for a member of this Society, must have a frank, honest, open heart, above anything dirty or mean, and must be a professed lover of one or more of the female sex. No haughty, self-conceited person, who looks upon himself as superior to the rest of the club ; and especially, no mean-spirited, worldly mortal, whose only will is to heap up money, shall upon any pretence whatever, be admitted."

Meetings were held once a month and in due time other names were added to the roll of membership, David Sillar, the Davie of the familiar Epistles, being among the number.

Among the questions debated during the winter months of this year were : " Whether is a young man of the lower ranks of life likeliest to be happy, who has got a good education, and his mind well-informed ; or he who has just the education and information of those around him ? " " Whether is the savage man or the peasant of a civilised country in the most happy situation ? " and " Whether between friends, who have no reason to doubt each other's friendship, there should be any reserve ? "

The Club continued in existence for some years after the poet had left Ayrshire, but latterly dissensions, and ill feeling among the members, led to its termination.

BACK OF THE WORLD, THE. See Kelly Burn (The).

BALLARAT, VICTORIA, AUSTRALIA.

Statue unveiled 21st April, 1887. The oration was delivered by the Hon. John Nimmo, M.P. Mr. John Udney, of Carrara, Italy, was the sculptor. The pedestal is thirteen feet high. On the plinth is the word " Burns," and on the front panel is the inscription—" Born near Ayr, Scotland, January, 25, 1759. Died at Dumfries, July 21st, 1796." The other panels are inscribed with appropriate quotations from the poet's poems. The statue stands on Sturt Street, facing the Post Office.

BALLOCHMYLE.

On the Ayr, about two and a half miles from Mauchline. The seat at one time of Sir John Whitefoord, afterwards occupied by Claude Alexander, a brother of Miss Wilhelmind Alexander in whose honour the song "The Lass of Ballochmyle" was composed. The song was sent to Miss Alexander, 18th November, 1786, accompanied by a letter in which Burns said: "I had roved out as chance directed, in the favourite haunts of my muse, the banks of Ayr, to view Nature in all the gayety of the vernal year. The evening sun was flaming o'er the distant western hills: not a breath stirred the crimson opening blossom, or the verdant spreading leaf. 'Twas a golden moment for a poetic heart. Such was the scene, and such was the hour—when, in a corner of my prospect, I spied one of the fairest pieces of Nature's workmanship that ever crowned a poetic landscape or blest a poet's eye. . . The inclosed song was the work of my return home; and perhaps it but poorly answers what might have been expected from such a scene."

BANKS O' DOON, THE.

There are three versions of this song, the first beginning "Sweet are the Banks, the Banks o' Doon," the second "Ye Flowery Banks o' Bonnie Doon," while the third and most popular one begins " Ye Banks and Braes o' Bonnie Doon."

See also under DOON, THE.

BANNOCKBURN. See under " Bruce's Address to his Army at Bannockburn."

BARD'S EPITAPH, A.

Of this beautiful epitaph, which Burns wrote for himself, Wordsworth says : " Here is a sincere and solemn avowal—a public declaration from his own will—a confession at once devout, poetical, and human— a history in the shape of a prophecy ! "

BARSKIMMING.

The residence, in Burns's time, of Sir Thomas Miller, of Glenlee, who in 1766 was appointed Lord Chief-Justice of the Court of Session with the title of Lord Barskimming. The estate was next to Ballochmyle, near Mauchline, and was well-known to the poet.

BARRE, VERMONT, U.S.A.

Statue unveiled 21st July, 1899. Mr. J. Massey Rhind was the sculptor. Mr. Wendell Phillips Stafford delivered the oration at the unveiling. The four carved panels on the die represent " The Cottar's Saturday Night," Burns's Cottage, " Tam o' Shanter," and Burns at the Plough.

BATTLE OF BOTHWELL BRIDGE, REFERENCE TO.

" For my own affairs, I am in a fair way of becoming as eminent as Thomas à Kempis or John Bunyan ; and you may expect henceforth to see my birth-day inserted among the wonderful events, in the Poor Robin's and Aberdeen Almanacks, along with the Black Monday, and the Battle of Bothwell Bridge "—Letter to Gavin Hamilton, 7th December, 1786.

The Battle of Bothwell Bridge was fought in Lanarkshire, 22nd June, 1679. Here the Scottish Covenanters were defeated by the Royalist forces, under the command of the Duke of Monmouth.

BATTLE OF SHERIFFMUIR.

This song is simply an improved version of one written by the Rev. John Barclay (1734-1798) who resided at one time in Edinburgh. Sheriffmuir is about two and a half miles from Dunblane in Perthshire. The battle was fought 13th November, 1715, between Government troops under the command of the Duke of Argyll, and those of the Jacobites under the command of the Earl of Mar. Both sides claimed the victory.

D

BEGBIE'S INN, KILMARNOCK.

This was a small place in the poet's time and is still to the fore, standing in Market Lane, the second opening to the left going down King Street.   It is now the Angel Hotel. The Laigh Kirk (q.v.) immortalized in " The Ordination," is near by and worshippers were wont, it is said, to troop

> " Aff to Begbie's in a raw
> An' pour divine libations."

in allusion to the single mode of progression rendered necessary by the contracted Bridge over the Marnock which led to the celebrated " Begbie's."

BELFAST STATUE.

Occupies a prominent position in the Free Library and Art Gallery on Royal Avenue.   The statue is a replica of that at Ayr, by George A. Lawson, R.S.A.   On the pedestal is the inscription " Robert Burns, 1759-1796.   Presented by his countrymen and admirers in Belfast."

BENNALS, THE.

A farm in the West of Tarbolton parish, near Afton Lodge and a short distance from Lochlea.   It was occupied in Burns's time by William Ronald and his family.   See the poem " The Ronalds of The Bennals."

BEUGO ENGRAVING OF BURNS, THE. See under Portraits of Burns.

BIBLE, HIGHLAND MARY'S.

In two volumes; is in the Monument at Alloway. The date on the title page is 1782, and the bookseller's price, five shillings and sixpence, is marked on volume one. On the fly-leaf of the first volume is written, in the Poet's handwriting: " ' And ye shall not swear by My Name falsely: I am the Lord.'—Levit. xix. 12." In the second volume: " ' Thou shalt not forswear thyself, but shall perform into the Lord thine oath.'— Matt. v. 33." And in both volumes is written, " Robert Burns, Mossgiel," with his Masonmark appended. In one of the volumes is preserved a lock of Highland Mary's hair.

These volumes came into possession of Mary's mother, and were kept in the family. William Anderson, mason, Renton, near Dumbarton, a grandson, took them with him to Canada in 1834. Circumstances forced him to part with them, after being assured they would be carefully treasured beyond the risk of loss or destruction. A party of gentlemen in Montreal bought them for £25, and sent them to the Provost of Ayr for presentation to the Monument. On Thursday, 24th December, 1840, they were formally presented to Provost Limond, at a dinner in honour of the occasion; and on the Poet's birthday, 25th January,

1841, were delivered to the custodier of the Monument, at a public dinner, in the Burns Arms Inn, Alloway.

BIBLE, THE ARMOUR FAMILY.

Containing the record of the marriage of James Armour with Mary Smith, December 7th, 1761, and the register of the births of their children, Jean coming second, born February 25th, 1765. The imprint of the title page reads: " Edinburgh, printed by Adrian Watkins, 1756." The Bible is now in the Burns House, Mauchline.

BIBLE, THE " BIG HA'."

This belonged to the poet's father, and is celebrated in " The Cottar's Saturday Night." It is now in the Cottage Museum at Alloway. It was purchased on the 12th July, 1921, at Sotheby's Auction Rooms for four hundred and fifty pounds. It bears the imprint, " Edinburgh : Printed by Alexander Kincaid, MDCCLXII." A " ha' Bible," was so called from the fact of its occupying a place usually in the hall of a large mansion house. When the family, including the servants, assembled for Divine Worship it was carried into the parlour or the room where the services were to be conducted.

BIBLE, THE POET'S FAMILY.

Is now in the Cottage Museum at Alloway. It has the imprint, " Edinburgh : Printed by John Reid, 1766." It was purchased 15th December, 1904, from Bernard Quaritch, the famous bookseller, for seventeen hundred pounds. The Bible was willed by Jean (Armour) Burns to her eldest son, Robert, from whose possession it passed into that of William Nicol Burns, the poet's second surviving son. He in his turn gave it to his niece (who lived with him), the late owner, Mrs. Sarah E. M. T. Burns Hutchison. The Bible contains the following entries on the reverse of the title of the New Testament in the handwriting of Robert Burns himself :

" Robert Burns was born at Alloway in the Parish of Ayr—Janry. 25th, 1759.

Jean Armour his Wife was born at Mauchline, Febry. 27, 1767.

September 3rd, 1786, were born to them twins, Robert their eldest Son at a quarter past Noon, and Jean since dead, at fourteen months old.— March 3, 1786, were born to them twins again two daughters, who died within a few days after their birth.—August 18th, 1789, was born to them Frances Wallace, so named after Mrs. Dunlop of Dunlop ; he was born at a quarter before Seven forenoon.—April 9th, 1791, between three and four in the morning, was born to them William Nicol, so named after William Nichol, of the High School, Edinburgh.—November 21st, 1792, at a quarter past Noon, was born to them Elizabeth Riddel, so named after Mrs. Robert Riddel of Glenriddel."

There is also an entry by James Glencairn Burns and two by William Nicol Burns.

BIBLIOGRAPHY.

Burns Calendar, The. A Manual of Burnsiana, relating Events in the Poet's History, Names associated with his Life and Writings, a Concise Bibliography, and a Record of Burns Relics, with engraved vignette portrait. Kilmarnock, 1874. Edition limited to 600 copies, each one numbered and signed by James M'Kie.

The Bibliography of Robert Burns, with Biographical and Bibliographical Notes, and Sketches of Burns Clubs, Monuments and Statues. By James Gibson, Kilmarnock. 1881. Edition limited to 600 copies, each one numbered and signed by James M'Kie.

Bibliotheca Burnsiana. Life and Works of Burns ; title pages and imprints of the various editions in the Private Library of James M'Kie, Prior to date, 1866. Kilmarnock, 1866.

The Printed Works of Robert Burns. A Bibliography in Outline. By W. Craibe Angus, Glasgow : Privately Printed, 1899.

BIELD INN, THE.

A noted wayside tavern between Edinburgh and Dumfries patronized by the poet on his journey to and from the capital.

BLACK BULL INN, THE, ARGYLE STREET, GLASGOW.

This was a popular hostelry in the poet's time and was patronized by him on his visits to the city. It is said that the inn was erected by the " Highland Society " as an investment, its first tenant being James Graham, valuer. From its doors every morning at 8 o'clock a coach started for Edinburgh, where it was due to arrive the same evening. The inn was discontinued in 1851, and part of the building was turned into a warehouse for Messrs. Mann, Byars & Co. A Memorial Tablet has been placed in the front wall with the inscription :— " Robert Burns lodged here when this Building was the Black Bull Inn. He visited Glasgow June, 1787, February and March, 1788. Scottish Burns Club Tablet." The Tablet was designed by the well-known Glasgow architect, Mr. Ninian MacWhannell.

BLACK MONDAY, REFERENCE TO.

" For my own affairs, I am in a fair way of becoming as eminent as Thomas à Kempis or John Bunyan ; and you may expect henceforth to see my birth-day inserted among the wonderful events, in the Poor Robin's and Aberdeen Almanacks, along with the Black Monday, and the battle of Bothwell Bridge."—Letter to Gavin Hamilton, 7th December, 1786.

Black Monday, Easter Monday, April 14, 1360, was so called on account of a terrible storm which occurred on that date, while an English Army was before Paris, and in which they suffered a great loss both in men and horses.

BLUE GOWNS, THE.

An order of licensed beggars in Scotland, now extinct. The members were also known as " The King's bedesmen," probably from some ancient religious order. The former name was derived from the dress or cloak usually worn by the members. The cloak along with a metal badge on which were the words " Pass and repass," were presented to them each King's birthday, and is said to have been supplied to them by Royalty. The badge conferred on its owner the privilege of pursuing his calling throughout the country in spite of all laws then in force against mendicity. Sir Walter Scott has much to say concerning this order in connection with Edie Ochiltree in " The Antiquary."

BOGHEAD.

Lies about a mile west of Lochlea in the parish of Tarbolton. In Burns's time, the place was occupied by James Grieve, locally known as the Laird of Boghead. Burns was on very friendly terms with the Laird and occasionally visited at his mansion. One of his earliest epitaphs is that beginning " Here lies Boghead among the dead," not a very complimentary composition.

BOLTON.

The parish of Bolton lies about three miles South by West of Haddington. The seat of Lord Blantyre, Lennoxlove, is in the immediate neighbourhood. In the Churchyard of the Parish Church is the burial place, wherein were interred the remains of the poet's mother, his brother Gilbert, and others. The record on the tombstone reads :

ERECTED.

By Gilbert Burns, Factor, at Grants Braes,
In Memory of his Children.
ISABELLA, who died 3rd July, 1815,
in the 7th year of her age,
AGNES, who died 14th Septr., 1815,
in the 15th year of her age,
JANET, who died 30th Octor., 1816
in the 18th year of her age ;

And of his Mother,
AGNES BROWN, who died 14 Janry., 1820,
in the 88th year of her age ;
whose mortal remains lie all buried here.
Also of other two of his Children, Viz. JEAN, who
died on the 4th of Jany., 1827, in the 20th year of her
age and JOHN, who died on the 26th Febry., 1827,
in the 25th year of his age.   GILBERT BURNS,
their Father, died on the 8th April, 1827, in the 67th
year of his age.

Also buried here, ANNABELLA, sister
of GILBERT BURNS, who died March 2nd,
1832, Aged 67.

The two-century old hearse that carried the remains of mother, son, and daughter can still be seen by pilgrims to the shrine, on applying to the party in charge of the grounds.

BOSTON, MASS., U.S.A., STATUE.

Unveiled 1st of January, 1920, by Governor, now ex·President Calvin Coolidge.

Colonel Walter Scott of New York City delivered the oration. The memorial is in the
form of a broad pylon flanked on either
side by low walls, and in the centre stands
the bronze figure of the Poet. The cost of
the memorial was nearly sixteen thousand
dollars, and credit for the raising of the funds
and in bringing the project to a successful
issue belongs to the members of the Burns
Memorial Association of Boston. The sculptor was Mr Henry H. Kitson of Quincy, Mass.

BRAES OF BALLOCHMYLE, THE. See under
" Ballochmyle."

BRIGS OF AYR, THE. Inscribed to John Ballantyne, Esq., Ayr. See also under "Auld
Brig of Ayr."

In the autumn of 1786, a new bridge was
begun to be erected over the river at Ayr,
in order to supersede an old structure which
had long been found unsuitable, and was
then becoming dangerous ; and while, the
work was being proceeded with, under the
chief magistracy of Mr. Ballantyne, the poet's
generous patron, he seized the opportunity
to display his gratitude by inscribing the poem
to him. The idea of the poem appears to
have been taken from Fergusson's " Dialogue
between the Plainstanes and the Causeway : "
the treatment of the subject is, however,
immeasurably superior to the older piece,
and peculiarly Burns's own.—Gunnion.

The poem first appeared in the Edinburgh edition of the poems, 1787.

BROW.

On the shore of the Solway Firth, a few miles from Dumfries. It consists of two or three cottages by the side of a country road running parallel to the Firth ; off from which cottages there goes a strip of smooth grassy ground leading to the margin of the Firth itself, also grassy in the main till the sands and ooze are reached, but broken into ridges and dotted with salt-water pools. Close to the cottages, and in the middle of the strip of verdant ground leading from them to the Solway, is a saline well called " The Brow Well," now a mere muddy splash enclosed within a wall, but still resorted to for its supposed medicinal virtues, and once of greater local fame on that account. It was on the 4th July, 1796, that Burns, then in the last stage of emaciation and debility, after six months of his fatal illness, harassed for money, and out of countenance with most of his former friends, was taken, by medical advice, from Dumfries to Brow, for such benefit as might still be possible for him from the Brow Well, country air, and sea bathing. For exactly a fortnight he tried the vain experiment ; but on the 18th of July he returned to Dumfries, to die there on the 21st. Brow

will ever retain a sad interest for the lovers of
Burns. It was here that the poet penned
his final letter to his friend, Mrs. Dunlop, and
from here he committed to the world's keeping the last of all his poetical conceptions,
" Fairest Maid on Devon Banks."

Mr. J. Taylor Gibb, Mauchline, is the
author of an excellent poem entitled " At
Brow and Afton," which appeared in the
" Burns Chronicle " for 1921, and from which
we quote a few lines :—

> " Oh, could that shady bower but speak,
>   It, too, might tell the story of the ending of a life
>   That struggled with the things that tell—
>   Those eternal things, which the great Father of us all
>   Has but too few, and that in measure small revealed
>   In life's great garden, sometimes rudely kept,
>   By those whose work is but to keep and tend."

BRUAR FALLS.

" In Athole. Exceedingly picturesque
and beautiful, but the effect is much impared
by the want of trees and shrubs." R.B.

The Bruar is a small stream, a tributary
of the Garry and runs a few miles west of
Blair Athole, near the line of road between
Perth and Inverness. Burns visited the
Falls while on his Highland Tour in 1787.
After leaving, and while in Inverness he wrote
his " Humble Petition of Bruar Water," a
poem of eleven stanzas, addressed to the Duke
of Athole through whose estate the Bruar
flowed :—

" Let lofty firs, and ashes cool,
   My lowly banks o'erspread,
And view, deep-bending in the pool,
   Their shadows' wat'ry bed :
Let fragrant birks, in woodbines drest,
   My craggy cliffs adorn ;
And, for the little songster's nest
   The close embow'ring thorn."

" Bruar Water no longer mourns the absence of ' lofty firs and ashes cool,' " writes Professor Walker at a later date. " The Duke complied with the poet's suggestion and caused a great number of trees to be planted which have greatly added to the charms of the scene. But the Tay Bridge Gale of 1879, made sad havoc, which has only been partially repaired.

BRUCE'S ADDRESS TO HIS ARMY AT BANNOCKBURN.

" There is a tradition," says the poet, in a letter to Thomson, enclosing this glorious ode, that the old air, " Hey tutti taitie " was Robert Bruce's march at the battle of Bannockburn. " This thought, in my yesternight's evening-walk, warmed me to a pitch of enthusiasm on the theme of liberty and independence, which I threw into a kind of Scots Ode, fitted to the air, that one might suppose to be the gallant royal Scot's address to his heroic followers on that eventful morning." "This ode," says Professor Wilson, "the grandest out of the Bible—is sublime!" "Why should we speak of Scots Wha hae wi' Wallace bled," writes Thomas Carlyle, "since all know of it from the king to the meanest of his subjects? It should be sung with the throat of the whirlwind. So long as there is warm blood in the heart of Scotchmen or man, it will move in fierce thrills under this war-ode, the best we believe, that was ever written by any pen." Bannockburn was fought, 24th June, 1314, between the Scots and the English and, as is well-known, resulted in Robert Bruce winning the Scottish crown. Historians say that the Scottish troops numbered 30,000 against 100,000 on the English side. Bannockburn is a small village about two and a half miles south from Stirling. It derives its name from a small stream or burn that flows through it on its way to the Forth. "Here," says the poet in the Journal of his Highland Tour, "no Scot can pass uninterested. I fancy to myself that I see my gallant, heroic, country-men coming o'er the hill, and down upon the plunderers of their country, the murderers of their fathers; noble revenge and just hate glowing in every vein, striding more and more eagerly as they approach the oppressive, insulting, blood-thirsty foe. I see them meet in gloriously triumphant congratulation on the victorious field, exulting in their heroic royal leader, and rescued liberty and independence."

BUCHANITES, THE.

"We have been surprised with one of the most extraordinary phenomena in the moral world, which, I dare say, has happened in the course of this last century. We have had a party of the 'Presbytery Relief,' as they call themselves, for some time in this country. A pretty thriving society of them has been in the burgh of Irvine for some years past, till about two years ago, a Mrs. Buchan from Glasgow came and began to spread some fanatical notions of religion among them, and in a short time made many converts. . . . Their tenets are a strange jumble of enthusiastic jargon; among others, she pretends to give them the Holy Ghost by breathing on them, which she does with postures and practices that are scandalously indecent. They have likewise disposed of all their effects, and hold a community of goods, and live nearly an idle life, carrying on a great farce of pretended devotion in barns and woods, where they lodge and lie all together, and hold likewise a community of women, as it is another of their tenets that they can commit no moral sin. I am personally acquainted with most of them, and I can assure you the above mentioned are facts."—Burns in a letter to his cousin, James Burness, 3rd August, 1784.

The Buchanites as they were called were gradually expelled from throughout Ayrshire. We hear of them in other parts of Scotland, in Ireland, England and in America, but the group became widely scattered and in the course of time became extinct. Mrs. Buchan died in May, 1791. Joseph Train, in 1846, published a little book, entitled " The Buchanites from first to last," to which we refer any one further interested in the subject.

BUCHAN'S DOMESTIC MEDICINE.

A very popular book, especially throughout Scotland in the time of Burns. Published in 1769 it speedily ran through many editions until 80,000 copies had been disposed of—quite a remarkable sale for a book in those days.

In " Death and Doctor Hornbook," Death refers to the fact that Hornbook has " Grown sae weel acquaint wi' Buchan."

BUCKSKINS.

A term applied to the American troops during the Revolutionary War. It is used by Burns in his " Ballad On The American War."

BUFF AND BLUE, THE.

Formerly the colours of the Whig party. At the time the song, " Here's a Health to them that's awa," in which occurs the lines :—

—It's guid to support Caledonia's Cause
And bide by the Buff and the Blue—

was written, the Whig party was in power and Charles James Fox was Prime Minister.

BUNYAN, JOHN, REFERENCE TO.

" For my own affairs, I am in a fair way of becoming as eminent as Thomas à Kempis or John Bunyan ; and you may expect henceforth to see my birth-day inserted among the wonderful events, in the Poor Robin's and Aberdeen Almanacks, along with the Black Monday, and the battle of Bothwell Bridge "—Letter to Gavin Hamilton, 7th December, 1786.

BURNEWIN.

Burn the wind—the Blacksmith—an appropriate title.—Dr. Currie.

Burns makes use of the name in the tenth stanza of " Scotch Drink."

BURNS, BURNESS.

The name Burns or Burness is probably derived from the Anglo-Saxon Beorn, a chief, with the affix nes denoting possession.— Rev. Charles Rogers.

E

BURNS FEDERATION, THE.

Instituted at Kilmarnock, 1885.   Motto, " A Man's a man for a' that."

Objects :—

To strengthen and consolidate by universal affiliation the bond of fellowship existing amongst the members of Burns Clubs and kindred Societies.

To purchase and preserve MSS. and other relics connected with the Poet.

To repair, renew, or mark with suitable inscriptions, any buildings, tombstones, etc., interesting from their association with Burns.

To encourage and arrange School Competitions in order to stimulate the teaching of Scottish History and Literature.

The Council consists of Hon. Presidents, Hon. Vice-Presidents, Presidents, two Vice-Presidents, Hon. Secretary, Hon. Treasurer, Editor of the " Burns Chronicle," and the Auditors, all of whom are elected annually, also any three members of, and nominated by, each affiliated Club. The Annual Conference is held on the second Saturday of September, at such place as may be agreed upon. The Federation has now been in existence for forty-four years, and during that period has accomplished a great deal of useful and valuable work along the lines for which it was organized.

BURNS COTTAGE, ALLOWAY, THE.

Universally known as "The Auld Clay Biggin," was erected wholly or mainly by the poet's father in 1757. It stands on a portion of ground that comprises seven acres purchased 22nd June, 1756 by William Burnes from Dr. Alexander Campbell of Ayr, on an annual feu or ground rental. The Cottage consists of two rooms—a but and a ben—and here in the "but" or kitchen, on the 25th January, 1759, was born Robert Burns, and here he spent the first seven years of his life, or until 1766 when the family removed to Mount Oliphant (q.v.) two miles away. "It was, with the exception of a little straw, literally a tabernacle of clay," said John Murdoch. "In this mean cottage, of which I myself was at times an inhabitant, I really believe there dwelt a larger portion of content than in any palace in Europe. The 'Cottar's Saturday Night,' will give some idea of the temper and manners that prevailed there."

Since then the Cottage has seen many changes, the father having let it to various parties until 1781, when it and the ground were bought by the Incorporation of Shoemakers in Ayr, for one hundred and sixty pounds. "That body," says Mr J. C. Dunlop, "also let the land and the buildings, and the first of their tenants, one of their own members, at some date before 1800, turned the cottage into an ale-house, and an ale-house it remained during the whole subsequent period of their ownership." In 1881 the property passed into the hands of the Alloway Burns Monument Trustees. "As soon as they came into occupation," continues Mr. Dunlop, " the Trustees earnestly set about making their property a worthy memorial of the Poet, and their energies have been steadily directed to the careful preservation of the original structure, and to the acquisition of genuine, well-authenticated relics of the Poet and his family. Their first action was to decree the withdrawal of the sale of alcoholic liquor that had increased the value of the property to the previous proprietors, but had tended to degrade the associations of the place. Later they set about the restoration of the Cottage to its original condition ; this involved the removal of the buildings that had been adjoined by the Incorporation of the Shoemakers to the ' Clay Biggin ' of William Burnes, and the restitution of the parts that had been altered to fit in with these additions." The Cottage and grounds are now in excellent order, and, as every one knows, are visited by thousands of people annually, from all parts of the world. Much has been written about the Cottage, but the most authoritative book on the subject is the story of the birthplace of Robert Burns from the feuing of the ground by William

Burnes in June 1756 until the present day. By James M'Bain (Member of the Institute of Journalists). With numerous illustrations. (Glasgow 1904).

" The compilation of this small volume," says Mr. Bain in his preface, " was undertaken chiefly with a view to setting at rest the doubts which one still finds lingering in the minds of many who are devoted admirers of Burns, as to whether the Cottage at Alloway, in which so much homage is still rendered to the memory of the poet, is the actual cottage in which he was born."

A small book entitled " The Auld Clay Biggin," by the present editor, was published at Kilmarnock in 1925. It contains a considerable amount of prose and verse by various authors, and was intended as a literary souvenir of a visit to the Cottage.

BURNS CHRONICLE. See under Annual Burns Chronicle.

" BURNS IN EDINBURGH, 1787." See under Paintings by Charles Martin Hardie, A.R.S.A.

BURNS'S " HOWFF." See under Globe Tavern.

BURNS'S PASSIONATE PILGRIM; or, Tait's Indictment of the Poet, with other Rare Records.   Glasgow, 1904.

A little volume of special interest for students of Burns, on account of its featuring Tait's verses on the Poet, David Siller and others.

"BURNS'S   TAVERN." See   under   Dowie's Tavern.

BULLERS OF BUCHAN, THE.

Referred to by Burns in his election ballad, addressed to "R. Graham, Esq., of Fintry," is an appellation given the huge vertical well in the rocky coast near Peterhead. The poet visited the "Bullers" while return- ing from his Highland Tour.

C

" CA IRA."   (" It Will Go.")

A popular song of the people during the French Revolution. It was sung in 1789 by the Insurgents as they marched to Versailles. The words are inferior to the music, the latter having been composed, it is said, by a drummer who was engaged in a minor part of the Opera Beaucourt.

The song was called for one night at a theatre party in Dumfries while Burns was present, but there was no response to the call. A disturbance followed, however, which was much commented on by the townspeople at the time, and Burns, fearing that his loyalty would again be called in question, wrote to Robert Graham of Fintry (5th June, 1792) disclaiming all connection with the entire proceedings, excepting that he unfortunately happened to be present.

CA' THE YOWES TO THE KNOWES.

The old version of this song beginning " As I gaed down the water side," is indebted to Burns for the fourth and fifth stanzas. The song, as improved by him, was sent to Johnson for insertion in the " Museum." The poet's own version beginning " Hark the Mavis' evening song," was written for and appeared in Thomson's " Selected Melodies of Scotland."

CALEDONIA'S BARD.

"I went to a Mason-lodge yesternight," Burns writes in a letter to John Ballantyne from Edinburgh, 14 January, 1787, "where the Most Worshipful Grand Master Charters, and all the Grand Lodge of Scotland visited. The meeting was most numerous and elegant ; all the different lodges about town were present in all their pomp. The Grand Master who presided with great solemnity, and honour to himself as a gentle-man and Mason, among other general toasts gave, ' Caledonia and Caledonia's Bard, brother B—— ' which rung through the whole Assembly with multiplied honors and repeated acclamations. As I had no idea such a thing would happen, I was downright thunderstruck, and trembling in every nerve, made the best return in my power. Just as I had finished some of the Grand Officers said, so loud as I could hear, with a most comforting accent, ' Very well indeed,' which set me something to rights again."

The Lodge in which this incident took place was St. Andrew's, at the time quite a renowned Masonic centre in Edinburgh.

See also under, "Scottish Bard."

CALEDONIAN HUNT, THE.

An association composed principally of noblemen and gentlemen of Scottish ancestry, whose chief tie was their common interest in field sports, as well as in races, balls, and assemblies for social and other purposes. Many of the members were quick to realize that Burns was no ordinary individual and gladly took him under their care, thus greatly befriending and encouraging him while in Edinburgh.

" A motion being made, by the Earl of Glencairn, and seconded by Sir John White-foord in favour of Mr. Burns, Ayrshire, who had dedicated the new edition of his poems to the Caledonian Hunt, the meeting was of opinion that in consideration of his superior merit, as well as of the compliment paid to them, Mr. Hagart should be directed to sub-scribe for one hundred copies, in their name, for which he should pay Mr. Burns twenty-five pounds, upon the publication of his book." —Excerpt from Minute of the Caledonian Hunt, held at Edinburgh on the 10th January, 1787.

" Though much indebted to your goodness, I do not approach you, my Lords and Gentle-men, in the usual style of dedication, to thank you for past favours ; that path is so hack-neyed by prostituted Learning, that honest Rusticity is ashamed of it. Nor do I present this ' Address ' with the venal soul of a ser-vile Author, looking for a continuation of those favours : I was bred to the Plough and am independent. I come to claim the common

Scottish name with you, my illustrious
Countrymen ; and to tell the world that I
glory in the title.   I come to congratulate my
Country, that, the blood of her ancient heroes
still runs uncontaminated ; and that from your
courage, knowledge, and public spirit, she may
expect protection, wealth, and liberty.   In
the last place, I come to proffer my
warmest wishes to the Great Fountain of
Honour, the Monarch of the Universe,
for your welfare and happiness."—Excerpt
from the " Dedication to the Noblemen and
Gentlemen of the Caledonian Hunt " of the
First Edinburgh Edition of the poems.

The poet was enrolled a member of the
Caledonian Hunt, 10th April, 1792.

CALF, THE.

The title of a small humorous poem by
Burns, composed on the Rev. James Steven,
after listening to a sermon preached by him
on the text, " And ye shall go forth, and grow
up, like calves of the stall " (Malachi, 4th
chapter and 2nd verse).   Gilbert Burns
writes, " The poet had been with Mr. Gavin
Hamilton in the morning, who said jocularly
to him, when he was going to church, in
allusion to the injunction of some parents to
their children, that he must be sure to bring
him a note of the sermon at mid-day : this
address to the reverend gentleman on his
text was produced."   But Burns himself

says regarding it : " The poem was nearly an extemporaneous production, on a wager with Mr. Hamilton, that I would not produce a poem on the subject in a given time. Mr. Steven was known by the name of " The Calf " ever afterwards.

CAMBUSDOON MSS.

Contained in a volume of sixteen pages in the handwriting of the Poet which belonged to Sir James Baird, Bart. A full description of the eight pieces will be found in the Burns Chronicle, volume 15.

CARLISLE, ENGLAND.

A Bust of the Poet was unveiled at Tullie House, 21st July, 1898. The sculptor was Mr. D. W. Stevenson, R.S.A. On the pedestal is engraved " Robert Burns. 1759-1796. Centenary Commemoration Bust. Presented to Tullie House, by Admirers of the Poet, 21st July, 1898."

Burns while on his Border Tour, accompanied by Robert Ainslie, made a stop at Carlisle and put up at the Malt Shovel Inn. Rickergate. From here he wrote a humorous letter (June 1st, 1787) in the Scottish dialect to his friend Nicol—" Kind Honest-Hearted Willie."

The Carlisle Burns Club was instituted 1889 ; Federated 1895. In 1893, The Burns Federation held its Annual Conference in the City.

CARLYLE'S ESSAY ON BURNS.

First published in "The Edinburgh Review," December, 1829.

CARLYLE ON BURNS.   By John Muir, Glasgow, 1898.

A most interesting book on the subject by one who is an authority on all matters connected with Robert Burns.

"In addition to this Essay (Carlyle's), there are to be found scattered throughout Carlyle's writings and collateral books—English and foreign—numerous passages on Burns, which are known only to the students of the by-ways of literature. It has been my aim to collect, translate and arrange these passages in such a form, and with such editorial helps, as may assist the general reader to understand the true value and significance of the fragments."—*From the Preface.*

CASSILIS DOWNANS.

"Certain little, romantic, rocky, green hills, in the neighbourhood of the ancient seat of the Earls of Cassilis."—Burns.

About a mile from the little village of Dalrymple. Here the wonderful imagination of Burns makes the fairies hold their revels on Hallowe'en :—

> "Upon that night, when fairies light
> On Cassilis Downans dance."

CASTLE GORDON.

One of the finest mansions north of the Firth of Forth, is a seat of the Duke of Richmond, but was formerly the seat of the Dukes of Gordon. It lies in the vicinity of Fochabers, Elginshire, in a beautifully wooded park, generally of level ground and covers a large area. Burns, who visited there during his Highland Tour in 1787, left on record his impression of the place in his song—" Castle Gordon." The last stanzas of the song reads :—

> " Wildly here, without controul
>   Nature reigns and rules the whole ;
>   In that sober pensive mood,
>   Dearest to the feeling soul,
>   She plants the forest, pours the flood,
>   Life's poor day I'll musing rave
>   And find at night a sheltering cave,
>   Where waters flow and wild woods wave
>   By bonie Castle Gordon."

CASTLE OF MONTGOMERY, THE. See Coilsfield.

CATALOGUE OF THE BURNS EXHIBITION. See under Memorial Catalogue, etc.

CATRINE HOUSE.

The seat of Professor Dugald Stewart, the philosopher. The town of Catrine stands on the banks of the river Ayr, about two miles from Mauchline and was founded about 1787. Burns was introduced to the Professor in October, 1786, and each learned in time to place a high value on the other's genius. Burns dined with the Professor and Lord Daer at Catrine House (consult poem " Lines on Meeting Lord Daer "), shortly after the publication of the Kilmarnock edition of the poems, and they met each other frequently afterwards in Edinburgh.

" A sweet little place on the banks of the Ayr, belonging to Professor Dugald Stewart, where he used to reside during the interval of his labours in the University (as his father had done before him) till banished from it by the erection of a Cotton-Mill Village immediately adjoining."—Gilbert Burns.

CENTENARY OF THE POET'S BIRTH.

" On that memorable Tuesday evening, the 25th day of January, 1859, the principal meeting held in Edinburgh took place in the Music Hall, and was presided over by Lord Ardmillan, who gave " The Immortal Robert Burns " in a most eloquent speech ; Lord Neaves proposed ' The Biographers of Burns and Mr. Robert Chambers ; ' Professor Blackie gave ' The Memory of Sir Walter Scott,' and Mr. James Ballantyne read his own verses composed for the occasion, beginning :—

> ' I dreamed a dream o' sitting here,
> Delighted wi' our canty cheer,
> While sangs and speeches charmed the ear
>   And heart by turns,
> When lo ! as frae some heavenly sphere,
>   Descended Burns.'

There also was held in the capital a Grand Citizen Banquet, which took place in the Corn Exchange, and which was presided over by Mr. D. M'Laren. A Workingmen's Festival was held in the Dunedin Hall, and a Fruit and Cake Soiree in the Queen Street Hall, at which Professor George Wilson took the chair.

At the magnificent meeting held in the City Hall, Glasgow, Sir Archibald Alison, the historian of Europe, was in the chair. The croupiers were Robert Dalgleish, M.P., Peter Cunningham, son of 'Honest Allan,' the biographer of Burns ; Alex. Baillie Cochrane, of Lamington ; Henry Glassford Bell and Walter Buchanan, M.P.

Supporting the chair on the right was to be seen Colonel Burns—son of the poet—Sir David Brewster, Samuel Lover and others. On the chairman's left was Judge Haliburton, R. Monckton Milnes, M.P. (afterwards Lord Houghton), Dr. Norman MacLeod, etc.

In one of the reports of this meeting the writer of the article says : ' Perhaps we are not wrong in saying the general literature of the United Kingdom was better represented than at any of the numerous festivals which have been got up.' At this meeting Colonel Burns, in the course of his speech, said : " My mother told the late Mr. M'Diarmid of Dumfries that my father once said to her— ' Jean, one hundred years hence they'll

think mair o' me than they do now.' "
The musical part of the evening's programme
in the City Hall was provided by a few old
Glasgow favourites, Messrs Stembridge, Ray,
Robinson, John Muir, and Fulcher.

At the Tontine Reading Room, Glasgow,
a meeting was also held, and in Carrick's
Royal Hotel, Glasgow, Dr. (then Mr. James)
Hedderwick occupied the chair, with such
artistic and literary luminaries to grace the
festal board as Daniel Macnee, R.S.A. (he was
not knighted then); Alexander Smith, author
of ' A Life Drama,' and William Cross, author
of ' The Disruption.'

In the King's Arms Hall, Trongate,
Glasgow, the genial ' Caleb,' Prince of
Ramblers, Hugh Macdonald, occupied the
chair, and had for company Robert Burns
Thomson and James Thomson, grandsons
of the poet; William Simpson, the Crimean
artist, and others.

At Tarbolton, in the earlier part of the
day, a procession was formed to visit some of
the scenes rendered prominent from the poet's
connection with them. It proceeded to the
hill from which the town takes its name,
and wound round the artificial mound of
Druidical formation, from the summit of
which a view can be obtained of Lochlea,
where he lived for seven years; of Boghead,
the residence of the rough, ready-witted
Rankine; of Spittle-side, where the brother

Davie of the poet dwelt ; while the road wends its way round the Willie's Mill to the scene of ' Death and Dr. Hornbook.'

The procession then visited ' Mary's Thorn,' remarkable as the trysting place of Burns and Highland Mary ; their farewell meeting place on the Fail and the castle of Montgomerie, where the procession pauses, and members of the company sang several of the poet's songs. In the afternoon a dinner was given in the town.

At Mauchline at 2 o'clock, to the strain of a band playing ' There was a lad,' the procession marched to Mossgiel, and according to the newspaper reporter, when the good folks of Mauchline that day got the first glimpse of the flag that waves above the farm building at Mossgiel, ' They raised a shout which made the very welkin ring.' They visited also Nance Tinnock's, the birthplace of Jean Armour, Johnny Pigeon's, Poosie Nancie's, and other places, known through the bard's life and works. There was a dinner in the Institution Rooms at 5 p.m., the chair being occupied by William Brown, Esq., Greenockmains. There were present at that meeting various contemporaries of Burns—Matthew Lerrie, who was a servant boy with Gavin Hamilton when Highland Mary was with him, and when the poet used to call ; James Hamilton, who remembered being sent with a letter from the poet to Jean Armour, with

F

strict injunctions to deliver it to no person but Jean; William Patrick, who was once a servant boy at Mossgiel during Burns's tenancy; also George Patrick and John Lambie, who were present but too frail to take any part in the proceedings.

At Kilmarnock they had also a procession, after which came the dinner, presided over by Archibald Finnie, Esq., of Springfield, then the worthy Provost of 'Auld Killie.' At that dinner the chairman read the prize poem composed for the occasion by the late Archibald M'Kay, author of the beautiful song 'Be kind to Auld Grannie.'

In Ayr, as it will be readily understood, that was a great day. At noon the Freemasons marched in procession to the Old Church, where services were conducted by the Rev. F. Rae, after which they again formed, and being joined by the representatives of various trades they marched through the town, doffing their hats as they passed the house occupied by the Misses Begg, who were at the window, and acknowledged the compliment, evidently with full hearts. There was a banquet given in the County Hall, at which presided Sir James Fergusson, Bart., of Kilkerran, with Professor Aytoun, croupier. In the Assembly Rooms a soiree was held, over which presided the Rev. Wm. Buchanan.

To our thinking, no meeting held on that memorable evening surpassed the gathering that took place beneath the rafters which had sheltered, one hundred years before, Mary (Brown) Burness and her infant son, that night given to the world as one of the Almighty's special gifts of the eighteenth century. We refer, of course, to the cottage demonstration at Alloway, the spot of the poet's birth. The meeting was presided over by one of Burns's biographers, Rev. P. Hately Waddell, then of Girvan, a man who would concede to no one in admiration and appreciation of the poet and his works. He was supported that night by a company of eighty; it has been a marvel since where they all found accommodation. Near the chairman sat George Gilfillan. The croupier was Robert Story, the Northumberland poet, and there was also present a genuine Scottish poet, in the person of Robert Leighton, the author of ' Scotch Words,' etc. The great treat of the evening, however, was the speech of the chairman, when he gave ' The Memory of Burns.' It was said to be the finest speech delivered by any speaker on that historical day."—D. Walker Brown, in " The Burns Scrap Book."

A large volume extending to over six hundred pages, and containing a history of the meetings held throughout the world with the addresses delivered on the occasion, was published by Messrs. A. Fullarton & Co., Edinburgh and London, towards the end of 1859. The book bears the title, " Chronicle of The Hundredth Birthday of Robert Burns. Collected and Edited by James Ballantine, author of The Gaberlunzie's Wallet, etc."

CENTENARY OF THE POET'S DEATH. 21st JULY, 1896.

The Centenary was celebrated throughout Scotland and elsewhere with solemn and impressive ceremonies. Public meetings were held at Ayr, Dumfries, Glasgow, Mauchline, Irvine, Edinburgh and other large centres. A very long procession proceeded to the Mausoleum and on arrival there reverently deposited wreaths sent from all parts of the world. The Earl of Rosebery was the principal speaker of the celebration in Dumfries and Glasgow, and on both occasions His Lordship delivered very notable addresses on the Poet and his time.

CESSNOCK.

A small stream about two miles from Lochlea farm. It runs about nine miles N.N.W. to the Irvine. It was on a farm by its banks that Elison Begbie resided when Burns fell in love with her. He addressed several letters to her, besides making her the heroine of the song, "The Lass of Cessnock Banks" and probably two or more others.

CHEYENNE, WYOMING, U.S.A., STATUE.

See under Wyoming.

CHICAGO, ILLINOIS, STATUE.

Unveiled 26th August, 1906, by Miss Barbara Williamson. The oration, in the form of an original poem, was read by the author, the Hon. Wallace Bruce. The statue is of bronze, the work of W. G. Stevenson, R.S.A., and is over ten feet high. The figure is said to follow the lines of the sculptor's marble in Kilmarnock. The pedestal is twelve feet high and has four bronze panels with illustrations from "Tam o' Shanter," "The Twa Dogs," "The Cottar's Saturday Night," and Burns at the plough. On the base is the name Burns, and underneath it the line, "A Man's a Man for a' that." The statue occupies a prominent position in Garfield Park.

CHILDREN OF BURNS AND JEAN ARMOUR.
See under Family, The Burns.

CHLORIS MEMORIAL, THE.

This consists of a Celtic Cross of gray granite and was unveiled in the Preston Street Cemetery, Edinburgh, by the Rev. George Murray, on the 25th May, 1901. The sculptor was Mr. Stewart M'Glashen. A panel in front of the shaft has an admirable reproduction of the poet's crest. The Cross, with its Celtic adornments and chaste beauty, which stands about the middle of the cemetery to the south of the walled-in graves there, and under the shades of a friendly birch, is very much admired. It carries in black letters the inscription : " This stone marks the grave of Jean Lorimer, the ' Chloris ' and ' Lassie wi' the lint-white locks,' of the poet Burns. Born, 1775 ; died, 1831. Erected under the auspices of the Ninety Burns Club, Edinburgh, 1901.

CLARINDA EPISODE, THE.

This has been touched upon and written up from various angles by every biographer of the poet since the day on which he died, and the Burns-Clarinda correspondence has been published in different forms, while the songs and poems inspired by the event are to be found in every edition of the poet since that issued by Dr. Currie in 1900 (q.v.). Agnes M'Lehose (Clarinda) was born in Glasgow, 17th April, 1759, and died 23rd October, 1841. From a brief account of her life in " Who's Who In Burns," we learn that

" Burns was introduced to her at a party held in the house of a Miss Nimmo in Edinburgh on the 7th December, 1784, and the two immediately became infatuated with each other. Anxious to know more of such an extraordinary genius as Burns, Mrs. M'Lehose invited him to tea at her rooms the following evening. An unlucky accident the next morning, however, not only prevented the poet from keeping the appointment that evening, but confined him to his own rooms for many days afterwards. That he was greatly disappointed at not being able to meet the lady is

shown by a letter addressed to her at this time —
' I never met with a person in my life whom I more
anxiously wished to meet than yourself. To-
night I was to have that very great pleasure. I
was intoxicated with the idea, and if I don't see
you again I shall not rest in my grave for chagrin.'
to which Mrs. M'Lehose at once replied : ' You
shall not leave town without seeing me if I should
come along with good Miss Nimmo and call for
you. I am determined to see you.' This led to a
correspondence between the two that was later
carried on under the names of Sylvander and
Clarinda, and from that time until the day in February, 1788, when Burns was compelled by circumstances to take his departure from Edinburgh,
letters, poems, and meetings between them were
of daily occurrence. ' Burns was not attracted
to Clarinda solely by her misfortunes,' writes Dr.
Peter Ross. ' She was a beautiful woman, accomplished beyond most women in her station of life,
sprightly in her manners, agreeable in her conversation, and possessing considerable poetic ability
as well as excellent literary taste. If we were to
judge of her relations with Burns by the code of
morals which is presumed to prevail in our day,
were her letters and his to be presented as proofs of
wrongdoing under present conditions, they might,
we freely admit, give rise to conjecture. But we
must remember they were written at a time when
people were more outspoken than now, when
manners were not so straitlaced, when people
talked more freely concerning many matters than
they now dare to think of them. We should
also remember that Mrs. M'Lehose, as a married
woman, had no need of comporting herself with the
reserve that would be natural in a spinster, that her
disposition was inclined to be gay and happy, and
her desire was to forget the sad position in which
she was placed by her husband's selfish conduct.

On the advice of her friends and especially at the suggestion of her husband, Mrs. M'Lehose in 1792 sailed from Leith to rejoin the latter, but on her arrival at Kingston she found he had a coloured mistress as well as a brood of children, and she returned home in the same ship that she had sailed out in. She saw no more of Mr. M'Lehose. He died at Kingston in 1812."

Burns had sufficient to occupy his attention after he settled on Ellisland and we hear little of Clarinda after that.—Among the immortal effusions produced by the Episode are : " The Dearest o' the Quorum," " Clarinda, Mistress of my Soul," " Fair Empress of the Poet's Soul," " Gloomy December," " My Nannie's Awa'," " My Lovely Nancy," and " I Burn, I Burn."

A small volume, entitled " The Poems of Clarinda," was issued by Mr Eneas Mackay, Stirling, in 1929.

CLARINDA MEMORIAL TABLET.

Unveiled in the Canongate Churchyard, Edinburgh, Saturday, 10th June, 1922. The Tablet is of Ravelstone stone, with moulded surround and sill, enclosing an oval bas-relief in bronze of the head of Clarinda. This was taken from the Miers silhouette and is the work of the well-known sculptor, Mr. H. S. Gamley, R.S.A., Edinburgh. The credit for the Memorial is due to the members of The Ninety Burns Club, Edinburgh, who some years previous erected the Memorial Shaft in Preston Street Cemetery, over the resting place of another immortal heroine—Chloris. (q.v.).

CLOUT THE CALDRON.

"A tradition is mentioned in the Bee that the second Bishop Chisholm of Dunblane used to say, that if he was going to be hanged, nothing would soothe his mind so much by the way, as to hear 'Clout the Caldron' played. I have met with another tradition that the old song :—

> Hae ye onie pots or pans
> Or onie broken chanlers ?

was composed on one of the Kenmure family, in the Cavalier times, and alluded to an amour he had, while under hiding, in the disguise of an itinerant tinker. The air is also known by the name of 'The Blacksmith and his Apron,' which, from the rhythm, seems to have been a line of some old song to the tune."—Burns to Johnson.

CLUDEN.

A small stream running about seven miles E.S.E. to the River Nith at Lincluden. It is distant about one and a half miles from Dumfries.

"COFFIN, THE." See Dowie's Tavern Johnnie.

COILA.

From Kyle in Ayrshire—so called from Coel Hen, a Pictish King.

COILSFIELD. See also under Fail.

Poetically termed by Burns, " Montgomerie Castle," in his song, " Highland Mary." The residence in the poet's time of Colonel Hugh Montgomerie, afterwards Earl of Eglinton. The estate is about six miles from Ayr, on the road to Mauchline and on the right bank of the Faile, a small tributary of the river Ayr. It was here Mary Campbell was employed in the capacity of dairy-maid, and here by the Faile the memorable parting of the lovers took place

" Ye banks and braes, and streams around
    The castle o' Montgomerie,
Green be your woods, and fair your flowers,
    Your waters never drumlie !
There simmer first unfauld her robes,
    And there the langest tarry ;
For there I took the last fareweel
    O' my sweet Highland Mary."

Tradition asserts that the name Coilsfield was derived from the belief that Coilus (i.e., Coel Hen), King of the Picts, was buried in the neighbourhood.

There was in ancient times a " Montgomery Castle," which lay in the parish of Tarbolton although only about a hundred yards from the residence of Colonel Montgomerie. The ruins of it were razed to the

ground when the foundation for Coilsfield
was laid in 1806.

COILUS.

More correctly Coel Hen, King of the
Picts, from whom the district of Kyle is said
to take its name.

"COMIN' THRO' THE RYE."

"Comin' Thro' the Rye" is one of the
old songs rewritten by Burns. It belongs to
the rustic lyrical group, which includes "Corn
rigs and barley rigs," "The lea rig," and even
"Clean pease strae." Students of Scottish
song know he meant a rye field in the
verses we know as the definitive form of the
song. Many poets before Burns sung of
"Rye," even with capital letters; and in
every case they referred to a field of rye.
Clearly, as in the old lilts, the episode is
founded on "a walk in the field." The tune
or air would no doubt furnish the first form of
the song; but, like many another proto-
type, it is lost in the mists of Scottish antiquity.

The song "Comin' thro' the Rye" has
been said to concern the "Rye River" or
stream, but there is no stream of particular
prominence in Scotland by the name of
"Rye."

COMMON-PLACE BOOKS, THE POET'S.

First one begun April, 1783, and ends abruptly October, 1785.

The following constitute the Title, Introduction and Specimens of the " Observations " as recorded in the book.

" OBSERVATIONS, HINTS, SONGS, SCRAPS of POETRY, &c., by ROBERT BURNESS ; a man who had little art in making money, and still less in keeping it ; but was, however, a man of some sense, a great deal of honesty, and unbounded good-will to every creature rational and irrational. —As he was but little indebted to scholastic education, and bred at a plough-tail, his performances must be strongly tinctured with his unpolished, rustic way of life ; but as I believe they are really his own, it may be some entertainment to a curious observer of human nature to see how a Ploughman thinks, and feels, under the pressure of Love, Ambition, Anxiety, Grief, with the like cares and passions, which, however diversified by the Modes and Manners of life, operate pretty much alike, I believe, in all the Species.

' There are numbers in the world, who do not want sense, to make a figure ; so much as an opinion of their own abilities, to put them upon recording their observations, and allowing them the same importance which they do to those which appear in print.'—Shenstone.

' Pleasing when youth is long expir'd to trace
The form our pencil or our pen design'd !
Such was our youthful air and shape and face !
Such the soft image of our youthful mind.'
                                        —Ibidem.

A second similar "Common Place Book" was begun at Edinburgh in April, 1787. The items included in it are undated, being "Fragments, Miscellaneous Remarks, etc." This Book, or Journal, is also known as "The Edinburgh Journal."

CONCORDANCE.

A Complete Word and Phrase Concordance to the Poems and Songs of Robert Burns, incorporating a glossary of Scotch words, with notes, index, and appendix of readings, compiled and edited by J. B. Reid, M.A., Glasgow, 1889.

> "This Concordance claims to be not only a complete Verbal but also a complete Phrase Concordance (The Concordance contains over 11,400 words, and 52,000 quotations)—the first instance in which this combination has been attempted. In view of the fact that no poet, except Shakespeare, is more quotable than Burns, the aim has been to give every quotation in sufficient fulness to serve the purpose of the literary man, the public speaker, or the conversationalist. This fulness of the quotations also makes it easy to determine from the context the various shades of meaning in which any word may be used. The Text adopted is that of the First Editions, edited by the Poet himself . . . . The Glossary will be useful to those Scotsmen whose acquaintance with their native tongue has become vague and shadowy, as well as to those who are ignorant of the Scottish language ; and, as incorporated, will save some trouble."—Extract from Preface.

CORSINCON.

A hill (height about fifteen hundred and forty-seven feet) in New Cumnock parish, about twenty-five miles from Ellisland. At its foot the Nith crosses from Ayrshire into Dumfriesshire. It is mentioned by the poet in one of the most beautiful and passionate of the songs addressed to his wife, " O,were I on Parnassus Hill."

COTTAR'S SATURDAY NIGHT, THE.

Gilbert Burns gives the following distinct account of the origin of this poem :—"Robert had frequently remarked to me that he thought there was something peculiarly venerable in the phrase, ' Let us worship God ! ' used by a decent, sober head of a family, introducing family worship. To this sentiment of the author, the world is indebted for ' The Cottar's Saturday Night.' When Robert had not some pleasure in view in which I was not thought fit to participate, we used frequently to walk together, when the weather was favourable, on the Sunday afternoons— those precious breathing times to the labouring part of the community—and enjoyed such Sundays as would make one regret to see their number abridged. It was in one of these walks that I first had the pleasure of hearing the author repeat ' The Cottar's Saturday Night.' I do not recollect to have read or heard anything by which I was more highly electrified. The fifth and sixth stanzas and the eighteenth thrilled with peculiar ecstasy through my soul. The cottar, in the ' Saturday Night,' is an exact copy of my father in his manners, his family devotion, and exhortations ; yet the other parts of the description do not apply to our family. None of us were ' at service out among the farmers roun',' Instead of our depositing our ' sair-won penny-fee ' with our parents, my father laboured hard, and lived with the most rigid economy, that he might be able to keep his children at home, thereby having an opportunity of watching the progress of our young minds, and forming in them early habits of piety and virtue ; and from this motive alone did he engage in farming, the source of all his difficulties and distresses."

COURT OF EQUITY, THE.

This was the title of a burlesque secret association or bachelors' club, the members of which met at intervals in the Whitefoord Arms Inn at Mauchline. The professed object of the association was, " to search out, report, and discuss the merits and demerits of the many scandals that crop up from time to time in the village " and to determine what punishment, if any, should be imposed in each case. The officers of the association were known and addressed by judicial titles. Burns was " Perpetual Presi-

dent," John Richmond, " Clerk of the Court,"
James Smith, "Procurator Fiscal," and
William Hunter, was "Messenger at Arms."
The association soon became extinct after the
Burns family removed from the neighbourhood. Among the poet's writings is a poem
entitled "The Court of Equity," but it is
never included in his works, although George
Gebbie in his edition (Philadelphia, 1886)
publishes a portion of it. The Manuscript
is in the British Museum.

CRAIGIEBURN.

A beautiful locality in the neighbourhood
of Moffat, Dumfriesshire, where the parents
of Jean Lorimer (Chloris) resided and where
she was born in 1775. The name is derived
from a little stream which at this point joins
the river Moffat. "Craigieburn Wood" is
one of the galaxy of fine songs inspired by the
heroine.

CREED OF BURNS. See under Religion.

CRITICISMS AND EARLY REVIEWS. See under
Reviews.

CROCHALLAN FENCIBLES, THE.

A short time before Burns's introduction
to Edinburgh society, says Dr. D. M'Naught,
William Smellie, Lord Newton, Charles
Hay, and a few more wits of the Parliament

House had founded a convivial club called
" The Crochallan Fencibles " (a mock allusion
to the Bonaparte Volunteer movement),
which met in a tavern kept by a genial old
Highlandman named " Dannie Douglas,"
whose favourite song " Cro Chalien "
suggested the dual designation of the Club.
Smellie introduced Burns as a member in
January, 1787. Cleghorn also appears to
have been on the muster-roll of this rollicking
regiment, which supplies a key to much of
Burns's correspondence with him. How the
revelry of the boon companions was stimulated and diversified may be as easily imagined
as described.

CROOK INN, THE.

Situated on the highway between Dumfries and Edinburgh. Frequented by the
poet on his way to and from the Capital.

CULLODEN.

Five miles east of Inverness. Here on a
part of the ground called Drummossie Moor
the celebrated battle was fought, 16th April,
1746, between the troops of the Duke of
Cumberland and those of Prince Charlie.
Burns while on his northern tour, accompanied
by Nicol paid a visit to the spot, 6th September, 1787, and made mention of the fact in his
Journal.

G

CURRIE'S EDITION OF BURNS, DR.

The Works of Robert Burns; with an account of his life and a criticism on his writings. To which are prefixed some observations on the character and condition of the Scottish peasantry. Four volumes, 8vo. Liverpool, 1800.

Edited by Dr. James Currie. Volume I. Life of Burns, Criticism, etc. II. General Correspondence. III. Published and Additional Poems. IV. Letters to Thomson and Additional Songs.

Published 12th April, 1800, for the benefit of the poet's family in an edition of two thousand copies. Eight editions followed until 1815 when the copyright expired. The work as published by Dr. Currie remained a favourite with the public for many years, but gradually much adverse criticism on his life of the poet began to appear and, not without good reason, has continued up till the present time.

"Currie was engaged in arranging and collecting this miscellaneous mass of materials, and in writing the "Life" for over a period of three years; and the only assistance he received was when, under a threat of flinging the whole thing up, Gilbert Burns and Syme came down to Liverpool and stayed a fortnight under the doctor's roof. It was in the summer of 1800 that the work, in four volumes, at last appeared. Two thousand copies were printed at thirty-one shillings and sixpence each, which realized fourteen hundred pounds—for the benefit of the Poet's family. Its appearance was greeted with universal favour, for the tact and delicacy, and the skill and discretion with which under difficult circumstances, he had accomplished his task. At least, nothing to the contrary ever reached his ear, and he died some five years after at Sidmouth, whither he had travelled from Bath, under the grateful impression that his benevolent exertions had been crowned with entire success."—Dr. William Findlay.

D

DAER, LORD.

In 1786, Professor Dugald Stewart resided in a villa at Catrine, on the Ayr, a few miles from the poet's farm ; and having heard of his astonishing poetical productions, through Dr. John Mackenzie, he invited Burns to dine with him, accompanied by his medical friend. The poet seems to have been somewhat alarmed at the idea of meeting so distinguished a member of the literary world; and to increase his embarrassment, it happened that Lord Daer (son of the Earl of Selkirk), an amiable young nobleman, was on a visit to the professor at the time. The result, however, appears to have been rather agreeable than otherwise to the poet, who has recorded his feelings in the poem, " Lines on Meeting with Lord Daer."

DALGARNOCK.

According to Burns this was " a romantic spot near the Nith, where are still a ruined church and a burial ground." The place is referred to in " Last May a braw wooer."

DALRYMPLE.

About four miles from Ayr. Here Burns when he was nearly fourteen years of age attended school for some time along with his brother Gilbert. The schoolhouse has long since disappeared, the site being now occupied by the Free Church. The little village has a neat appearance and is romantically situated, the Doon flowing smoothly along at its southern end.

DALSWINTON HOUSE AND LOCH.

Dalswinton House was built by Patrick Miller (Burns's friend and landlord while he occupied Ellisland) on what was once the site of the Red Comyn's Castle. The estate is on the Nith, directly opposite the farm of Ellisland. On Dalswinton Loch the first steam boat was launched by Miller, and Burns is said to have been one of the passengers. This important event took place 14th October, 1788.

DEATH OF BURNS. THE REAL CAUSE. See " Burns from a New Point of View."

(By Sir James Crichton-Browne, London, 1926).

" Burns's death was not an accidental event, but the natural consequence of a long series of events that had preceded it . . . .Burns died of endocarditis, a disease of the substance and lining membrane of the heart, with the origination of which alcohol had nothing to do, though it is possible that an injudicious use of alcohol may have hastened its progress. It was rheumatism that was the undoing of Burns. It attacked him in early years, damaged his heart, embittered his life, and cut short his career."

" Reliance upon the several vindications pronounced by Jean Armour, by the somewhat unstable Gilbert, by Supervisor Findlater and by others was not enough," says the Burns Chronicle, 1927. " A strictly scientific analysis of the evidence for and against is what Sir James Crichton-Browne set himself to accomplish. With painstaking care he has followed up every reference made by the Poet to the malady which afflicted him almost from infancy, which at times distorted his mind, and subjected him to the fits of morbidity so often mentioned in his letters and poems, and which ultimately destroyed his body before middle age had overtaken it. From the ever-recurring mention of his bodily torturings, which were ever accompanied by fits of that ' melancholia which transcends all wit,' Burns himself makes abundantly clear just precisely what it was that pursued him to the grave. Sir James Crichton-Browne has followed the trail like a sleuth. Nothing appears to have escaped him. Every source of information has been tapped, every mine exhausted, every avenue blocked until it yielded up any secret it might possess. . . . .

" Sir James Crichton-Browne proves his case beyond the shadow of a doubt, and by the same method of patient research and logic he demolishes the sometimes malicious and sometimes merely ignorant slanders concerning the alleged intemperance of the Poet while at Ellisland and Dumfries."

DEATH AND DOCTOR HORNBOOK.

According to Gilbert Burns, " the schoolmaster of Tarbolton parish "—John Wilson— " to eke out the scanty subsistence allowed to that useful class of men, had set up a shop of grocery goods. Having accidentally fallen in with some medical books, and become most hobby-horsically attached to the study of medicine, he had added the sale of a few medicines to his little trade. He had got a shop bill printed, at the bottom of which, overlooking his own incapacity, he had advertised that advice would be given in " Common disorders at the shop gratis." Robert was at a Mason meeting in Tarbolton, when the dominie made too ostentatious a display of his medical skill. As he parted in the evening from this mixture of pedantry and physic, at the place where he described his meeting with Death, one of those floating ideas of apparition he mentions in his letter to Dr. Moore crossed his mind : this set him to work for the rest of his way home." The ridicule caused by the poem, and a dispute with the heritors of Tarbolton regarding his salary, resulted in the removal of Wilson to Glasgow, where he again engaged in teaching. In 1807, he was elected Session Clerk to the Gorbals, then a suburb of Glasgow. He is described at this time as a decent, dumpy, elderly gentleman, dressed in black, with just enough of corpulency to give him " a presence ; " and a pair of stout legs, inclined to be crooked, the attractions of which were fully developed through the medium of black tights and black silk stockings. He became quite prosperous in his latter years, and was able to acquire a competency before his death, which occurred 13th January, 1839. Burns, in writing the satire, bore no ill-feeling towards Wilson, and the poem was intended to be nothing but a piece of humorous poetical fiction. Nor did Wilson resent it to any great extent when it was first read by him. Indeed, " many a time in his latter days," says Scott Douglas, " he was heard over a bowl of punch to bless the lucky hour when, as dominie of Tarbolton, he provoked the castigation of Robert Burns."

DEATH AND DYING WORDS OF POOR MAILIE.

" The circumstances of the poor sheep," says Gilbert Burns, " were pretty much as Robert has described them. He had, partly by way of frolic, bought a ewe and two lambs from a neighbour, and she was tethered in a field adjoining the house at Lochlea. He and I were going out with our teams, and our two younger brothers to drive for us, at mid-day when Hugh Wilson, a curious-looking,

awkward boy, clad in plaiding, came to us
with much anxiety in his face, with the information that the ewe had entangled herself
in the tether, and was lying in the ditch.
Robert was much tickled with Hughoc's
appearance and postures on the occasion.
Poor Mailie was set to rights, and when we
returned from the plough in the evening, he
repeated to me her ' Death and Dying Words,'
pretty much in the way they now stand."

DEIL'S AWA WI' THE EXCISEMAN, THE.

Lockhart gives the following interesting
account of this song :—This spirited song
was composed on the shores of the Solway,
while the poet and a party of his brother
excisemen were engaged in watching the
motions of a suspicious-looking brig, which
had put in there, and which, it was supposed,
was engaged in smuggling. The day following that on which she was first seen, the vessel
got into shallow water, and it was then discovered that the crew were numerous, and not
likely to yield without a struggle. Lewars
accordingly was despatched to Dumfries for
a party of dragoons, and another officer proceeded on a similar errand to Ecclefechan,
leaving Burns with some men under his
orders, to watch the brig and prevent landing
or escape. "Burns manifested considerable im-
patience while thus occupied, being left for
many hours in a wet salt marsh with a force

which he knew to be inadequate for the purpose it was meant to fulfil. One of his comrades hearing him abuse his friend Lewars in particular, for being slow about his journey, the man answered that he also wished the devil had him for his pains, and that Burns in the meantine would do well to indite a song upon the sluggard. Burns said nothing ; but after taking a few strides by himself among the reeds and shingle, rejoined his party, and chanted to them the well-known ditty."

DE LOLME ON THE BRITISH CONSTITUTION.
See Dumfries Public Library.

DENVER, COLORADO, STATUE.

Unveiled 4th July, 1904, by Miss Jane Morrison. The oration was delivered by the Hon. John D. M'Gilvray and the invocation by the Rev. James D. Rankin of the Presbyterian Church, a direct descendant of the Burns family. The statue is of bronze, the work of W. G. Stevenson, R.S.A., and is over ten feet high, while the pedestal measures a little over sixteen feet in height. The name " Burns," in prominent letters is on the third block of the base and underneath are the lines by Isa Craig Knox :

> " A poet, peasant-born,
> Who more of Fame's immortal dower
> Unto his country brings, than all her kings."

The credit for the erection of the statue is due to the members of the Denver Caledonian Club.

DETROIT, MICHIGAN, U.S.A., STATUE.

Unveiled 23rd July, 1921, by Colonel Walter Scott, of New York City. The statue is a replica of the one in Ayr, executed by Mr. George A. Lawson, R.S.A., and stands in Cass Park. To Mr. Edward Goodwillie of Detroit, the principal credit for the erection of the statue is due. It was he who originated the plan and worked indefatigably to carry it, amidst many difficulties, to a successful issue. As one writer claimed, " the Monument is not only one to our National Bard ; it also represents a monument to Scottish perseverance and steadfast fidelity to a herculean task." " The Fiery Cross " for September, 1921, in its notice of the unveiling, said : " In 1912 Goodwillie organized the Burns Club, and has been its president continuously. At the same time Mrs. Goodwillie ably seconded her husband's efforts by forming the Jean Armour Club, which under her presidency has laboured all these years wholeheartedly for the success of the great work. Inspiring and cheery when the hours were darkest, only the indomitable courage of the Scot could have carried the work through the dark days of 1914. When the war clouds swept over us and the storm broke over the world, Detroit was a border city, and, when the call to arms sounded the Scots crossed to Canada and cast in their lot with the motherland. The sons and daughters of Scotia gave themselves and all they had to the cause, and the statue had to take second place. But when the storm clouds had been swept away, their work was resumed and carried to a successful finish. We, as Clansmen, must feel proud that, in spite of the tremendous handicap, Scottish grit made possible what Major Couzens said was the greatest day Detroit had ever seen."

DEVON, THE.

A small stream that rises in the Ochil Hills and joins the river Forth at Alloa. The Falls near the village of Crook of Devon, are rugged and romantic, while the foliage and scenery along the banks are extremely beautiful and abundant. It was at Harviestoun in Clackmannanshire, near the Devon, that Burns, while on his Highland Tour in 1787, was introduced to Charlotte Hamilton, and it was she who inspired the song, " The Banks of the Devon," as well as the last song that the poet composed, " Fairest Maid on Devon Banks." These two songs have immortalized the Devon.

DICK, JAMES C.   The Songs of Robert Burns.

Now first printed with the melodies for which they were written.   A study in Tone-Poetry.   With Bibliography, Historical Notes and Glossary.   London, 1903.

Contents : Love Songs, Personal, General, and Humorous ; Connubial ; Bacchanalian and Social ; Patriotic and Political ; Jacobite ; and Miscellaneous.

The most complete collection of data in connection with the tunes of Burns's songs in existence.

DOON, THE.

This river flows from Loch Doon on the borders of Ayrshire and Kirkcudbrightshire, and separates the Ayrshire districts of Carrick and Kyle.   Immortalized by Burns in his song, " The Banks o' Doon " (q.v.)—" Ye banks and braes o' bonnie Doon."   He was born almost on its banks, and it is frequently mentioned in his writings, notably in " Tam o' Shanter."   There is a great wealth of scenery all along its course.   It terminates in the Firth of Clyde, about two miles from Ayr.

DOONHOLM.

In the poet's autobiography he tell us : " For the first six or seven years of my life, my father was gardener to a worthy gentleman of small estate in the neighbourhood of Ayr."

This gentleman was Dr. William Fergusson, of Doonholm, a retired London physician, who became Provost of Ayr. The estate of Doonholm is on the river Doon, in the parish of Ayr, and is romantically situated. An avenue of elms, said to have been planted by William Burness, adds considerable beauty to the place.

DOUGLAS, ALBERT (Washington, U.S.A.).

Index to the Burns Chronicle, from No. 1 (1892) to No. XXX (1921). (With Portrait). Dumfries, 1921.

" With obvious propriety I dedicate this index and my work upon it to Duncan M'Naught, one of the founders of the Burns Federation, for long its honoured president, and for some thirty years the wise and able editor of the Burns Chronicle."—From the Preface.

DOWIE'S TAVERN, LIBERTON WYND EDINBURGH, JOHNNIE.

A favourite howff of the poet, during his stay in the Scottish Capital. Here he is said to have spent many happy hours in the company of Allan Masterton, William Nicol and others. In a small room, christened either by himself or some wit " The Coffin," he composed a few of his songs, " O Poortith Cauld " being among the number. The tavern was for many years a rendezvous for Edinburgh lawyers and writers and was specially noted for such delicacies as North Loch trout and Welsh rabbits, in addition to all kinds of " Guid Scotch drink." Dowie was well liked by his patrons. " Mine host," says a recent writer, " decked out with his cocked hat, knee and shoe buckles and cross-headed cane, was none too grand to draw the cork of his brown ale and fill for his guests the long slender glasses. His tavern was a house of much respectability. He was himself a conscientious, worthy man, and the majority of his customers were social, but neither intemperate nor debauched in their enjoyments. The moment twelve o'clock struck in St. Giles's, not another cork would he draw. In answer to the demand for ' Another bottle, John '—his reply invariably was : ' Gentlemen, 'tis past twelve and time to go home.' "

Dowie died in 1817. He left a considerable fortune to his son, a Major in the army at the time. The place was known for many years afterwards as " Burns's Tavern." It was demolished many years ago.

DRUMLANRIG CASTLE.

Lies about seventeen miles from Dumfries, on the right bank of the river Nith and close to the town of Thornhill. It dates back to 1679 and its site on a terrace overlooking the river is very grand and imposing. In the poet's time the Castle was the residence of

William, fourth Duke of Queensberry, a nobleman to whom Burns was politically and otherwise bitterly opposed. In this connection
see his poems " On the Duke of Queensberry,"
" Verses on the Destruction of the Woods near
Drumlanrig," and " How shall I sing Drumlanrig's Grace ? "—John M'Murdo, the poet's
friend, was Chamberlain to the Duke for many
years.

DRUMMOSSIE MOOR. See Culloden.

DUMFRIES.

Queen of the South. A royal and
parliamentary burgh on the banks of the
Nith. Distant from Edinburgh nearly
seventy-one miles. In early times
the city suffered much from border
wars and raiders, as well as from
trained English troops sent against it in 1448,
1536, and 1570. It was here in the ancient
Franciscan friary, that Robert Bruce in 1306
slew the Red Comyn. Many years elapsed
before the neighbourhood was entirely free
of border warfare, but gradually peace prevailed, and to-day Dumfries is a beautiful and
prosperous city of about twenty thousand
inhabitants enjoying all modern inventions
and improvements, and is commercially noted
for its output of fine tweeds, hosiery and
woollen goods of all descriptions. It is also
celebrated the world over, for its connections

and memories of Robert Burns and perhaps more especially so on account of the mortal remains of the poet being for ever entrusted to its care.

Burns and his family took up their residence in Dumfries towards the end of 1791. " With a tearful eye," says Allan Cunningham, " he had bade a final adieu to pleasant Ellisland, leaving nothing there but a putting-stone, with which he loved to exercise his strength, a memory of his musings that can never die, and three hundred pounds of his money sunk beyond redemption in a speculation from which all had augured happiness." " A great change it must have been," writes Principal Shairp, " to pass from the pleasant holms and broomy banks of the Nith at Ellisland to a town home in the Wee Vennel of Dumfries. It was, moreover, a confession visible to the world of what Burns himself had long felt, that his endeavour to combine the actual and the ideal, his natural calling as a farmer with the exercise of his gift as a poet, had failed, and that henceforth he must submit to a round of toil, which neither in itself nor in its surroundings, had anything to redeem it from commonplace drudgery. He must have felt, from the time when he first became Exciseman, that he had parted company with all thought of steadily working out his ideal, and that whatever he might now do in that way must be by random snatches. To his proud spirit the name of gauger must have been gall and wormwood, and it is much to his credit that for the sake of his wife and children he was content to undergo what he often felt to be a social obloquy."

Burns was no stranger, however, to Dumfries when he settled there. His first appearance in the city was on the 4th June, 1787, when he arrived on the invitation to be made a burgess. The ticket issued to him reads :— "The said day, 4th June, 1787, Mr. Robert Burns, Ayrshire, was admitted burgess of the burgh, with liberty to exercise and enjoy the whole immunities and privileges thereof, as freely as any other does, may, or can enjoy, who being present accepted the same, and gave his oath of burgess-ship to his Majesty and the burgh in common form."

The first home occupied by the family consisted of three rooms on the second floor of a three storey house in the Wee Vennel. Here they remained for about eighteen months, after which they moved into a self-contained house in Mill Street, now appropriately named Burns Street. For an account of these houses see under " Dumfries Houses occupied by Burns."

On taking up his residence in Dumfries, Burns was well received by the townspeople and the neighbouring gentry. While devoting the necessary time to his duties as

Excise Officer, he also found opportunity to enter into the social and political activities of the town, and he soon became a welcome guest, whether in the cottage, the mansion or at the tavern.   In a letter written during the first year at Dumfries, to show how his time was being occupied, he says : " Hurry of business, grinding the faces of the publican and sinner on the merciless wheels of the Excise, making ballads, and then drinking and singing them ; and above all, correcting the press of two different publications."   " But besides these duties by day and the convivialities by night, there were other calls on his time and strength," says Principal Shairp, " to which Burns was by his reputation exposed. When those of the country gentry whom he still knew were in Dumfries for some hours, or when any party of strangers passing through the town had an idle evening on their hands, it seems to have been their custom to summon Burns to assist them in spending it ; and he was weak enough on receiving the message, to leave his home and adjourn to the Globe, the George, or the King's Arms, there to drink with them late into night, and waste his powers for their amusement. . . . . .   It would have been well if, on these occasions, the pride he boasted of had stood him in better stead, and repelled such unjustifiable intrusions.   But in this, as in so many other respects, Burns was the most inconsistent of men."

Yet with all these social faults, as they may be termed, in addition to the many uncongenial duties connected with the Excise, he never neglected the Muse, and the number and quality of matchless songs produced during the Dumfries period is simply marvellous. But this was not all. For Thomson's "Select Melodies" and Johnson's "Scots Musical Museum," he continued to furnish original and other matter until within a few days of his death, and without the help which he rendered to those two publications at the time, they would probably be practically unknown to-day.

"Duncan Gray," "What can a young Lassie," "Ae fond Kiss," "O wert thou in the cauld blast," "My Love is like a red red Rose," "Auld Lang Syne," "Flow gently sweet Afton," "The Lassie wi' the lint white locks," "O whistle and I'll come to ye my lad," "A Man's a Man for a' that," "Bruce's Address," "The Soldier's return," "Love will venture in," and many others were the work of what has been termed "The dark days of Dumfries."

"Had Burns done nothing more than elevate the ministrelsy of his native country, he would have done a grand service to what is now the land of song, and earned an undying place in its literature," writes Dr. Peter Ross

in " All About Burns." " Scotland had many
song-writers before Burns, but most of their
songs were of the lips ; Burns's lyrics were of
the heart, went to the heart, and were sung
back from the hearts of those who re-uttered
them. ' The song,' writes Carlyle, ' he sings
is not of fantasticalities ; it is a thing felt,
really there. The prime merit of his singing,
as of all in him, and of his life generally, is
truth.' In another place Carlyle classes
Burns as the greatest man of his century, and
ascribes to him all the attributes of pre-
eminence among men—the greatness of the
seer, a prophet, a leader ; and all that high-
standard greatness is now accorded to the
bard of Ayr by the world at large. But with
Dumfries came the end. It is the custom,
as well it might be, to lament the untimely
death of the poet ; a man is so young at thirty-
seven, has apparently so many more years
of his life in him that to be cut off at that age
seems pitiful. In Burns's circumstances, in
the helpless condition of his wife and
family it was especially pitiful. There
was no sign of mental weakening as the
light of life neared the socket. The light
the life gave out was as clear and pure, purer
even than it had ever been, yet the signs of
doom were evident to many from the beginning of the Dumfries period, some four years
before the end. Burns's early death had
been foretold from his boyhood, and had he
been merely a wise man he would have pre-

pared for it.   He never had himself any hope of length of days, but it was only for a year before he passed away and particularly after the death, in the autumn of 1795, of his little daughter, Elizabeth, who seems to have been his especial pet, that he himself had an admonition that the end was rapidly coming, that his constitution was shattered beyond hope. rheumatic fever and irregular hours fostered by remorse, despondency and, it must be confessed, a desire to be blind to the future, made up a combination that even the strongest frame would not be proof against, and when hope fled from his breast the end advanced with rapid strides.   Like his father his last hours were embittered by the importunities of creditors, and amid it all his once independent spirit broke down.   Nine days before he died he penned his last song— " Fairest Maid on Devon Banks "—and laid aside his harp forever.   Appeals for help to George Thomson, the recipient of so many of his songs, and to a cousin in Montrose, were his last efforts with his pen, excepting a piteous message to his wife's father to send Mrs. Armour to her daughter's bedside. Then he surrendered himself to the gloom that was now gathering so fast ; delirium set in, and with scathing, muttered words on his lips against a petty creditor, who, he imagined, was threatening him with legal proceedings, the greatest of Scotland's poets went out beyond the darkness and the veil, and took his place among the immortals.

He died on July 21st, 1796, and on the 25th, four days later, Dumfries gave him a grand funeral, a sort of public pageant with military, a band playing "The Dead March," and sympathizing spectators lining the streets— bestowed on the inanimated clay the respect that had been withheld from the Man. There is no doubt that his fate was mourned in Dumfries, and that the hearts of the people went out in the profoundest sympathy to his widow, who, as the melancholy procession was wending its way to St. Michael's Kirk- yard, gave birth to a son. But the wail of Dumfries was nothing to be compared to that of Scotland when it was known that the sweetest of her singers had departed. With true Scottish sympathy—practical and easily understood—no time was lost in putting the widow and little ones beyond the reach of want, and then commenced the pæan of praise which is still heard, and is still gathering in volume, for the rare life that had been vouchsafed to Scotland, for that genius which had interpreted Scotland to the world as it had never been interpreted before.

There are numerous places of special inter- est in and around Dumfries to the lover or student of Burns which will amply repay a visit. The Mid Steeple; the houses in which he lived, and especially the one in which he

died ; the Mausoleum ; St. Michael's Churchyard ; the Globe and other taverns ; the
Town Hall ; the Burns Statue, etc.

The Burns Federation held its Annual
Conference in the city in 1899 and again in
1924.

Dumfries Burns Club.

Instituted 18th January, 1820 ; federated
1913 ; number 226. The special features
of the Club are—To maintain the Burns Mausoleum in good repair and provide for its proper
supervision—To discharge the obligations
laid upon the Club by the testamentary disposition of Colonel William Nicol Burns with
respect to Burns's House and the Mausoleum
—To celebrate in suitable manner the Anniversary of the Poet's birth, and to honour his
memory in such other ways as may be from
time to time determined—To foster a knowledge of the life and works of Burns by means
of an annual competition amongst local
school children, prizes being awarded to the
successful competitors. The club has been in
all respects a successful organization from
the first and has carefully and honourably
fulfilled the trusts given to its charge. The
present membership is about two hundred
and fifty.

DUMFRIES, BURNS HOWFF CLUB.

Instituted 1889; federated 1899 ; number 112 ; 130 members. Meets in the Globe Hotel first Wednesday of each month during the winter. A well-established and progressive club and deeply interested in all matters connected with Burns and the city.

DUMFRIES. Houses occupied by Burns.

The first house occupied by Burns and his family on their settling in Dumfries about the end of 1791, consisted of three small rooms, one stair up, in a three-storey building situated in the Wee Vennel, now named Bank Street. The central room, about the size of a small bed closet, was furnished and fitted up by the poet as a study. On the ground floor John Syme had his office for the distribution of stamps, while the top storey served as a residence for the family of George Hough, a well-known blacksmith in the town. On the opposite side of the street resided Captain Hamilton, the poet's landlord, a gentleman of many sterling qualities, who frequently invited the poet and his wife to join him at a Sunday dinner. The house in Bank Street is still standing, but alterations have been made from time to time in the interior. Late in 1793, the family moved to a self-contained house in Mill Street (now appropriately named " Burns Street"), the rental for which was eight pounds per annum.

It consisted of two storeys and contained the usual kitchen, parlour and three or four small rooms. According to the testimony of Robert Burns, junior, given to Mr. Robert Chambers, " the house in Mill Street was of a good order, such as were occupied at that time by the better class of burgesses ; and his father and mother led a life that was comparatively genteel. They always had a maid-servant, and sat in their parlour. That apartment, together with two bedrooms, was well furnished and carpeted ; and when good company assembled, which was often the case, the hospitable board which they surrounded was of a patrician mahogany. There was much rough comfort in the house, not to have been found in those of ordinary citizens ; for the poet received many presents of game and country produce from the rural gentlefolk, besides occasional barrels of oysters from Hill, Cunningham, and other friends in town ; so that he possibly was as much envied by some of his neighbours as he has since been pitied by the general body of his countrymen." " The second storey of the house contained two rooms, the smaller one being the bedroom in which the poet died. This room is now set aside as a Museum for Burns relics as well as for the sale of souvenirs. The place is kept in excellent order by the present caretaker, and is in charge of the Dumfries Burns Club. The house adjoins the building known as the Industrial or Ragged School, and in a niche in front of this building the late Mr. William Ewart, M.P. at one time for the Dumfries burghs, caused to be placed a bust of the poet and the inscription : ' In the adjoining house to the North, lived and died the Poet of his Country and of Mankind, Robert Burns.' "

DUMFRIES PUBLIC LIBRARY.

A public library had been established by subscription among the citizens of Dumfries in September, 1792, and Burns, ever eager about books, had been from the first one of its supporters. Before it was a week old he had presented to it a copy of his poems. He does not seem to have been a regular admitted member till 5th March, 1793, when "the committee, by a great majority, resolved to offer to Mr. Robert Burns a share in the library, free of any admission money (10s 6d) and the quarterly contributions (2s 6d) to this date, out of respect and esteem for his abilities as a literary man ; and they directed the secretary to make this known to Mr. Burns as soon as possible, that the application which they understood he was about to make in the ordinary way might be anticipated." This is a pleasing testimony to Burns as a citizen and member of society. His name appears in September as a member of committee—an honour assigned by vote of the members. He presented to the library four volumes of books, as some acknowledgment for his being elected a free member of the library. One volume—" De Lolme on the English Constitution "—has an inscription in the Poet's handwriting on the fly leaf : —" Mr. Burns presents this book to the Library, and begs they will take it as a creed of British liberty, until they find a better.— R.B. " Fearing the inscription might be quoted to his prejudice, he pasted the fly-leaf to the engraving. Another volume—" The Statistical Account of Scotland," by Sir John Sinclair. (Vol. XII.) At page 652, under the head " Balmaghie," reference is made to several persons who suffered as martyrs for the Covenant. The simple statement seems to have struck a responsive chord in the Poet's breast for he has left a remembrance of the famous " Solemn League and Covenant " verse, pencilled as a foot note, on the margin.

DUMFRIES STATUE.

The work of Mrs. D. O. Hill of Edinburgh, a sister of Sir Noel Paton. Unveiled by Lord Rosebery, 6th April, 1882. The figure is pure white marble, rising nine feet in height, and representing the poet in a half sitting attitude, resting against a tree trunk. The right arm is placed over the heart, while the left holds a cluster of daisies. The dress is such as he might have worn while following the plough at Mossgiel. The monument is embellished by numerous figures, including the ever faithful Luath, a bonnet, a shepherd's pipe, a book, thistles, and a couple of mice. On the South face of the pedestal is the inscription :—" Erected by the inhabitants of Dumfries (With the aid of many friends) as a loving tribute to their fellow-townsman, the National Poet of Scotland. 6th April, 1882." The other panels contain mottoes from the works of the poet, representing patriotism, philanthropy and philosophy.

The monument occupies a prominent position in Church Place, at the head of the High Street, and is quite a centre of interest for the thousands of Burns lovers and others, who annually visit the historical and now celebrated town.

As it stands, the monument is, no doubt, an ornament to the town, but as a " Burns Memorial," it has been severely criticised by various authorities. In " Robert Burns and Dumfries," by Philip Sulley, the Hon. Secretary of the Dumfries Centenary Celebration, 1896, the author says : " ' This statue of our greatest King of Song '—and a poor statue it is. The commission was given to Mrs. D. O. Hill, sister of Sir Noel Paton. Her small model was sent to Italy to be carved in marble, of considerable more than life size, ' by Carrara artists.' Such a production could scarcely be a success, and this is far from it. The limbs are disproportioned, and while there may be a certain resemblance in face and feature, the expression is stolid, vacant, meaningless, certainly not the inspired, commanding look of Burns. The base is crowded with inartistic, paltry details—a bonnet, shepherd's pipe of an Italian type, mice, daisies, and thistle, while the alleged collie defies description."

DUMFRIES VOLUNTEERS. See under Volunteers.

DUNCAN GRAY.

There are two versions of this popular song, the first beginning " Weary fa' you Duncan Gray," being simply the old song remodelled by Burns for the " Museum." The second version, which has been termed " a masterpiece in poetic lore," is wholly original except the first and third lines. Burns says in regard to the air of the song :— " Duncan Gray is that kind of light-horse gallop of an air which precludes sentiment. The ludicrous is its ruling feature." The Hon. Andrew Erskine, wrote to Burns: "' Duncan Gray' possesses native, genuine humour. ' Spak o' lowpin ' o'er a linn,' is a line in itself that should make you immortal."

DUNDEE STATUE.

Unveiled 16th October, 1880. The sculptor was Sir John Steell, R.S.A. Engraved on the pedestal is the verse beginning, " Thou ling'ring star," and on the base is the inscription, " Inaugurated 16th October, 1880."

DUNEDIN, NEW ZEALAND.

Statue unveiled 24th May, 1887, by Miss Burns, a great-grand-niece of the poet and a grand-daughter of the Rev. Dr. Burns. The oration was delivered by the Governor of New Zealand, Sir George Gray. The statue is a replica of Sir John Steell's work for New York, Dundee, and London. It was subscribed for by the Scottish residents of Dunedin and the surrounding neighbourhood. The pedestal bears the inscription " Robert Burns, 25th January, 1759—21st July, 1796."

DUNOON, HIGHLAND MARY STATUE. See under Highland Mary Statue at Dunoon.

DUNFERMLINE.

A royal burgh in Fifeshire, 16 miles N.W. of Edinburgh. The principal attraction in the town is the Abbey, founded in 1072, and in which were interred the bodies of Robert Bruce, and other Scottish Kings. There are many modern fine buildings throughout the city, and the Public, or, Carnegie Library with its notable and exceedingly valuable collection of Burnsiana is quite a feature in itself. Most of the Burnsiana is the celebrated Murison Collection of books and manuscripts. This collection, after being purchased by Sir Alexander Gibb, was presented by him to the Library and here every facility is provided for the convenience of admirers and students of the poet to consult them. The staple industry of the burgh is damask linen, known everywhere for its superiority over other linens.   It was in Dunfermline in 1650 that Charles II. signed the Covenant.   The place is entirely changed since the day on which the poet and his friend, Dr. James M'Kitterick, visited it in 1787. " At Dunfermline we visited the Abbey Church now consecrated to Presbyterian Worship. Here I mounted the cutty stool, or stool of repentance, while Burns addressed to me a ludicrous reproof and exhortation, parodied from one that had been delivered at one time in Ayrshire. In the church, two broad flagstones marked the grave of Robert Bruce, for whose memory Burns had more than common veneration. He knelt and kissed the stone with sacred fervour, and heartily execrated the worse than Gothic neglect of the first of the Scottish heroes."

The Burns Federation honoured the town by holding its annual conferences within its borders in 1909 and again in 1921. The Dunfermline United Burns Club is a select body of men who meet in annual session in the Masonic Temple each January. The Club was instituted in 1818 and federated 1896. Its number on the Federation Roll is 85.

DUNS.

Burns, while on his Border Tour in 1787, made stops at least on two occasions. In his Journal he writes—" Sunday May 6th, Went to Church at Dunse," and "Wednesday, May 16th, Dine at Dunse with the Farmers' Club company—impossible to do them justice." His calling at the town a second time would indicate that he had been well received on his former visit.

Duns is the centre of a great farming district. It was founded in 1588 and derives its name from an even older town which was situated near the top of Duns Law, a hill which rises at one point to a height of six hundred and thirty feet. It is a cleanly town with wide streets, a Public Library opened in 1875 ; public schools, etc. Both the town and the district figure to a large extent in the old border wars. The spelling Dunse was officially altered in 1882 to Duns.

E

EARNOCK MSS., The.

Consists of the correspondence between Messrs Cadell & Davis and Gilbert Burns in connection with the latter's edition of his brother's works. Also correspondence concerning Dr. Currie's edition and Cromek's " Relics of Burns," in addition to letters, etc. from William Roscoe, T. Stewart, George Thomson, Mr. Riddell and others. These manuscripts were contained in three volumes and belonged to Sir John Watson, Bart., of Earnock. After Sir John's death in 1889 the volumes were sold by auction and taken to America. A full account of the contents of the volumes will be found in the " Burns Chronicle," vols. 7 and 8.

ECCLEFECHAN.

A small village in Dumfriesshire. Noted as the birthplace of Thomas Carlyle.

Burns visited the village on at least two occasions of which we have a record. On one of these he was snow bound and employed part of the time in writing the following letter to George Thomson.

Ecclefechan, February 7, 1795.

My Dear Thomson,—You cannot have any idea of the predicament in which I write you.   In the course of my duty as Supervisor (in which capacity I have acted of late) I came yesternight to this unfortunate, wicked, little village. I have gone forward, but snows of ten feet deep have impeded my progress : I have tried to *gae back the gate I cam again,* but the same obstacle has shut me up within insuperable bars. To add to my misfortune, since dinner, a scraper has been torturing cat-gut, in sounds that would have insulted the dying agonies of a sow under the hand of a Butcher, and thinks himself, *on that very account,* exceeding good company. In fact, I have been in a dilemma, either to get drunk, to forget these miseries, or to hang myself, to get rid of them ; like a prudent man (a character congenial to my every thought, word, and deed), I, of two evils, have chosen the least, and am very drunk, at your service !

I wrote you yesterday from Dumfries. I had not time then to tell you all I wanted to say ; and, Heaven knows, at present I have not capacity.

Do you know an air—I am sure you must know it—" We'll gang nae mair to yon town ? " I think, in slowish time, it would make an excellent song. I am highly delighted with it ; and if you should think it worthy of your attention, I have a fair dame in my eye to whom I would consecrate it; try it with this doggerel, until I give you a better. You will find a good set of it in Bowie's collection.

There is also a song by Burns entitled " The Lass of Ecclefechan," beginning, " Gat ye me, O gat ye me."

Mr. John Muir, F.S.A. Scot. in 1896, published a very interesting little book entitled " Burns at Galston and Ecclefechan," which is now out of print and very scarce.

EDINA.

A poetical form of the name, Edinburgh. The first to so designate the Scottish Capital was George Buchanan (1506-1582). Burns adopted it for his " Address to Edinburgh," and Byron uses it in his " English Bards and Scotch Reviewers."

EDINBURGH.

Burns arrived in Edinburgh from Mossgiel on Tuesday evening, 28th November, 1786, and immediately arranged to lodge with his old Mauchline friend, John Richmond, in Baxter's Close, Lawnmarket. He was fresh from the applause that had greeted his Kilmarnock volume, and the principal object of his visit to the Scottish Capital at this time, was to secure a publisher for a new, and enlarged edition of his poems. The first few days after his arrival were spent in loitering about the city, visiting the Castle, Arthur's Seat, Holyrood Palace, the Parliament Buildings and other places of interest.

Before leaving Ayrshire, he had dined with Professor Dugald Stewart at Catrine House and had been introduced by him to Sir John Whitefoord and to Lord Daer. These gentlemen were now in Edinburgh, and he felt assured that their influence would be invaluable to him, especially in his search for a publisher. In due time, he, therefore, made his presence in the city known to them, and they at once introduced him to other influential persons, and he soon found himself the centre of an ever increasing circle of admiring friends. About this time a very favourable notice of his poems appeared in the " Lounger," written by Henry Mackenzie, author of " The Man of Feeling," and this very materially helped in increasing his reputation as one of the best of all the poets born in Scotland. Invitations to dine with persons prominent in society, and to visit at Masonic Assemblies began to pour in on him, and at one of the latter he was hailed by the presiding officer as " Caledonia's Bard " (q.v.), an unexpected honour which he dearly appreciated at the moment. In the homes of society he took his place at the table without hesitation, and he astonished the company around him by the correctness of his expression, the soundness of his opinions and the brilliancy of his humour. Even the Duchess of Gordon acknowledged that he was the only man she ever met whose conversation carried her off her feet, while others wondered and were unable to comprehend how an unlettered ploughman, as he was called, could move them to tears or laughter without any seemingly great effort on his part.

" It needs no effort of imagination," says Mr. Lockhart, " to conceive what the sensations of an isolated set of scholars (almost all either clergymen or professors) must have been in the presence of this big-boned, black-browed, brawny stranger, with his great flashing eyes, who, having forced his way among them from the plough-tail at a single stride, manifested, in the whole strain of his bearing and conversation, a most thorough conviction, that, in the society of the most eminent men of his nation, he was exactly where he was entitled to be ; hardly deigned to flatter them by exhibiting even an occasional symptom of being flattered by their notice ; by turns calmly measured himself against the most cultivated understandings of his time in discussion ; overpowered the " bon mots " of the most celebrated con-vivialists by broad floods of merriment, impregnated with all the burning life of genius ; astounded bosoms habitually enveloped in the thrice-plied folds of social reserve by compelling them to tremble—nay to tremble visibly—beneath the fearless touch of natural pathos ; and all this without indicating the smallest willingness to be ranked among those professional ministers of excitement, who are content to be paid in money and smiles for doing what the spectators and auditors would be ashamed of doing in their own persons, even if they had the power of doing it."

Writing to Gavin Hamilton on the 7th December, Burns says :

> " For my own affairs, I am in a fair way of becoming as eminent as Thomas à Kempis or John Bunyan ; and you may expect henceforth to see my birth-day inserted among the wonderful events in the Poor Robin's and Aberdeen Almanacks."

Among the more prominent persons to whom Burns had been introduced, was the Earl of Glencairn, a man to whom he always acknowledged himself as greatly indebted, and this nobleman who had considerable influence with William Creech, the Edinburgh publisher, induced the latter to undertake the publishing of the new volume of poems. He also prevailed upon the members of the Caledonian Hunt to subscribe for a hundred copies of the work, while various parties gladly helped the matter along by subscribing for ten, twenty and fifty copies each, and in the beginning of April (1787), what is known as the " First Edinburgh Edition of Burns " made its appearance. Nearly fifteen hundred copies at least had already been subscribed for and the entire edition of three thousand copies was exhausted within a few weeks. From this source the poet received altogether some four hundred pounds, and of this sum he advanced one hundred and eighty to help his brother Gilbert who was still struggling with the farm at Mossgiel. " This fact," writes Dr. Peter Ross, " is not very prominently remembered by the maligners of his character, but we cannot help thinking that, even in a Christian land, one man as soon as he earned a few hundred pounds, giving nearly half of it to assist a struggling brother, is an action seldom heard of." "The volume was published by subscription ' for the sole benefit of the Author,' says Principal Shairp, "and the subscribers were so numerous that the list of them covered thirty-eight pages. In that list appeared the names of many of the chief men of Scotland, some of whom subscribed for twenty—Lord Eglinton for as many as forty-two, copies. Chambers thinks that full justice has never been done to the liberality of the Scottish public in the way they subscribed for this volume. Nothing equal to the patronage that Burns at this time met with had been seen since the days of Pope's Iliad."

After making one or two trips to the Highlands and other parts of Scotland while awaiting a final settlement with his publisher Burns turned his thoughts towards procuring a farm, and in due time leased that of Ellisland (q.v.), near Dumfries, where later and in anticipation of much domestic happiness he settled down with the wife of his choice—Jean Armour.

During the visit to Edinburgh the celebrated Clarinda episode (q.v.) occurred, but this had no lasting effect on the poet after he entered upon the occupancy of Ellisland farm, although he paid her a final visit, shortly after he went to live in Dumfries.

Among the poems and songs produced while in Edinburgh, exclusive of those inspired by Clarinda, were the " Address to Edinburgh," " Address to a Haggis," the " Birthday Ode," " Verses to Miss Logan," the first version of " The Banks o' Doon," " Reply to the Gudewife of Wauchope House," and the inscription on the tombstone of Robert Fergusson.

EDINBURGH JOURNAL, The. See Common-Place Books.

EDINBURGH MONUMENT.

Not among the largest by any means but among the most interesting must be reckoned the Burns monument, which occupies a high position near its yet higher neighbour, the Nelson monument, on Calton Hill. The Burns monument was built in 1830 for the purpose of containing a marble statue of the poet by Flaxman (q.v.). The building, of freestone, is a circular temple on a quadrangular basement surrounded by a peristyle of twelve Corinthian columns which support an entablature and cornice. Over this is a cupola, a restoration of the monument of Lysicrates at Athens. The whole is surmounted by a tripod supported by winged griffins. The extreme height of the structure is fifty feet the twelve outside columns are fourteen feet high and the twelve inside columns are ten feet high. The latter are of freestone painted to represent variegated marble. The cost of the monument and statue was three thousand three hundred pounds sterling, not a large sum considering the result attained.

ELBOW TAVERN, The. Mauchline.

One of the places mentioned as a resort which the poet frequented in his day, but now only a memory. While there is no doubt that such a tavern did exist at the time, there is positively no direct evidence connecting Burns or his name, or any of his friends' names, with it in any way. The place where it stood is still pointed out to the curious in such matters when visiting the now famous little town.

ELLISLAND.

The farm of Ellisland is romantically situated on the banks of the Nith, six and a half miles N.W. from Dumfries. In 1777 it was one of three farms belonging to Patrick Miller of Dalswinton, and extended to one-hundred and sixty acres. It was an ideal location in all respects for a poet to dwell on, but it was other than what a practical farmer at the time would have decided on, for his particular purpose. The soil was stony and impoverished, while the dwelling house,

and other small buildings, were dilapidated
and greatly in need of repairs. Burns became
possessed of the farm on the 13th of June,
1788, but did not begin to occupy it until
late in the following summer. The lease
was to run for seventy-seven years at fifty
pounds per annum for the first three years, and
seventy pounds per annum for the remain-
der of the term. Three hundred pounds,
is said to have been allowed by the landlord,
towards the expense of a new dwelling house
and repairs on the other buildings. The
story is told of how the poet with his wife
(in compliance with an old custom or tradition) walked arm in arm, smiling to each other,
to the new home, proceeded by a young servant girl, bearing a Bible on which was placed
a bowl of salt, a ceremony intended to pro-
pitiate the Fates, and bring good luck and
prosperity to the new household.

After the first few months, it seems, Burns
began to entertain serious doubts as to his
making Ellisland a successful and paying
farm. According to Robert Heron, " a lease
was granted to the poetical farmer at the
annual rent which his own friends declared
that the due cultivation of his farm might
easily enable him to pay. But these friends,
being Ayrshiremen, were little acquainted
with the soil, with the manures, with the
markets, with the dairies, with the modes of
improvement in Dumfriesshire ; they had

estimated his rental at Ayrshire rates, so that contrary to his Landlord's intentions he must pay more for Ellisland than Ellisland was worth." Burns, we know, was a diligent farmer. He worked early and late, in the beginning at any rate, to make Ellisland yield a living with a margin for emergencies, but the fates seemed combined to defeat him at every turn. He once remarked that " the soil was a mixture of boulders and loam and after a shower of rain had fallen on a field of new-sown barley, it looked like a paved street." He at last relinquished the idea of farming and resolved to turn his holdings into a dairy farm to be conducted by Mrs. Burns, and he made application to Mr. Graham of Fintry, Commissioner of Excise in the district, for an appointment as exciseman, a request that was at once complied with, for shortly afterwards he was appointed to the charge of ten parishes. About the end of 1790 he had concluded that " Ellisland was altogether a ruinous business," and he decided to surrender his lease and move into a smaller home. He therefore applied for a new appointment in the Dumfries district so that he could get away from farm life altogether. His salary of fifty pounds a year, he argued to himself, would be sufficient to support his little family until he would be promoted to a higher position. In the meantime, " Fifty pounds a year, and a pension for widows and

orphans, you will allow, is no bad settlement,"
he wrote to Lady Glencairn. Again his friend,
Graham of Fintry, was applied to and he
secured for the poet an appointment in the
Dumfries Division of Excise, with a salary
of seventy pounds a year, besides other per-
quisites. "I may perhaps see you about
Martinmas," he wrote to his friend Peter Hill,
about this time, "I have sold to my landlord
the lease of my farm and as I roup off ever-
thing then, I have a mind to take a week's
excursion to see old acquaintance . . . I am
now ranked on the list as a supervisor . . . the
appointment is worth from one to two
hundred a year, according to the place of the
country in which one is settled. I have not
been so lucky in my farming. Mr. Miller's
kindness has been just such another as
Creech's, his meddling vanity, a busy fiend,
still making work his selfish craft must mend."

In December, 1791, Burns and his family
took final leave of Ellisland and went to
reside in a house in the Wee Vennel, Dumfries
(q.v.).

Among the many warm friendships that
the poet found during his stay at Ellisland were
the members of the Riddell family and Captain Grose. His Muse had been prolific to a
wonderful extent while there and among the
more prominent of the compositions of this
period are " Tam o' Shanter," " Of a' the
Airts the wind can blaw," " O were I on

Parnassus Hill," " Epistle to Hugh Parker,"
" Auld Lang Syne," " I hae a wife o' my ain,"
" Address to a wounded Hare," " Address to
the Toothache," " Willie brewed a peck o'
Maut," " Lament on Mary Queen of Scots "—
sufficient to have rendered his name immortal,
had he never written another line.

ELLISLAND FARM FOR THE NATION.

An interesting announcement, which will
be read with interest by Scots at home and
abroad, was made at the annual dinner of the
Edinburgh Burns Club on 25th January, 1923, that Ellisland, the well-known
Dumfriesshire farm associated with Scotland's
national poet, has been presented to the
nation.

Ellisland was purchased in 1921 by Mr.
George Williamson, a former President of
the Club, whose death occurred but a few
months afterwards. It was one of his last
public-spirited acts to instruct his brother,
Mr. John Williamson, a member of the Edinburgh Burns Club, to have the property
handed over to the nation as a permanent
centre of Burns interest and repository for
Burns relics.

The Rev. Dr. Wallace Williamson, the
Dean of the Thistle and Chapel Royal, who
made the intimation, narrated how the late
Mr. George Williamson, thirty years ago,
remarked to his brother, that if Ellisland ever

came into the market it would be an interesting place to secure for the nation. Some
time ago an intimation appeared in the Press
that the property was for sale, and immediately
afterwards came the announcement that it
had been purchased by Mr. George Williamson. Before his death Mr. Williamson took
steps to put into concrete form the desire
which he himself had expressed so many years
ago, and he told his brother what his wishes
were in regard to Ellisland. Dr. Wallace
Williamson congratulated the Edinburgh Club
on the honour of announcing this gift to the
nation. Ellisland, after certain things, necessary and fitting, were done, was to be handed
over to the burgh of Dumfries as the property
of the nation, to remain for ever in the national
possession a centre for Burns interests. A
farmhouse, suitable for residence, was to be
built, but in no respect were the buildings, as
they were in Burns's time to be interfered
with, and the authorities of the burgh of Dumfries, the Sheriff, and other legal officers, and
others, were to be the permanent trustees of
the property on behalf of the nation. He
thanked Mr. John Williamson, who was
present with them that night, and expressed
gratitude for what the late Mr. George
Williamson had done to make this great gift
possible

An interesting feature of the menu card for
this dinner was a striking illustration of

Ellisland, showing its beautiful situation on the river Nith.

EPISTLE TO DAVIE, A brother Poet.

David Sillar, to whom this epistle was addressed, was a native of Tarbolton, a poet and scholar. " Among the earliest of Robert's poems," says Gilbert Burns, " was the epistle to Davie. Robert often composed without any regular plan. When anything made a strong impression on his mind, so as to rouse it to any poetic exertion, he would give way to the impulse, and embody the thought in rhyme. If he hit on two or three stanzas to please him, he would then think of proper introductory, connecting, and con- cluding stanzas ; hence the middle of the poem was often first produced. It was, I think, in the summer of 1784, when, in the interval of harder labour, Robert and I were weeding in the garden, that he repeated to me the principal part of this epistle. I believe the first idea of Robert's becoming an author was started on this occasion. I was much pleased with the epistle, and said to him I was of opinion it would bear being printed, and that it would be well received by people of taste ; that I thought it at least equal, if not superior, to many of Allan Ramsay's epistles, and that the merit of these, and much other Scottish poetry seemed to consist principally in the knack of the expression; but here there was a strain of interesting sentiment, and the Scotticism of the language scarcely seemed affected, but appeared to be the natural language of the poet; that, besides, there was certainly some novelty in a poet pointing out the consolations that were in store for him, when he should go a-begging. Robert seemed well pleased with my criticism."

EXCISE.

Burns entered on active service as an Exciseman in the autumn of 1789. He was promoted to Dumfries, 3rd Division, 28th July, 1790; recommended for Examiner, 27th January, 1791; promoted to Dumfries 1st Division, 26th April, 1792; and appointed Temporary Supervisor, December, 1794; was still in the service at the time of his death, 21st July, 1796.

> "The facts of Burns's Excise career are simple enough," writes Mr. R. W. Macfadzean. "In December, 1787, he wrote to the Earl of Glencairn, 'I wish to get into the Excise.' Early in 1788 'Kind Old Sandy Wood,' the surgeon who treated his crushed limb, interested himself with Graham of Fintry to get him the appointment, with the result that his name was at once put on the list. In April he was the bearer of the Board's order for his instruction for six weeks in his future duties to Mr. James Findlay, officer, Tarbolton. (This document is quaint reading to Revenue Officers now-a-days.) In the end of May, 1788, Burns, having finished his instructions, went to Ellisland with his commission in his pocket. He did not,

however, get employed till the following year, and was promoted to a division on 28th July, 1790. All available evidence proves that Burns earnestly desired the appointment. His farming had failed, his cultivation of the Muses had not met with the reward it merited, and the Excise appointment probably saved him and his from great privation.

Every proof exists that he became an energetic and faithful officer, and that he bore his commission with fidelity to the last. Only one passing cloud darkened his official escutcheon, and far too much was made of it by his biographers, Lockhart and Cunningham.

Before the French Revolution movement degenerated into the Reign of Terror, it awakened the sympathy of all earnest Liberals in this country, and few people will now affirm that his participation in this feeling did not do the poet credit.

In the spring of 1792 he committed the indiscretion of sending four rusty old carronades, which he had captured with the smuggling brig in the Solway, to the French Government. This practical joke had serious consequences. They were stopped at Dover, and an inquiry was ordered to be made into ' Mr. Burns's ' political opinions. The result was a verbal caution. His loyalty was never really doubted, and until the date of his fatal illness he was a zealous Volunteer in the Dumfries corps.

Sufficient publicity has, perhaps, not been given to the fact that about 35 years ago great additional light was thrown upon Burns's official career. Mr. James Macfadzean, now superannuated Collector of Glasgow, was at that time engaged at Somerset House in the removal of old stores to the new wing ; when he discovered among the books of the Scottish Board several in which the name of the poet, Robert Burns appeared.

There were five pages in different books which

contained his name—and these were—First, a
scheme of the Dumfries District, in which the
poet's name occurs in three separate stations ;
second, a list of persons recommended for pro-
motion to the rank of supervisor, with dates of
appointment, etc., containing the poet's name ;
third, a similar list of later date, where there
appears opposite the poet's name the impressive
entry—" Dead." (It is interesting to notice here
that the next man on the list—James Lindsay—
was appointed supervisor of Dunblane District
on the 10th August, 1797, proving that if the poet
had lived in all probability he would have received
the appointment.) Burns's names remained on
the list till his death, and he was aware of the fact.
In 1795 he wrote to Patrick Heron :—" I am on the
the supervisor's list, and as we come on there by
precedency, in two or three years I shall be at the
head of the list, and appointed of course. Fourth,
a page, Letter B., from an alphabetical register in
which the official characters of the officers were
recorded at the head office. The poet's character
is here given, ' Never tryed—a poet,' with the
subsequent interlineation—' turns out well.'
Fifth, a page, Letter B., from a similar register,
compiled three years later. Burns's character
given here is, ' The poet—does pretty well.'
From an inspection of the characters given on the
register it is evident that they were drawn out with
great candour, and that of Burns, it is pleasing to
observe, is about the average.

Probably the most important book found was a
' Register of Censures,' embracing the whole period
of the poet's service. It appeared to be a faithful
record of everything of this kind issued by the
Board, from cautions for trifling irregularities to
dismissals. This volume was carefully searched
by Mr. Macfadzean, and, as all lovers of Burns will
be glad to know, the poet's name was conspicuous
by its absence.

EXHIBITION.

The Burns Exhibition, comprising Portraits, Pictures, Manuscripts, Books and Relics, was held in the Galleries of The Royal Glasgow Institute and Fine Arts, 175 Sauchiehall Street, Glasgow, from the 15th of July till the 31st of October, 1896. The undertaking was well patronized, and was managed with entire success ; such a complete collection of objects was shown as had never before been brought together in connection with any one man of mark.

The Exhibition was under the patronage of Her Majesty the Queen. Sir James Bell, Bart., Lord Provost of Glasgow, was President, while many of the nobility and men prominent in all ranks of life, acted as Vice-Presidents, or as Members of the General Committee.

A voluminous " Memorial Catalogue of the Exhibition " was issued in 1898, by Messrs William Hodge and Company, Glasgow. In an Introductory Note to the Catalogue, Mr. James Walker says :

" The conception of the Exhibition arose with Mr. Craibe Angus of Glasgow. In the actual carrying out of the idea into practical shape, the Council of the Burns Federation played a most important part, and with their knowledge of the situation helped to make the Exhibition possible. Mr. Craibe Angus and Captain David Sneddon, the Secretary of the Federation, acted from the outset as the Honorary Secretaries of the undertaking. To these gentlemen and to Mr. Andrew J. Kilpatrick, the Chairman of the Royal Glasgow Institute, who was chairman of the Burns Exhibition, Mr. Patrick S. Dunn, also of the Institute, who filled the position of Vice-Chairman, Mr. D. M'Naught, editor of the ' Burns Chronicle,' and to the various members of the Executive Committee, the success of the Exhibition is due. The public of Scotland are much indebted to the owners of Burns Relics, who made so generous a response to the Committee's applications for loans . . . The Exhibition was done well, and having been done once, has been done once for all, at least as far as the next one hundred years are concerned.'' The book is profusely illustrated with 120 fine plates of relics, portraits and paintings, manuscripts, books, furniture, etc., either belonging to or relating in some other way to the Poet.

Of great interest, not only to the Burns collector but to everyone of Scottish descent. As the catalogue shows, the exhibition aimed at bringing together all the portraits, the pictures, the books, the relics that illustrate the life of the National Poet of Scotland. Contains an exhaustive bibliography, no less than 1,473 items being mentioned, including 10 copies of the Kilmarnock, 1786, Poems. Collations are given of the rarer books.

F

FAIL OR FAILE. See also under Coilsfield.

A very small stream occasionally alluded to as the Faile Burn. It runs about five miles S.S.E. to the River Ayr. It was near the junction of the two waters that the parting of Burns and Highland Mary is said to have taken place, and here a small memorial has been erected in honour of the event.

FALL OF FYERS (or FOYERS), The.

Near Loch-Ness in Inverness-shire. Visited by Burns 5th September, 1787, while on his Highland Tour, and which impressed him so much that he composed the lines entitled, " Written with a Pencil, standing by The Fall of Foyers," before he resumed his travel. The Foyer is a small stream which runs about fourteen miles North of Loch Ness and traverses a wild high glen. Foyers House adjoins it.

FALL RIVER, MASS., U.S.A.

A white marble bust of the poet, a replica of a study of Burns by Fidardo Landi, adorns the Reading Room of the Public Library. It stands on a pedestal which bears the following inscription :—" Burns Presented by The Fall River Caledonian Society and their friends, 1899."

FALLS OF MONESS.

Burns visited the Falls of Moness in the course of his Highland Tour and was so captivated with their romantic beauty that he composed the song " The Birks of Aberfeldy " on the spot. " I composed these Stanzas," he writes, " standing under the Falls of Moness at or near Aberfeldy." The Falls are in the neighbourhood of the village, adjacent to the river Tay, in a deep chasm behind Moness House. When visited by Burns, the property belonged to a family named Fleming ; later it was purchased by the Breadalbane family.

FAMILY, THE BURNS.

The children of Robert Burns and Jean Armour who survived infancy were :

>Robert, born 3rd September, 1786, died 14th May, 1857.
>
>Frances Wallace, born 18th August, 1789, died 9th July, 1803.
>
>William Nicol, born 9th April, 1791, died 21st February, 1872.
>
>Elizabeth Riddel, born 21st November, 1792, died September, 1795.
>
>James Glencairn, born 12th August, 1794, died 18th November, 1865.
>
>Maxwell, born 25th July, 1796, died 23rd November, 1799.

Three children died in infancy and were buried in the Mauchline Churchyard.

FERINTOSH.

The name of a celebrated brand of whisky at one time distilled and sold free of revenue duty. " For services and expenses on the public account at the Revolution, Forbes of Culloden was empowered by an Act of the Scottish Parliament, in 1690, to distil whisky on his barony of Ferintosh, in Cromartyshire, free of duty." This grant was declared abolished in 1785 and the estate of Forbes was awarded twenty-one thousand, five hundred and eighty pounds as compensation.

> " Thee, Ferintosh ! O sadly lost !
> Scotland, lament frae coast to coast !
> Now colic grips, an' barkin hoast
>   May kill us a' :
> For loyal Forbes' charter'd boast
>   Is ta'en awa ! —" Scotch Drink."

FESTIVAL IN HONOUR OF THE POET'S SONS.

This was celebrated with great success on Tuesday, 6th August, 1841, in Ayr, and along the banks of Bonnie Doon. The Earl of Eglinton presided at a Banquet held in a pavilion into which were crowded some two thousand or more admirers of the Poet. Among those present at the time were the three sons of the Poet, Mrs. Begg and her three children, Mrs. Thomson (Jessie Lewars), Sheriff Glassford Bell, Professor William Aytoun, and a company of distinguished persons of the period, from far and near. Professor Wilson (" Christopher North ") was croupier, supported by Sir Archibald Alison.

FIVE CARLINES, THE.

An election ballad occasioned by a contest for the Dumfries burgh in 1789. The principals were Sir James Johnston of Westerhaugh and Captain Patrick Miller of Dalswinton. The five carlines were the burghs of Dumfries, Annan, Kirkcudbright, Sanquhar and Lochmaben.

FLAXMAN STATUE, THE.

Originally designed for the Edinburgh Monument (q.v.), and now stands in the Scottish Portrait Gallery, Edinburgh. The statue is of marble, and the Naysmith portrait has evidently been followed, but the general appearance of the poet is too classic and as such has been subjected to much adverse criticism. The poet is represented standing with his hands crossed in front, the right one holding a cluster of daisies. The folds of a plaid fall from the left shoulder and he is attired in knee breeches. The inscription " Robert Burns, Born near Ayr, 25th Jan., 1759. Died at Dumfries, 21st July, 1796," is in front of the plinth. As a piece of sculpture the statue is exquisite and perfect in all details. " The Flaxman Marble is a fair example of the sculptor's mastery of technique," writes Edward Pennington in ' The Art Journal ' for 1897. The chiselling is superb. In certain passages a desire may arise for finer discrimination, a more sensitive appreciation of the subtleties of the texture, but as a whole the statue is the product of a highly accomplished sculptor who found a keen delight in the practice of his art. The plaid is arranged in shepherd fashion, its disposal being skilfully devised to break the lines of the under folds."

FLOW GENTLY, SWEET AFTON. See under Afton Water.

FREDERICTON, N.B. CANADA, STATUE.

A replica of the Chicago one by W. G. Stevenson, R.S.A. The height is ten and a half feet, and the pedestal twenty feet. The figure is of bronze. The unveiling ceremonies were celebrated on the 18th October, 1906, the oration being delivered by Governor Fraser of Nova Scotia. There are four bases to the statue, the top one displaying the name, "Burns," in raised letters, while the four panels of the pedestal contain scenes from "The Cottar's Saturday Night," "The Daisy," "John Anderson My Jo, John," and a wreath. The statue occupies a prominent position opposite the entrance to the Parliament Building in Fenety Avenue.

FREEMASONRY.

In the last quarter of the eighteenth century Freemasonry in Scotland was at the height of its popularity. In the ranks of the Order were to be found the Scholars, the Philosophers and the Gentry of that day. From 1781 to 1796 Robert Burns was an ardent Mason, and no doubt found great pleasure in the meetings among the Brethren of the Mystic Tie.

He was initiated July 4th, 1781, in St. David's Lodge No. 174, Tarbolton. Passed and Raised in the same lodge on October 1st, 1781. Less than a year after his initiation, dissensions arose in St. David's Lodge, and a disruption took place, the old members of St. James' Kilwinning Lodge, No. 178, who had amalgamated with St. David's (with Burns among them) seized the properties of the St. James Lodge and reopened it. To the new lodge Burns adhered with all the ardour of new love and light. This was a memorable event in the life of the Poet, he was enthusiastically devoted to the Order. To one so brimful of human nature Masonry held out an irresistible hand of fellowship. "Burns, beyond question," says Hunter in his " Lectures on Freemasonry," derived considerable advantage from Masonry. It is evident, from the statements which he has placed on record, that it contributed greatly to his happiness in admitting him into close and intimate fellowship with the wise, intelligent, and social, and furnishing him with opportunities for enjoying the " feast of reason and the flow of soul " in the most rational and ennobling manner. It presented him also with one of the best fields that he could find for the improvement of his mind and the display of his talents. In no other society are all the members treated with so much indulgence, and placed on a footing of so much equality. In the Masons' Lodge, merit and worth are sure to be appreciated, and to meet with appreciation and respect. When the young and humble ploughman of Lochlea joined the Lodge of Tarbolton, he was still in a great measure unnoticed and unknown ; but no sooner did he receive the stamp of Freemasonry, than he took his place with Sir John Whitefoord of Ballochmyle, Jas. Dalrymple of Orangefield, Sheriff Wallace of Ayr ; Gavin Hamilton, writer, Mauchline ; John Ballantine, Provost of Ayr ; Professor Dugald Stewart of Catrine ; Dr. John M'Kenzie of Mauchline ; William Parker, Kilmarnock ; and a whole host of Ayrshire worthies, high and low. By coming in contact with these men his manners were refined, his intellectual energies stimulated, and his merits acknowledged and applauded. Alexander Wood, the tailor ; Manson, the publican ; Wilson, the schoolmaster ; Humphrey, the " noisy polemic ; " and all the meaner brethren, seem very soon to have discovered his high intellectual qualities, for they were not long in raising him to the second highest office in the Lodge—an office that caused him, on ordinary occasions, to occupy the master's chair, and perform the work of initiation.

It was within the closed portals of the various lodges of which he was a member, particularly Canongate Kilwinning Lodge, No. 2, Edinburgh, who not only made him a member, but, it is claimed, crowned him Poet Laureate (q.v.) of their lodge, that he met and made many life-long friends other than those he had made in Ayrshire, amongst them William Creech, the publisher, and Alexander Naysmith, the painter, to whom, by the way, we are indebted for the one authentic portrait of Burns, Henry Mackenzie, author of "The Man of Feeling," and many others.

Burns was elected Deputy Master of St. James' Lodge, on July 27th, 1784, a position he filled for four years with great credit to himself and honour to the Fraternity. In the following years he received Honorary membership from many lodges throughout Scotland, but his first Hon. membership was given by St. John's Kilwinning, Kilmarnock, on October 26th, 1786. Immediately after the publication of the Edinburgh Edition of his poems he, with Brother Robert Ainslie, went on his Border Tour, and in the little village of Eyemouth, Berwickshire, on the evening of

May 19th, 1787, in St. Ebb's Lodge No. 70
those two young brothers received the
Royal Arch degrees.   On taking up his
residence in Dumfries Burns became a
member of St. Andrew's Lodge No.
179, December 27th, 1788, and filled
some minor offices in the following years.
He was elected Senior Warden in 1792.   His
last visit to this lodge was just three months
before his death.

The humblest item in the creative plan of
the Great Architect of the Universe was dear
to Robert Burns.   " The tethered yowe, the
wounded hare, the wee mouse wi' its house
laid bare, the daisy that he could'na spare,
a' touched the heart o' Robin."—James
M'Murdo.

" Let us see who were the friends Burns
acquired in Edinburgh Masonic circles, and
we will at once understand the important
service they rendered to him during that
memorable winter in the annals of Scottish
literature," writes Dr. Peter Ross in " All
About Burns."   " We will also be able to see
that the magnificent reception he met with
was owing to his Masonic connections, and to
the enthusiasm which he had infused into the
breasts of the ' sons of light,' as well as to the
kindly, fraternal feelings they entertained for
one of their number who more than all other
men seemed to be endowed with true manhood, and who had proclaimed, in words that

sank deep into all hearts and lingered lovingly
on every tongue, the dignity of labour, the
majesty of work. Highest in rank, Masonically, was Francis Charteris, Lord Elcho, the
Grand Master. Then followed Lord Tor-
phichen, a name which is associated with the
history of Masonry from the very first period ;
Archibald Montgomery, Earl of Eglinton ;
James Cunningham, Earl of Glencairn—
through whose influence the Caledonian Hunt
became the patrons of the second edition of the
poems ; Patrick Miller of Dalswinton (who
will ever be remembered in connection with
the early history of steam navigation) ; he
was more than a mere sentimental admirer of
the bard, for, after having met him in Canongate Kilwinning and learning of his circumstances, he sent him anonymously a ten-pound
note—a generous and timely gift ; he also
afterwards offered Burns the choice of a farm
at Dalswinton on his own terms, but the poet
selected Ellisland (q.v.)—a true friend certainly, worthy in every way of the couplet,
in which Burns has enshrined his memory ;
Dalrymple of Orangefield ; Sir William Forbes
of Pitsligo, a famous Edinburgh banker, who
would have been Lord Pitsligo had his fore-
bears attended to their own business instead
of marching out with Prince Charlie in the
rebellion of 1745 ; James Burnet, Lord Monboddo, one of the Lords of Session, a zealous
believer in what is now known as the Dar-

winian theory long before Darwin was born, and one of the most curious characters which that cabinet of curiosities—the Edinburgh Court of Session—has furnished to the world ; Professor Dugald Stewart, the greatest of Scottish philosophers, who was chaplain of Kilwinning Lodge ; Frances Napier, Lord Napier, an officer who figured in the war of the American Revolution under General Burgoyne ; William St. Clair, Earl of Rosslyn, in whose family the Grand Mastership of Scotland was long hereditary. There were hundreds of lesser degree, including very many advocates and writers, such as Alexander Cunningham and William Dundas. Any one who knows Edinburgh must be aware that such legal gentry form the real backbone of its society. The scholastic profession also was represented by its leading lights. Among these was William Nicol, one of the masters in the High School, and, what is of infinitely more consequence now, one of the heroes of that grandest of all bacchanalian songs,

' Willie brew a peck o' maut.'

Allan Masterton, another of the heroes of the song, was also a teacher in the High School and a brother in the craft.

" Such were the leading men, so far as position and social standing were concerned, who met Burns in Masonic circles, and through whom he became the fashionable hero of the season. They took, from the first, a warm personal interest in him, his poetry, and his fortunes. With such friends to give him a brotherly grip and to stand by him as brothers, is it a wonder that in the most fashionable parlours he was received with the honours usually awarded to distinguished strangers? Certainly not. But the wonder is that he, so recently a petty farmer in a remote county, could at once take his place in such circles and hold his own against all comers— ministers, teachers, lawyers, soldiers, litterateurs, and men of the world—and that he charmed and fascinated the most aristocratic and refined dames with as much ease as he had won the hearts of the dairy-maids and farm lassies in his own native Coila."

A very interesting little book on this subject is " Robert Burns as a Freemason," by William Harvey. Published by T. M. Sparkes, Dundee, 1921. In the preface to the book Mr. Harvey says: " The association of the national bard with the brethren of the mystic tie forms one of the most picturesque aspects of the poet's short and interesting career. Burns was a ' keen ' Mason, by which I mean not that he was facile in the use of grip, word, and sign, but that he found much pleasure in the gatherings of the ancient and honourable fraternity of free and accepted Masons and fellows of the Craft, and spent many a happy hour in what is described

L

masonically in Scotland as ' Harmony,' and
elsewhere as ' The Fourth Degree.' A goodly
number of his acquaintances were Freemasons,
and it is not too much to say that not a few
of them derive any immortality they enjoy by
living in the shadow of his fame.

" In the following pages I have sought to
gather up the scattered references to Freemasonry that are found in the record of the
poet's life, and to weave the whole into a more
or less connected narrative. I have
endeavoured to adhere closely to my subject,
and my constant aim has been accuracy in
matters of fact. I hope the book will appeal
not only to Freemasons, but also to lovers of
Burns both at home and abroad."

FRIARS' CARSE.

The residence, in the poet's time, of Captain Robert Riddell. The estate situated on
the river Nith is about one mile from Ellisland. Soon after the poet's arrival at the
latter place he became acquainted with the
Captain, and in a short time the acquaintance
had ripened into so close a friendship that the
poet was presented with a key to the grounds,
to enter and leave as he pleased. Here the
poet was introduced to Captain Francis
Grose, to whom we are indirectly indebted for
" Tam o' Shanter." It was also at Friars'
Carse that he made the acquaintance of the
beautiful Deborah Davies, whom he later

immortalized by the song, " Bonnie Wee Thing." Here also was held the famous drinking contest for the Whistle (q.v.) and celebrated by the poet in verse, along with other well-known poems composed either while loitering through the grounds or sitting in the " Hermitage," a substantial little stone building used by the Captain as a retreat when he wished to be alone to commune with his own thoughts. For further particulars regarding Captain Riddell and the poems composed in connection with Friars' Carse— see Riddell, Captain Robert, in " Who's Who In Burns."

G

GAELIC.

Dain, is Luinneagan, Robert Burns, eadar-theangaichte do'n Ghaidhlig Albannach. Songs and Poems of Robert Burns translated into Scottish Gaelic by Charles Macphater, Glasgow. Glasgow, Alexander M'Laren and Son. [1910.]

" The translator has, in these pages, given a rendering of Burns's works, as literal as his knowledge and command of his mother tongue permitted, and is hopeful that he has also given a faithful as well as tuneful reproduction of the many pieces of which the work consists."—Preface.

GALASHIELS STATUE.

Unveiled May 31, 1913, by Mrs Harry Murray of Glenmayne. The site of the memorial, which was donated by Mrs Scott of Gala for the purpose, is at the foot of Lawyers Brae at the junction of that street with Albert Place. The oration was delivered by Mr H. S. Murray. The bust which is of bronze was the work of Mr T. Doyle of Chelsea, while the granite work was carried out by the well known Scottish sculptor, Mr G. Sutherland. The pedestal has the word "Burns" on front, and the words "Braw, Braw Lads" are on the base. Mr George

Hope Tait was the Chairman of the proceedings. Provost Sutherland in an appropriate address accepted the custody of the memorial on behalf of the Town Council. Galashiels has a progressive Burns Club, and in 1913 The Burns Federation favoured the town by holding its annual convention there. A pleasing feature of the 1930 celebration of the Riding of the Marches, was the placing of a large laurel wreath on the brow of the poet, by a self-appointed committee consisting of William Baxter, Tranent, Thomas Rintoul, of Elphinstone, Alexander Robb of Edinburgh, and John D. Ross of Woodhaven, New York.

Galashiels is famous the world over for its manufacture of Scottish Tweeds. As early as 1581, wool was here manufactured into cloth. The town also contains dyeworks, iron foundries, engineering works, and boot factories.

GALA WATER.

There are two or three old songs sung to the air of Gala Water and according to Cunningham "the Poet had in his thought one of these which he brushed up for the 'Museum' when he composed his verses on Gala Water."

" Gala Water rises in Midlothian, through which county it flows as a clear pastoral stream nearly its entire course. It enters the shires Roxburgh and Selkirk in the neighbourhood of Galashiels, when it assumes more of the character of a river, and loses itself in the Tweed within two miles below that town, in the vicinity of Abbotsford."— Douglas.

GARPAL, THE.

A small tributary of the river Ayr. Burns makes mention of it in " The Brigs of Ayr : "

"Or haunted Garpal draws his feeble course."

"The banks of Garpal Water," he says, " is one of the few places in the West of Scotland where these fancy scaring beings, known by the name of Ghaists, still continue pertinaciously to inhabit."

GEDDES BURNS, THE.

" The volume known as ' The Geddes Burns,' is one of the most valuable and interesting Burns items in existence, second indeed only to the original Kilmarnock edition of 1786. The history of the volume from the time it left the author's hands until it passed into the possession of Mr. W. K. Bixby, of St. Louis, appears more like romance than reality. The volume is a copy of the first Edinburgh edition of Burns's Poems, which was formerly in the possession of Dr. John Geddes (1735-1799), a Roman Catholic Bishop residing in Edinburgh, elder brother of the more widely known Bishop Alexander Geddes, biblical critic, translator,

and poet, to whom Burns was introduced
at the house of Lord Monboddo in the winter
of 1786-87. Burns and the Bishop became
intimate friends, and when the poet left
Edinburgh on his Highland tour he borrowed
the Bishop's copy of his (Burns's) Poems
with the promise to jot down in it whatever
he thought would be worthy of Dr. Geddes's
perusal. The volume contains twelve poems
in the Poet's handwriting, in addition to which
the Poet wrote out in full the names left blank
in the printed text.

The volume appears to have afterwards
passed into the possession of the Bishop's
sister, Margaret Geddes, who was married
to John Hyslop, a surgeon residing in Fins-
bury Square, London. On the decease of
Dr. Hyslop and his wife, the volume passed to
their daughter, also named Margaret. Dr.
Henry Goadby, an English anatomist and
author of the ' Text Book of Vegetable and
Animal Physiology,' was an intimate friend
of this Margaret Hyslop, and on his leaving
London for America in 1838 she presented him
with the volume as a token of her regard. Dr.
Goadby settled in Detroit, and while resident
there became acquainted with Mr. James
Black, a native of Nairn, who held an official
position in that city. Mr. Black greatly
coveted the volume, and eventually it
came into his possession by purchase from the
widow of Dr. Goadby on the 12th December,

1863. It was exhibited by him to the members of the Burns Club of Detroit on May 1, 1867. From Mr. Black the volume passed into the possession of Mr. W. K. Bixby, President of the Burns Club of St. Louis, who caused it to be photographed and reproduced by lithographic and gelatine process in an edition of 473 copies, printed for the members (only) of the Bibliophile Society of Boston, Mass., in 1908."—George F. Black, Ph.D., in " Who's Who In Burns."

GENEALOGY OF ROBERT BURNS.

Genealogical and Historical Memoirs of the Poet, his Associates, those celebrated in his writings, and the Lineage of the Poet, by Rev. Charles Rogers, D.D., LL.D. ; with Life of the Poet, by Rev. J. C. Higgins, A.M., B.D., illustrated by a silhouette of Robert Burns and facsimiles, appendices, and index, 3 vols. cr. 4to. Edinburgh, Grampian Club, 1889-91 ; also Genealogical Memoirs of the family of Robert Burns, and of the Scottish House of Burns.—Edinburgh, 1877.

GIRVAN.

An ancient town about twenty miles S.W. from Ayr. Stands at the mouth of the river from which it derived its name, and is nearly opposite Ailsa Craig. It is a seaport with Post Office, two railroad stations, banks, hotels and churches of different denominations. It was at one time extensively engaged in the weaving trade, but farming and other branches of business now occupy the attention of its inhabitants. Burns in early life frequently passed through the little town on his way to and from Ayr.

GIRVAN, THE.

A small stream which rises in Straiton parish and runs through Ayrshire to the Firth of the Clyde nearly opposite Ailsa Craig. It is mentioned in connection with the poet while he resided on the farm of Lochlea. At one time he made use of the name in his beautiful song, "My Nanie O'." "Behind yon hills where Girvan flows," but this was afterwards changed to the "Lugar."

GLASGOW.

Burns visited Glasgow on three occasions and put up at the Black Bull Inn (q.v.), off Argyle Street. In one of his letters dated from the City, 18th February, 1788, to Clarinda, he says ; "My brother William too, the young saddler, has come to Glasgow to meet me, and here are we three spending the evening," and again, in a letter, also dated from the City and addressed to Mr. Robert Muir, Kilmarnock, he says, "I am on my way thence collecting small sums owing me for my first edition in the villages of Galston and Newmilns," while on the 20th March, the same year, he writes to his friend William Brown " regretting his being unable to send him a copy of " Jones' Directory."

A special attraction for visitors to the City is the great Monument (q.v.) erected in honour of the poet in George Square.

There are numerous Burns Clubs throughout Glasgow ; and the Burns Federation has honoured the City by holding its annual conference within its borders on no less than five times (1894, 1901-11-14 and 19).

The greatest of all the honours paid to the poet's memory on the Centenary of his death (1896) was the Burns Exhibition (q.v. under Exhibition) held in the Royal Glasgow Institute of Fine Arts, from the 15th July, to the 31st October, 1896.

GLASGOW STATUE.

Unveiled 25th January, 1877.—Mr. George E. Ewing, sculptor. The statue is nine feet high and stands on a pedestal of grey Aberdeen granite twelve feet high. On the front of the pedestal is the inscription : " Robert Burns. Born, 1759—Died, 1796." A panel on the left side has a representation of " The Cottar's Saturday Night," and on the right side, a representation of " Tam o' Shanter and the Witches," while the rear panel has a representation of " The Vision."

The movement for the erection of the statue, which is known as the National Tribute to the Memory of Burns, was begun in 1872. An appeal by the Waverley Burns Club of Glasgow for one shilling subscriptions was so successful that in a few months over two thousand pounds were realised. Lord Houghton delivered the oration at the unveiling ceremonies. Over thirty thousand people were collected around the statue in George Square at that time.

An excellent poem by John Macfarlane, entitled " A Poet King," written in connection with the unveiling ceremonies, was very favourably commented on by the public and the press.

GLENCAIRN MEMORIAL AT FALMOUTH.

An addition to the attractions of Falmouth was made in the Church of King Charles the Martyr, the parish church of Falmouth, by the erection of a marble tablet in memory of the Right Hon. James Cunningham, 14th Earl of Glencairn, the patron, benefactor and friend of Robert Burns. The ceremony of the unveiling and dedication on 30th October, 1922, was attended by the Mayor (Councillor John Harris) and the members of the Corporation, leading Scotsmen from all parts of Cornwall, and a large number of the principal residents of Falmouth. The hymn, " Our God, our help," was sung, and the lesson was read by Alderman R. J. Bowles, who had taken great interest in the arrangements.

The tablet—provided by the Burns Federation—is of white Sicilian marble, with moulded frame of dark green marble from Tepos. It was designed by Mr. Ninian Macwhannell, F.R.I.B.A., and executed by Messrs William Vickers & Company, Glasgow. It measures four by two feet and is inscribed in leaded letters:—

> To the glory of God and in Memory of
> The Rt. Hon. James Cunningham,
> Fourteenth Earl of Glencairn,
> The Friend and Benefactor of
> Robert Burns.

He died on 30th January, 1791, in his forty-second year, while returning from Lisbon to Scotland, and was buried in this church.

> " The bridegroom may forget the bride
>   Was made his wedded wife yestreen ;
> The monarch may forget the crown
>   That on his head an hour has been ;
> The mother may forget the child
>   That smiles sae sweetly on her knee ;
> But I'll remember thee, Glencairn,
>   And a' that thou hast done for me !"
>   —Burns.

The tablet is placed here by the Burns Federation, 1922.—Burns Chronicle, 1923.

GLENCONNER.

The name of a farm about two miles from the little village of Ochiltree in Ayrshire. It was occupied by Burns's friend, John Tennant, the "guid auld Glen," who had helped the poet to decide on his acceptance of the farm of Ellisland. The Burns and Tennant families were nearby neighbours at one time.

GLENRIDDELL MSS.

"It was at Friars' Carse (q.v.) that Burns first met Captain Grose; and here on Friday, the 16th October, 1784, was held the great "Whistle" contest. The following poems were composed by Burns, either on Captain Riddell, or bearing directly with Friars' Carse :—"Written in Friars' Carse Hermitage on Nithside" (two versions), "Impromptu to Captain Riddell, on returning a newspaper," "The Whistle," "Reply to a Note from Captain Riddell." "The Day Returns," and "Sonnet on the Death of Robert Riddell of Glenriddell." At Captain Riddell's request Burns made a selection from his unprinted poems, which he copied into a blank book and presented to his friend. At the end of a brief preface to his book, the poet wrote : 'Let these be regarded as the genuine sentiments of a man who seldom flattered any, and never those he loved.' There was also a volume of letters. On the death of Captain

Riddell, Burns made a request to the family for the return to him of these volumes, a request that was ultimately complied with. When Dr. Currie was writing his life of the poet, the volumes at his request were forwarded to him so that he could make copies or extracts from the letters, etc. For some reason they were never returned to the poet's family, and nothing further was heard of them until 1853, when Dr. Currie's daughter-in-law presented them to the Liverpool Athenaeum, presumably for safe keeping. The Manuscripts, writes Dr. George Fraser Black, in the "New York Library Bulletin," lay hidden away in a wooden box in the Liverpool Athenaeum untouched till 1873, when Mr. Henry A. Bright, a merchant in Liverpool, discovered them, described them in a small privately-printed volume, and got them placed in a glass-case in the library of the Athenaeum. They remained there till 1913, when the Athenaeum decided to sell them, and gave Messrs. Sotheby & Co., auctioneers, London, a six months' option on them at five thousand pounds.   Before the six months had expired, Messrs. Sotheby & Co. exercised the option. No intimation of the proposed sale reached the public until Messrs. Sotheby & Co. exercised their option, and it was only then that the matter was mentioned in the newspapers. On news of the sale becoming public, a very strong feeling of indignation was aroused

among admirers of Burns and public and
literary men at the Athenaeum's sordid action
in disposing of such a priceless relic. An
influential committee was formed in Scotland
to contest the right of the Athenaeum to dispose of the manuscripts, and the heirs of
Burns were communicated with ... Apparently
before the Scottish Committee could institute
proceedings the manuscripts were sold. In
November, 1913, they were offered by an
American dealer to Mr. John Gribbel, of Philadelphia, by whom they were purchased. Mr.
Gribbel's object in securing them was that
they might be sent to Scotland for perpetual
security. In September, 1914, Mr. Gribbel
executed a deed of trust by which the manuscripts were presented as a gift to the Scottish
nation, to be deposited and to remain forever
in Scotland. In the deed it was directed 'that
until there shall be founded or established
in Scotland a Scottish National Library or
similar institution,' the trustees' shall entrust
the custody of the said manuscripts for the
period of five years at a time alternately
to the Corporation of Edinburgh and the
Corporation of Glasgow .... with a view to the
said manuscripts being exhibited to the public
view at all reasonable times, and under
proper protection.' As the Advocates'
Library in Edinburgh has now, thanks to
the munificent gift of Sir Alexander Grant,
become the National Library of Scotland, the

manuscripts will find there a permanent home. Before sending the volumes to Scotland, Mr. Gribbel had facsimiles made of them (150 copies), which he generously distributed to public libraries, Burns Societies, and prominent students of the poet."—" Who's Who In Burns."

GLENTURRET.

A glen of Perthshire, through which Turret burn runs a course of eight and half miles when it falls into the Earn near the town of Crieff. It is mentioned by Burns in his song " Blythe was she."

GLOBE TAVERN or INN, DUMFRIES.

A congenial resort of the Poet who termed it his favourite " Howff." It was an old and much frequented hostelry when the Poet took up his residence in Dumfries, and it still remains one of the best and most frequented establishments of its kind in the ancient burgh, the " Queen of the South." It is situated a little off the High Street, opposite the head of the Assembly Street, and has undergone very few changes since the Poet's time, the windows, doors, stair railings, etc., remaining unaltered to this day. Two small panes of glass in a window of a room on the second storey still exhibit his handiwork ; the arm chair, always reserved for his coming in the evening, is still to the fore, as are also his punch bowl and toddy ladle, together with other valuable and authenticated relics connected with him and his companions.

For many years " The Globe " was conducted by Mr. and Mrs. Hyslop, persons much respected by the Poet and who occasionally figure in his correspondence. Here, too, at one time resided Anna Park, niece of Mrs. Hyslop, and heroine of the song " Yestreen I had a pint o' Wine."

GLOSSARY.

By John Cuthbertson. Complete glossary to the poetry and prose of Robert Burns, with upward of three thousand illustrations from English authors. Paisley, 1886.

" My endeavour has been to show to English readers that by far the greater number of the Poet's words for which a glossary is generally consulted are to be found in their own authors. For this purpose I have quoted upward of three thousand passages from English authors, besides words from old dictionaries and provincial glossaries . . . I do not know whether or not this volume has any philological value, but surely it cannot be altogether uninstructive to see so many words, most of them dead or dying, which have had new life breathed into them by the genius of Robert Burns. To have these words shown, as it were, in their shrouds, and then to behold them 'instinct with life,' in the

M

pages of the modern Poet, cannot fail to be interesting to many."—From the Preface.

GRACE, THE SELKIRK. See under Selkirk Grace, The.

GRANT'S BRAES.

This now famous shrine is situated a little more than a mile to the West by South of Haddington on the Bolton road.   It is the termination of a narrow neck of wooded land stretching along the North side of the road. At the West end it broadens out on the shoulder-like cliff.   On three sides the braes run down to the lower plain.   It was towards the close of the eighteenth century that Gilbert Burns and his family, with his mother and sister, Annabella, took up their residence in a pleasantly situated cottage on the edge of the braes by the roadside.   Gilbert was then factor of the East Lothian estates of Lord Blantyre, and the inmates of the little home doubtless enjoyed many pleasures and comforts.   It is indeed gratifying to know that the Mother of our beloved poet passed the latter years of her life amid pleasant surroundings, respected and honoured by her own and her son's children.

Mr. D. S. Allan, of Haddington, writing of Mrs. Burnes's life at Grant's Braes at this time, in the "Weekly Scotsman," June 23, 1928, says: "It was a pleasant lovely spot on the shoulder of a hill, surrounded on three sides with a belt of wood, and with its sunny southern outlook it was a restful, peaceful home ; ' far from the maddening crowd.' Here she spent nearly 20 years, the most peaceful of all her chequered life.

" Her early married life with all her little ones around her, was perhaps her happiest time ; but ever there hung over them the cloud of straitened means. Her wilful, righteous husband, with his high ideals for his children—ideals he found hard to attain to, even with all the application of his active brains, and strenuous muscular powers, would in earlier days detract from her happiness. But here, in this quiet, restful home, sheltered by her loving son and daughter, with no care or anxiety how to make ends meet, surrounded, too, by a happy group of grandchildren, pleasanter days were her lot.

"Grannie and Annabella must have been a much needed help in the Grant's Braes home, with its rapidly increasing home, till it housed six sons and five daughters. One can imagine there would be a great demand for the stockings and socks that the economical Grannie would knit, and many little breeches would need the patching skill of Aunt Annabella.

"One visualises the grandmother in the long winter evenings sitting surrounded by the ' young Gilberts,' with open ears and glistening eyes, as she crooned the old ballads she used to sing, or told in her gentle, melodious voice their uncle's touching stories of the modest daisy his plough had crushed, making his tender heart bleed, and would repeat from her wonderful memory those soulful lines :—

> " Wee modest crimson tipped flower,
>   Thou's met me in an evil hour ;
> For I maun crush among the stoure
>   Thy slender stem.
> To spare thee now is past my pow'r
>   Thou bonnie gem."

"And those other touching stories, pleasing to children—' The Mouse,'—' wee sleekit, cow'rin, tim'rous beastie '—whose home, to Burns's springing tears, his plough had ruined ; and the ' Wounded hare,' that raised his anger to boiling pitch ! . . ."

In after years the house was let to tenants, but in 1891 it was destroyed by fire, the walls taken down and carried away. To-day nothing remains but a few crumbling stones of the foundation, and these are covered over with a growth of weeds and wild flowers.

GREATER NEW YORK MASONIC BURNS CLUB, THE.

Instituted October 27th, 1927, at Brooklyn, N.Y. Over fifty members were enrolled at the first meeting. Federated December 17th, 1927, No. 381.

The Club started out with the hope of making Burns's Poems, Songs and Letters better known in New York and vicinity ; also to encourage the reading, and studying of Scottish Literature and Music generally.

The members belong to over fifty different Lodges, England, Ireland, and Scotland being represented, while a number of the members are from half-a-dozen States of the Union.

GREENOCK BURNS CLUB.

Instituted 1802. Federated, 1886. Membership, two hundred and fifty. The following information is quoted from "A Little Book of Burns Lore."

" The Mother Club " was instituted, and held its first anniversary meeting, in 1802. Since the year 1885, when it was re-formed and re-constructed on a wider and more useful basis, the club has never ceased to prosper in its membership, in its finances, in its mission. It has held meetings four times a year regularly, it has observed the Poet's anniversary without a single omission, it has had its delightful summer picnics, it has fostered the study of Scottish history and poetry (especially ballad poetry) among the rising generation by the presentation, after competition, of valuable prizes for knowledge and efficiency in recitation ; it has frequently contributed sums in aid of local charities, and it has kept alive a most desirable spirit

of Scottish nationality in the community. It
may be said to be the most cosmopolitan
society in the towns of Greenock and Port-
Glasgow—quite a number of prominent
gentlemen belonging to the latter place are
included in the membership. It is cosmopolitan in this respect, that in religion it knows
no creed or sect, in politics it recognises no
particular party. Thus it is that at quarterly
meetings, and also anniversary gatherings
on that night when

> " A blast o' Janwar win'
> Blew hansel in on Robin,"

Whigs and Tories a' agree. Conservatives
who think that politics begins and ends with
them, Liberals who imagine that they are the
salt of the earth, and Radicals who maintain
that they, and they alone, have the salvation
of the country in their hands—all these meet
on a common level of Caledonianism, with the
author of " Tam o' Shanter " as the " key-
stane " of the social arch. Snobbery is, as
far as may be, at a discount at a symposium
of Burns admirers. The Poet's spirit is then
in the air, and every man is as good as his
neighbour. Yet this feeling of democracy—
this tacit confession that a man's a man for
a' that—does not interfere with the fusion of
the Poet's devotees. The club has, in recent
years particularly, drawn about as much support from West-end mansions as from the flats

and half-flats of the shopkeepers and better class of clerks and workmen resident in every ward of the town.

The club has property, too, and a habitation, as well as a kenspeckle name. Its principal meeting room in Nicolson Street is a dream of beauty—a suggestion of the artist and the antiquary. Attractive, in some instances valuable, pictures in oil, water-colour, and photography of past hon. presidents and presidents, of prominent members of the club, of famous honorary members literally cover the walls. Among these are Professor Blackie, Lord Rosebery, Andrew Carnegie, Oliver Wendell Holmes, Lord Tennyson, Andrew Lang, Sir Noel Paton— one of whose pictures also graces the right side at the fireplace—Professor Masson, Sir Henry Irving, J. M. Barrie, Colin Rae Brown, Sir Andrew Lusk, Professor Schipper (Vienna), Professor Auguste Angellier (Lille), Rev. Dr. Hugh MacMillan, Dr. W. C. Smith (author of " Olrig Grange "), " Ian Maclaren," Professor Saintsbury, Right Hon. A. J. Balfour, J. Logie Robertson (" Hugh Haliburton "), C. Martin Hardie, R.S.A., Rudyard Kipling, Colonel John Hay (Washington), Sir Donald Currie, Neil Munro, Dr. Robertson Nicoll (of the " British Weekly "), Hon. J. H. Choate, Dr. John D. Ross, Sir Henry Craik, Colonel Scott, C.B., Sir James Sivewright, General Sir Archibald Hunter, Sir. Thos.

Lipton, Dr. Robert Caird, Sir George Reid, R.S.A., Sir Thomas Sutherland, Mr. Durward Lely, etc. The collection includes a number of canvases, chiefly in oil, of Scottish scenes, also a few local pictures, old spinning wheels, curling stones, besides other articles of interest relating to the time in which Burns lived. An old oaken brass-bound chest, placed near the well-stocked bookcase, contains the club's manuscripts, minute-books, and other papers and relics. The principal treasure, perhaps, in this chest is the original minute-book of the Greenock Club, the first entries in which are dated 1801, in the summer of which year the society was first formed. It is an Excise book, which belonged to Robert Burns, or rather was in his keeping and for his use as a Government servant. It is of the once familiar form, oblong and narrow in width, and bound in thick brown calf boards. The leaves have taken on an age-worn appearance, but otherwise the little volume is in a state of good preservation. On the first leaf, under the top cover, is the following inscription :—
" This book was found in the house of the late Mr. Robert Burns at his demise, and presented to the Burns Club of Greenock by Adam Pearson, Esq., of His Majesty's Excise, Edinburgh, A.D. 1801." On the second page is the following, in large and legible handwriting : " Greenock Burns Club and Ayrshire Society." The minutes in this book open

with an ode on the Poet composed by Mr. Neil Dougal, a prominent and gifted local musician of the early years of the last century, and the author of some psalm tunes long popular with Presbyterians, including the well-known " Kilmarnock." The long ode— oh, how lengthy and gushing these old odes on Burns usually were !—concludes as follows :

" Sae for his [Burns] sake, the dainty cheil,
   I wish his weans and widow weal,
      Gude grant them wealth
         O' milk and meal,
         For brose and bread,
   And bless them with a cosy beil
      Till they are dead."

Homely, yet quite expressive, and a trifle quaint ! This entry is signed by " Robert Barr," who appears to have acted as the first of the long list of secretaries. The next item in the minute-book, " Presented by Mr. Pearson, of Edinburgh," gives a brief account of the first " anniversary celebration," as it is called even in those early days. It says : " On Friday, 29th January, 1802, the club held their anniversary celebration of the birth of the Bard "—Greenock men were apparently at that time ignorant of the fact that Burns was born on the 25th of that month. The minute-writer goes on to say that about forty members sat down to a "sumptuous repast " in the White Hart Hotel, under the presi_

dency of Mr. John Wright, who proposed the
toast of the Poet, and recited an ode—the
usual long-drawn-out, winding, word-spun
ode. The book shows, as one turns over its
stained and yellow pages, that anniversaries
were held in 1803, 1804, 1805, and 1806, and
there were also enthusiastic meetings, invariably in July and at Hallowe'en. It ought to
be mentioned that in 1804 the anniversary of the birth was also held at
Alloway, in the house in which the Poet first
saw the light, Greenock Club being present by
deputation. Many entries in the book are
most interesting reading. For example, at
the January celebration of 1803 there is a
presentation of books to the society, along with
copy of " the new edition " of Burns's works,
from Mr. Archibald Campbell, brother to
" Highland Mary ; " in August, 1804, the
death of Admiral Duncan, of Camperdown
fame, is intimated and entered in the book.
At this meeting "Mr. Wright stated that he had
known Robert Burns intimately for three
years, and having been associated with him
in his profession he could from his personal
knowledge deny most emphatically that
Robert Burns was a man of intemperate or
dissolute habits." In 1806 the anniversary
dinner was held for the first time on 25th
January, the meeting taking place in the
" White Hart Inns," as the wording is. This
was a remarkable gathering, for much busi-

ness was transacted at it, and the minute is long and detailed. One entry has more than usual interest. It says that the club passed a message of sympathy with one of its members, Mr. Greer, and family, on " the loss of their gallant son and brother, who fell most nobly fighting for his King and country at the glorious Battle of Trafalgar." The member who proposed the motion of consolation said that " it seemed a very remarkable coincidence that while the son of one of their most esteemed members had died fighting gloriously "—Britishers were in those dangerous and stirring days jingoes unabashed and unashamed—" under Lord Nelson, the son of another member of the club had, while spared to return to his home and friends, assisted to carry the immortal and gallant Admiral from the deck mortally wounded." Details on this and a mass of other ancient and engrossing matters are in this wonderful Excise-book.

GREY-NECK STILL, A.

Erroneously printed in most editions of Burns's Works as, " A Grey-Neck ' Quill.' " The phrase occurs in " The Twa Herds " and alludes to the Rev. George Smith, who was at the time minister of Galston. In the manuscript copy of the poem—now in the British Museum—the brief sentence is plainly written by the poet, " I doubt he's but a grey-neck still." The phrase means one who is changeable, indifferent, or who lacks character.

GUDE-WILLIE WAUGHT.

" No expression of Burns has been more generally misunderstood than this. Hogg and Motherwell, Cunningham, Chambers, and Waddell, print it ' Gude Willie-Waught,' as if ' Willie-Waught ' were a separate word, and Chambers even glosses the fabricated compound ' draught.' There is no such word. ' Gude-Willie,' is a common Scotch adjective signifying with hearty good-will, friendly, and is antonym or opposite of ' ill-will,' signifying malicious. ' Waught,' is a word in every-day use for a hearty drink. The expression, then simply means a drink taken with hearty, mutual good-will."—J. Hunter.

H

HAGGIS.

Contrary to popular opinion, the Haggis is not originally a Scottish dish. Had it not been for Burns's poem in its praise it would probably be unknown in Scotland at the present day. It consists of the heart, lungs, and liver of a sheep or calf, minced with suet, and oatmeal and seasoned with salt, onions, etc. The whole is then boiled in the maw of the animal. The Haggis was a favourite dish among the English in olden times as witness the following extract from good old Gervase Markham's English Housewife, published originally in London in 1637: " This small Oat-meal mixed with blood, and the liver of either sheep, calf, or swine, maketh that pudding which is called the Haggas or Haggus, of whose goodness it is vain to boast, because there is hardly to be found a man that doth not affect them."—Dr. George F. Black.

HALLOWE'EN.

The thirty-first day of October. This in the old Celtic Calendar was the last day of the year, and witches, devils and other demons were supposed to be around on peculiar missions that night. It used to be celebrated with much mirth by the young people of both sexes, and it is still celebrated in some parts of the Old World, but generally speaking it is now a thing of the past. Robert Chambers in his 'Book of Days' has some interesting reading and information on the subject. It was in full sway throughout the West of Scotland during Burns's early days, and his poem " Hallowe'en " is one of his most humorous pen pictures of peasant life as it existed in his time.

HARDIE, CHARLES MARTIN, A.R.S.A. See under Paintings by.

HASTIE MSS., THE.

Consisting principally of the MSS. of the songs sent by Burns to James Johnson for insertion in " The Scots Musical Museum." The Collection is in The British Museum. (Addit. MS. 22,307.)

It is of great importance for the text of the songs, written, improved, or collected by Burns for Johnson's " Scots Musical Museum." The volume containing the manuscripts was bequeathed to the British Museum in 1858, along with the Poet's punch-bowl, by Archibald Hastie (1791-1857), who for some years was M.P. for Paisley.

HAWICK BURNS CLUB.

Instituted, 1878; federated, 1914, No. 239. About 300 members. Special features : To honour the name of Robert Burns ; to celebrate the anniversary of his birth and otherwise endeavour to perpetuate his memory ; to afford the members the means of social intercourse, mutual helpfulness, intellectual improvement and social recreation.

The Club now owns its own home—a handsome building in Albert Road—opened 28th April, 1928, by Sir Joseph Dobbie. The architect was Mr. George Scott. The new clubhouse is well equipped with all modern improvements and reflects credit on its officers and members. The first president of the Club was James Thomson, the author of " The Star o' Robbie Burns."

" HEE BALOU ! "

Words used to soothe a child—literally —" Ha ! be soothed," hence the opening of the song, " Hee Balou, my sweet wee Donald." The composition is an English translation of a Gaelic ditty which Burns heard while travelling in the Highlands, and appeared in the fifth volume of Johnson's Museum. The song evidently has reference to the time when cattle and other goods of the Lowlanders were looked upon as fair game by the Highlanders.

HENLEY AND BURNS ; or THE CRITIC CENSURED.

Being a collection of papers replying to an offensive critique on the life, genius and achievements of The Scottish Poet. Collected and edited by John D. Ross: Eneas Mackay, Stirling, 1901.

" The amount of feeling contained between the covers of this not very bulky volume is prodigious."—" Daily Record."

" There is one redeeming feature about the Essay—and only one—it was not written by a Scotsman. Thank Heaven for that! . . . So far I have failed to realize just why Mr. Henley should wish to belittle the ' Life, Genius, and Achievements ' of Burns in the manner he has done. His tirade of abuse was certainly uncalled for, especially when we consider that the poet has been dead for over a century, and the whole world to-day pays homage to his genius and greatness. As far as the Essay—if the thing can be called by so dignified a name—is concerned, there is absolutely not a scrap of new information in it. The matter is all second-hand, and, in addition to this, it is placed before the public in so peculiar a form that it is positively unreliable and misleading."—From the preface.

HERD'S COLLECTION.

Issued in 1770, and afterwards with additions in 1776, attends more to the taste of the antiquary. Very little is known of the life of honest David, and even the editorship of the two celebrated volumes cannot with certainty be given to him. All that is known is that he was a native of St. Cyrus, in Kincardineshire, that he was for many years a clerk to an accountant in Edinburgh, and died in June, 1810, aged 78 years. A notice of his death appeared in the "Scots Magazine" for July, 1810, and included the following sketch :— "He was a most active investigator of Scottish Literature and Antiquities, and enjoyed the friendship of nearly all the eminent artists and men of letters who have flourished in Edinburgh within these fifty years. Runciman, the painter, was one of his most intimate friends ; and with Ruddiman, Gilbert Stuart, Fergusson, and Robert Burns, he was well acquainted. His information regarding the History of Scotland was extensive. Many of his remarks have appeared in periodical publications ; and the notes appended to several popular works are enriched by materials of his own collecting. He was a man truly of the old school, inoffensive, modest, and unambitious, and in an extraordinary degree forming in all these respects a very striking contrast to the forward puffing and ostentatious disposition of the present age." Sir Walter Scott informs us that " His hardy and antique mould of countenance and his venerable grizzled locks procured him, amongst his acquaintances, the name of Greysteil." George Paton, who appears to have been co-editor of the Collection, was in the Customhouse. He carried on a most extensive correspondence with many of the most cele-

N

brated antiquarians of his time, amongst
others Bishop Percy, Gough, and Joseph Rit-
son. Herd's Collection, as it is commonly
called, was arranged in several divisions
according to the subject of the pieces, and a
glance at the pages of the present volume will
show how much old Scottish Song has been
indebted to it for preservation. Burns refers
to it on several occasions. Herd and Paton,
as far as we know, were model editors for
antiquarians : Scraps and Fragments were
printed exactly as they found them, as well as
complete songs, without the slightest regard
to rhyme or metre, decency or beauty.—Peter
Ross, LL.D., in " The Songs of Scotland "
(chronologically arranged).

HERVEY'S MEDITATIONS.

In one of Burns's letters to Clarinda (3rd
February, 1788) he says : " Did you ever meet
with the following lines spoken of Religion,
your darling topic ?

' 'Tis this my friend, that streaks our morning bright !
'Tis this that gilds the horror of our night !
When wealth forsakes us, and when friends are few ;
When friends are faithless, or when foes pursue ;
'Tis this that wards the blow, or stills the smart ;
Disarms affliction or repels its dart :
Within the breast bids purest rapture rise,
Bids smiling Conscience spread her cloudless skies.'

I met with these verses very early in life,

and was so delighted with them that I have them by me, copied at school."

"The lines," says George Gebbie, "are taken from one of several sets of recommendatory addresses in rhyme, prefixed to old editions of 'Hervey's Meditations,' a book that had an immense circulation in Scotland during the last century." They would also indicate that Burns in early life had carefully read the 'Meditations' more than once, as indeed was his custom when he managed to get hold of a book that interested him.

HIGHLAND MARY'S GRAVE.

Mary Campbell, the inspirer of "To Mary In Heaven," and other immortal creations of the poet's imagination, died at Greenock on the 20th of October, 1786, and a couple of days later her remains were laid in a plot of ground belonging to Peter Macpherson, a relative, in the West Kirk Burying Grounds. Here her grave remained unmarked as far as her name was concerned, for fifty-eight years, or until 1842 when a number of admirers of Burns subscribed sufficient funds for the erection of a small but appropriate monument to mark her resting place. To the spot annually come pilgrims from all parts of the world to pay their silent respects to the memory of her who in life was so dear to the poet. On account of the extension of the works of Messrs Harland and Wolff, Greenock, this company purchased the property of the old West Kirk, and the remains of Highland Mary were reverently removed and transferred on the 13th November, 1920, to the Greenock Cemetery. The new burial place is in a prominent part of the Cemetery, and the surroundings are respectful and praiseworthy. A brief sketch of the life of Mary Campbell will be found in " Who's Who In Burns."

HIGHLAND MARY STATUE AT DUNOON, THE.

Unveiled by Lady Kelvin of Dunoon Castle, Saturday, 1st August, 1896. The statue is of bronze, the work of Mr. D. W. Stevenson, Edinburgh, and stands on the Castle Hill, within a mile of where the heroine is said to have been born. The figure is that of a country maiden. The gown is kilted at the knee and on the feet are buckled shoes. The left hand held close to the breast, clasps a Bible and in the right hand is a satchel. The figure is depicted gazing in the direction of the Ayrshire coast.

The cost was provided for by subscriptions sent from far and near, and to Mr. Colin Rae Brown, chairman, as well as to the other members of the Committee having the matter in charge, much credit was due for the successful completion of what is universally regarded as one of the finest memorials of its kind in existence. The statue stands on a pedestal of Ballochmyle sandstone, designed by Mr. R. A. Bryden, Glasgow, and is an object of much interest whether viewed from on foot, or from the deck of a steamship, or other sailing vessel on the Clyde.

HOLY FAIR, THE.

" Holy Fair," says Burns, "is a common phrase in the West of Scotland for a Sacramental occasion," and his own well-known poem or satire by this name has reference to an assemblage of the kind which took place in the Mauchline Churchyard. The poem appeared in the Kilmarnock edition, and created quite a sensation in religious and other circles. Previous to its appearance in print, however, it was known through manuscript copies to numerous friends of the author. It is by far the ablest of the satires written in 1785, and his worst enemies, says some one, could not avoid confessing that it was as well deserved as it was clever. Scenes such as the poet described had become a scandal and a disgrace to the Church. The poem was met by a storm of abuse from his old enemies ; but, amid all their railings, they did not fail to lay it to heart, and from that time forward there was a manifest improvement in the bearing of ministers and people on such occasions. This is not the least of its merits in the eyes of his countrymen of the present day. Notwithstanding the daring levity of some of its allusions and incidents, the poet has strictly confined himself to the sayings and doings of the assembled multitude—the sacred rite itself is never once mentioned.

HOLY WILLIE'S PRAYER.

"The origin of this satire," says James Gunnyon, "may be briefly told as follows :— Gavin Hamilton, the special friend of the poet, had been denied the benefit of the ordinances of the church, because he was alleged to have made a journey on the Sabbath, and to have made one of his servants take in some potatoes from the garden on another Sabbath —hence the allusion to his "kail and potatoes" in the poem. William Fisher, one of the Rev. William Auld's elders, made himself somewhat conspicuous in the case. He was a great pretender to sanctity, and a punctilious stickler for outward observances. Poor man, he unfortunately merited the satire of the poet, as he was a drunkard, and latterly made too free with the church-money in his hands. Returning drunk to his home in Mauchline one night, he fell into a ditch and died of exposure." It is only just to add that there is no official record of the charge of his having made too free with money belonging to the church, and the statement that he died drunk in a ditch is not conclusively proved.

HONRESFELD COLLECTION.

"There has recently come into the ken of students of Burns a very important, but little known, collection of manuscripts which forms part of a library owned by A. J. Law, Esq., formerly M.P. for Rochdale. Many of these manuscripts yield valuable corrections of, and additions to, certain published letters and poems. Several of the manuscripts have never been printed ; while one, though in print, has never been suspected to have been a composition of Burns. [The poem here referred to by Mr. Cook is " The Queen o' the Lothians cam cruisin' to Fife."] Scotland and the far-flung Burns world owe Mr Law grateful thanks for kindly allowing those valuable items to be published in the *Burns Chronicle*. In the fifth volume of *Burnsiana* (1895, p. 31) there is an article by Mr. G. A. Aitken, entitled ' A collection of Burns Manuscripts ;' it deals with a great sale at Messrs. Puttick and Simpson's Rooms in London, on 2nd May, 1861. Mr. Aitken expresses the hope that his article ' will lead to the discovery and publication of some of the manuscripts dispersed so long ago.' Several of the manuscripts to which he refers are in the Law Collection."— Davidson Cook.

An account of the Burns Manuscripts by Mr Cook, will be found in the "Burns Chronicle," 1926-27-28.

HOWFF, BURNS'S.   See under Globe Tavern.

IBBETSON. THE, Portrait of Burns. **See under** Portraits of Burns.

INVERARAY.

When on his Highland Tour in 1787, the poet made a stop at Inveraray, probably with the intention of paying his respects to the Duke and Duchess of Argyll, who were among the subscribers to the Edinburgh edition of the poems. The Duke, at the time however, was entertaining a large number of guests at the Castle, and learning of this Burns sought shelter for the night at the Inn. He may not have received the attention here that he expected and before leaving next morning, he is said to have inscribed the epigram, beginning, "Whoe'er he be that sojourns here," on one of the windows.

Inveraray stands on the West side of Loch Fyne, thirty miles from Greenock. It dates back at least to the 14th century. It is the capital of Argyllshire.

IRVINE.

Six miles south of Kilmarnock, stands on the North side of the river Irvine and ranks as a seaport. It supports two weekly newspapers, has a railway station, and post office, in addition to many churches, schools, hotels,

etc. "The Royal Burgh of Irvine has many
and varied memories," writes the Rev. Henry
Ranken in the 'Burns Chronicle' for 1905,
"which carry back those who think of such
things at least seven centuries. She had her
days of humiliation in the war of Scottish
Independence, when in 1297, the 'Capitu-
lation of Irvine' was signed. But she had
her triumphs, too, and her comfortable reflection on her loyalty to Robert Bruce, for
we find her rewarded for her help by a charter,
granted by the hero of Bannockburn six years
before he dealt his crushing blow to English
pretensions. Her best claims to attention
lie, however, in the regions of peace, for she
can boast of having given birth to John Galt,
'the fore-runner,' if not 'the master,' of a recent school of Scottish fiction. James Montgomery, the Christian poet, and Eckford, the
designer of the American Navy, and a chief
'Senator of the College of Justice,' Lord
Justice-General Boyle." And while it
would be of considerable interest to continue
to trace the social, as well as the commercial
and other progress of the Burgh down to our
own day, yet our chief concern with it at present is centered in its connection with Robert
Burns and its direct bearing on his life at the
time he resided there.

Burns went to Irvine in the summer of
1781 for the express purpose of learning the
trade of a flax-dresser. Irvine was at that

time the emporium of the flax-dressing trade. Gilbert Burns says of this incident : " The stocking of a farm required a sum of money, Robert had no probability of being master of for a great while. He began, therefore, to think of trying some other line of life. He and I had for several years taken land of my father for the purpose of raising flax on our own account. In the course of selling it, he began to think of turning flax-dresser, both as being suitable to his grand view of settling in life and as subservient to the flax-raising." Burns himself continues the story in his letter to Dr. Moore :

" My twenty-third year," he said, " was to me an important era. Partly through whim, and partly that I wished to set about doing something in life. I joined a flax-dresser in a neighbouring country town to learn his trade. . . This turned out a sadly unlucky affair. My partner was a scoundrel of the first water, who made money by the mystery of thieving, and to finish the whole, while we were giving a welcome carousal to the New Year, our shop, by the drunken carelessness of my partner's wife, took fire and burned to ashes, and I was left, like a true poet, not worth sixpence. I was obliged to give up business ; the clouds of misfortune were gathering thick round my father's head ; the darkest of which was—he was visibly far gone in consumption. To crown all, *a belle fille*, whom I adored, and who had pledged her soul to meet me in the fields of matrimony, jilted me, with peculiar circumstances of mortification. The finishing evil that brought up the rear of this infernal file, was my hypo-

chondriac complaint being irritated, to such
a degree, that for three months I was in a diseased
state of body and mind scarcely to be envied by
the hopeless wretches who have got their sentence."
—Depart from me, ye cursed ! etc.

From this adventure I learned something of a
town life ; but the principal thing which gave
my mind a turn was I formed a bosom friendship
with a young fellow, *the* first created being I had
ever seen, but a hapless son of misfortune. He
was the son of a plain mechanic ; but a great
man in the neighbourhood- taking him
under his patronage, gave him a genteel
education, with a view of bettering his situation
in life. The patron dying .... just as he was
ready to launch forth into the world, the poor
fellow in despair went to sea ; where, after a variety
of good and bad fortune, he was a little before I
was acquainted with him set ashore by an
American privateer, on the wild coast of Con-
naught, stript of everything. I cannot quit this
poor fellow's story without adding, that he is at
this moment Captain of a large West Indiaman
belonging to the Thames.

This gentleman's mind was fraught with courage,
independence and magnanimity, and every noble,
manly virtue. I loved him ; I admired him to a
degree of enthusiasm, and I strove to imitate him.
I in some measure succeeded ; I had the pride
before, but he taught it to flow in proper channels
His knowledge of the world was vastly superior
to mine, and I was all attention to learn.
He was the only man I ever saw who was a
greater fool than myself where Woman was the
presiding star ; but he spoke of a certain fashionable failing with levity, which hitherto I
regarded with horror. Here his friendship did me
a mischief."

And this practically finishes the poet's connection with Irvine, for he at once returned to his home at Lochlea. " A good deal has been written, mainly upon conjecture, about the misfortunes of this episode of Irvine," writes Dr. Peter Ross, " but it all resolves itself into this, that Robert Burns was not a shrewd business man, and it was as well for Scottis poetry and song—for Scottish literature and nationality, in fact—that he was not. He had troubled mental communings at this crisis about his own immediate welfare ; he wrote a metrical ' Prayer on the Prospect of Death,' and tried his hand at paraphrasing some of the penitential Psalms ; sometimes, like so many Scottish youths in like circumstances, he thought he'd ' go and be a sodger ; ' but at such times the patient, wasting figure and the helpless ones at Lochlea came before his vision. So he accepted his evident destiny and duty, and like a true man, hied himself back to the farm and again held the plough."

It may be recalled that Burns's friend Dr. John Mackenzie was a resident of Irvine for a long period ; also that the grave of David Sillar, a " brother bard," is in the Irvine Kirkyard.

IRVINE STATUE.

Unveiled 18th July, 1896. The sculptor was Mr. Pittendrigh MacGillivray, R.S.A. Alfred

Austin, at that time Poet Laureate, gave the oration. The red granite pedestal bears the following inscription—" The Gift of John Spiers, Esq., to his Native Town," and the four panels represent " The Toil-worn Cottar," Burns and Highland Mary, the Poet being crowned with a Laurel Wreath, and the word " Burns."

The pedestal is twelve feet high and the statue is nine feet, the entire height of the Monument thus being twenty-one feet.

IRVINE, THE RIVER.

Rises in Lanarkshire, runs twenty-one miles westward between Cunningham and Kyle to the Firth of Clyde and has there a joint mouth with the Garnock in Irvine Harbour. Occasional references are made to the river in the poet's writings.

ISLE, THE.

After the lease for the farm of Ellisland had been signed, it became necessary for the poet to remain in the neighbourhood so he could superintend the repairs and alterations which were absolutely necessary on the house before he and his bonnie Jean could "settle down" in it. He accordingly took up his residence in a dilapidated old place called " The Isle," about one mile from Ellisland. Robert Chambers, about 1838, described it as " A small track of ground which had once been encircled by the waters of the Nith, partly through natural channels, and partly through an artificial trench. Here rises a small old dismantled tower, with more modern buildings adjoining to it on two of its sides, the whole forming the farm-buildings of ' The Isle ; ' for such is the name of the place, still retained, although one of the ancient water-courses is now only a rushy piece of ground. The place, which has an antiquated, and even somewhat romantic appearance, was the property of Mr. Newall, writer in Dumfries, whose family had lived in it during the summer, but only for a short time, in consequence of certain nocturnal sounds in the old tower having led to a belief that it was haunted. What added a little, or perhaps not a little, to the *eerieness* of the spot, was that the old burying-ground of Dunscore, containing the sepulchre of the dreaded persecutor, Grierson of Lagg, was in the immediate neighbourhood.''

When Jean, early in December, left Mauchline and joined her husband, she had to remain here until the following summer, before Ellisland was in proper condition to receive her.

J

JEDBURGH.

Stands on Jed river, between Hawick and Kelso, forty-six miles S.E. from Edinburgh. It dates from the ninth century and was in former times a favourite residential town with Scottish royalty. It figures in many border conflicts. Burns while on his Border Tour accompanied by his travelling companion Robert Ainslie reached Jedburgh on the 8th of May (1786). In his Journal he recorded that the town occupied a "charming romantic situation ; was presented by the magistrates with the freedom of the Burgh ; my heart is thawed into melting pleasure, after being so long frozen up in the Greenland bay of indifference, amid the noise and nonsense of Edinburgh ; Jed, pure be thy crystal streams, and hallowed thy sylvan banks ; took farewell of Jedburgh with some melancholy disagreeable sensations."

The Jedburgh Burns Club was instituted 1869, and Federated 1887. Membership, 75.

JENNIE GEDDES.

A mare purchased by Burns when starting on his Border Tour with Robert Ainslie in 1787. The name was assigned to her in honour, or in remembrance of the indignant old dame who threw her stool at the Dean of

Edinburgh's head, on the 23rd July, 1637, when the attempt was made to introduce a Scottish " Liturgy " into the services of St. Giles's. The mare became quite a favourite animal with the poet and he makes mention of her in letters to Mrs. Dunlop, John Richmond and others.

JERUSALEM TAVERN. A rendezvous of the poet in Dumfries.

JOHN O' GROAT'S HOUSE. See Maidenkirk.

JOLLY BEGGARS, THE. A Cantata.

' The Jolly Beggars,' for humorous description and nice discrimination of character, is inferior to no poem of the same length in the whole range of English poetry. The scene, indeed, is laid in the very lowest department of low life, the actors being a set of strolling vagrants, met to carouse and barter their rags and plunder for liquor in a hedge alehouse. Yet, even in describing the movements of such a group, the native taste of the poet has never suffered his pen to slide into anything coarse or disgusting. The extravagant glee and outrageous frolic of the beggars are ridiculously contrasted with their maimed limbs, rags, and crutches ; the sordid and squalid circumstances of their appearance are judiciously thrown into the shade. The group, it must be observed, is of Scottish character ; yet the distinctions are too well marked to escape even the southron. The most prominent persons are a maimed soldier and his female companion, a hackneyed follower of the camp ; a stroller, late the con‧ sort of a Highland ketterer or sturdy beggar,— 'but weary fa' the waefu' woodie!' Being now at liberty, she becomes an object of rivalry between a 'pigmy scraper with his fiddle' and a strolling tinker. The latter, a desperate bandit, like most of his profession, terrifies the musician out of the field, and is preferred by the damsel of course. A wandering ballad-singer, with a brace of doxies, is last introduced upon the stage. Each of these mendicants sing a song in character ; and such a collection of humorous lyrics, connected with vivid poetical description, is not, perhaps, to be paralleled in the English language. The concluding ditty, chanted by the ballad-singer at the request of the company, whose 'mirth and fun have now grown fast and furious,' and set them above all sublunary terrors of jails and whipping-posts, is certainly far superior to anything in the 'Beggar's Opera,' where alone we could expect to find its parallel ! In one or two passages of 'The Jolly Beggars,' the muse has slightly trespassed on decorum, where, in the language of Scottish song,

> 'High kilted was she,
>   As she gaed owre the lea.'

O

Something, however, is to be allowed to the nature of the subject, and something to the education of the poet ; and if, from veneration to the names of Swift and Dryden, we tolerate the grossness of the one, and the indelicacy of the other, the respect due to that of Burns may surely claim indulgence for a few light strokes of broad humour."—Sir Walter Scott.

The scene of The Jolly Beggars was Poosie Nancie's (q.v.) in Mauchline. John Richmond told Robert Chambers that one night, when Burns, ' Smith, the sleest pawkie thief,' and Richmond were coming up the street in a state of partial intoxication, their attention was attracted by the noise of revelry, issuing from this hostelry. At the instigation of Burns they went in, and entered *con spirito* into the scene of drunken frolic which they found going forward. Such was the source of the poet's inspiration, and such the scene, which a few touches of his pen have rendered immortal !

K

KELLY BURN, THE.

The Northern boundary of Ayrshire. Divides the parish of Largs from Renfrewshire for upwards of two miles and flows into the Firth of Clyde near Wemyss Bay. Further East the boundary is marked by " the Rowtin burn," and the locality is called " The back of the World." " The Carle of Kellyburn Braes," a humorous ballad by Burns appeared in the first volume of " Johnson's Museum."

KEMPIS, THOMAS A, Reference to.

" For my own affairs, I am in a fair way of becoming as eminent as Thomas à Kempis or John Bunyan ; and you may expect henceforth to see my birth-day inserted among the wonderful events, in the Poor Robin's and Aberdeen Almanacks, along with the Black Monday, and the Battle of Bothwell Bridge " —Letter to Gavin Hamilton, 7th December, 1786.

KENMURE CASTLE.

Situated at the head of Loch Ken near Galloway, in Kirkcudbrightshire, and dates back to the thirteenth or fourteenth century. It stands on a high round mount and is approached by an avenue of beautiful lime trees. The Castle at one time was the seat of the Earls of Kenmure. Burns and his friend Syme visited Kenmure in July, 1794, and enjoyed the hospitalities of the place for three days.

KERRY, THE. MINIATURE PORTRAIT OF BURNS. See under Portraits of Burns.

KILBAIGIE, or KILBAGIE.

A whisky so named from Kilbaigie distillery in Clackmannanshire. It is mentioned by Burns in the " Tinker's Song " of " The Jolly Beggars : "

> " And by that stowp ! My faith an' houpe,
> And by that dear Kilbaigie."

This whisky is said to have sold in Burns's time as low as one penny a gill, the revenue tax being exceedingly small on it.

KILLIECRANKIE.

Song. " The battle of Killiecrankie (fought 17th July, 1689) was the last stand made by the clans for James after his abdication. Here the gallant Lord Dundee fell in the moment of victory, and with him fell the hope of the party. General M'Kay, when he found the Highlanders did not pursue his flying army, said : ' Dundee must be killed, or he never would have overlooked this advantage.' A great stone marks the place where Dundee fell."—Burns.

KILMARNOCK.

Famous in the annals of Burnsiana as the home of the first, or as it is termed to-day, the " Kilmarnock Edition " of the Poet (q.v.) issued by John Wilson, Printer, 31st July, 1786. The town and much of the surrounding district is reminiscent of the spirit and time of Burns. Its population was then estimated at about three thousand souls; to-day it is close on forty thousand. It is about sixteen miles from Ayr and twenty miles from Glasgow. Kilmarnock, we read, derives its name, Kil-mo-Ernin (the Gaelic for church of my little Ernin) from the dedication of its church, about 1200, to an Irish Saint of the seventh century. In 1591 it was created a Burgh of Barony under the Boyd family, the ruling house of the district at the time. In the past it was noted far and wide for its manufacture of " Kilmarnock Cowls ; " to-day its commercial output consists of various kinds of woollen goods, boots, shoes, and carpets, hydraulic and nearly all other kinds of machines and machinery. It has churches, and schools of all denominations, a Town Hall, Court House, Corn Exchange, Public Library and Museum, a colossal Statue of Sir James Shaw and, perhaps the greatest of all, an imposing Burns Memorial situated in Key Park. Alex. Smith, celebrated poet and essayist, was born here in 1830 ; Died, 1867. Apart from these associations there are many tender memories of Covenanting times with the place. It is the home of the Burns Federation, instituted in 1885 and its local Burns Club has been in existence since 1808. Kilmarnock must be credited with having progressed rapidly in recent years, and to-day is one of the largest and most prosperous towns in the West of Scotland.

KILMARNOCK BURNS, THE.

Poems, chiefly in the Scottish Dialect, by Robert Burns.

> ' The Simple Bard, unbroke by rules of Art,
>   He pours the wild effusions of the heart ;
>   And if inspired, 'tis Nature's pow'rs inspire ;
>   Her's all the melting thrill, and her's the kindling fire.'
>
>   Anonymous.

Kilmarnock ; Printed by John Wilson, MDCCLXXXVI. Published, 31st July, 1786 ; price, three shillings ; stitched.

In his famous autobiographical letter, (August 2nd, 1787) to Dr. John Moore, the Poet says :

> " I weighed my productions as impartially as in my power ; I thought they had merit ; and 'twas a delicious idea that I should be called a clever fellow, even tho' it should never reach my ears— a poor negro-driver—or perhaps gone to the world of spirits, a victim to that inhospitable clime. I can truly say, that *pauvre inconnu*, as I then was, I had pretty nearly as high an idea of myself

and my works as I have at this moment. It was ever my opinion that the great, unhappy mistakes and blunders, both in a rational and religious point of view, of which we see thousands daily guilty, are owing to their ignorance or mistaken notions of themselves. To know myself had been all along my constant study. I weighed myself alone ; I balanced myself with others ; I watched every means of information, to see how much ground I occupied as a man and as a poet ; I studied assiduously Nature's design, where she seemed to have intended the various *lights* and *shades* in my character. I was pretty sure my poems would meet with some applause ; but at the worst, the roar of the Atlantic would deafen the voice of Censure, and the novelty of West Indian scenes would make me forget Neglect. I threw off six hundred copies, of which I had got subscriptions for about three hundred and fifty. My vanity was highly gratified by the reception I met with from the public ; besides pocketing (all expenses deducted) near twenty pounds."

Robert Heron, one of the poet's early biographers, writing of the reception accorded to the poems, says :

"It is hardly possible to express with what eager admiration and delight they were everywhere received. Old and young, high and low, grave and gay, learned or ignorant, all were alike delighted, agitated, transported. I was at that time resident in Galloway, contiguous to Ayrshire, and I can well remember, how that even ploughboys and maid servants would have gladly parted with the wages which they earned the most hardly, and which they wanted to purchase necessary clothing, if they might but procure the works of

Burns. A copy happened to be presented from a gentleman in Ayrshire to a friend in my neighbourhood ; he put it into my hands, as a work containing some effusions of the most extraordinary genius. I took it, rather that I might not disoblige the lender, than from any ardour of curiosity or expectation. ' An unlettered ploughman, a poet ! ' said I, with contemptuous incredulity. It was on a Saturday evening. I opened the volume by accident, while I was undressing to go to bed. I closed it, not till a late hour on the rising Sunday morn, after I had read over every syllable it contained."

To-day the " Kilmarnock Edition " is a very rare book and is greatly prized by Collectors, while Libraries and similar institutions vie with each other in their eagerness to obtain copies for which they are prepared to pay almost any price asked. The last recorded price is two thousand, four hundred and fifty pounds paid by Dr. A. S. W. Rosenbach of Philadelphia, for one in 1929. And Robert Burns reaped the golden harvest of twenty pounds from the first publication of the book !

KING KYLE.

The district between the rivers Ayr and Doon. Burns changed from this district to Stewart Kyle on leaving Mount Oliphant for Lochlea, in 1777.

KIRKOSWALD.

This town figures largely in the seventeenth year of Burns. Here he attended a school for a few months studying mensuration, surveying, dialling, etc. Smuggling was briskly carried on in the town and here he says he learned to look unconcernedly on a large tavern bill, meaning undoubtedly what constituted such an item to him at the time. " I went on," he says, " with a high hand in my geometry, till the sun entered Virgo— a month which is always a carnival in my bosom : a charming *Fillette*, who lived next door to the school, overset my trigonometry, and set me off in a tangent from the spheres of my studies. I, struggled on with my " sines " and " co-sines " a few days more ; but stepping out to the garden one charming noon to take the sun's altitude, I met with my angel,

> ' Like Proserpine, gathering flowers,
>   Herself a fairer flower.'

It was in vain doing any more good at school. The remaining week I stayed, I did nothing but craze the faculties of my soul about her, or steal out to meet with her, and the two last nights of my stay in the country, had sleep been a mortal sin—the image of the modest and innocent girl had kept me guiltless." And so he returned to Mount Oliphant.

Kirkoswald is now a quiet and law-abiding village. It has to a great extent retained its old time appearance and is probably much the same as it was in 1776. According to Robert Chambers, the classes which Burns attended, were held in a house in the Main Street opposite the Churchyard. Each house was provided with a strip of ground used as a kitchen garden and here it was the young poet espied the " Proserpine gathering flowers " of his lively fancy. The town is visited each year by a number of tourists and others. John Keats was a prominent visitor as far back as 1818.

" Oswald," says Mr. James L. Hughes, " was a son of the last King of the Heptarchy in England. He was brought up by the King of Carrick. He became a soldier and defeated the English, when they invaded Carrick where Kirkoswald now stands. He vowed the night before the battle that if the Lord would help him to win he would establish a shrine which was followed by a Kirk known as the Kirk o' Oswald."

" This church, planted on the site of the shrine erected by Oswald, King (and Saint) of Northumbria, about 625 A.D., is now a roofless ruin ; not unlike Alloway Kirk in appearance," says the Rev. James Muir in his interesting book ' Robert Burns Till His Seventeenth (Kirkoswald) year.' It ceased to be used in February, 1777, when the present church on the hill was opened for worship. Burns, therefore, worshipped in the ancient sanctuary in 1775, and it is not unlikely that King Robert the Bruce was baptised in it. The present church, designed by the famous architects, the brothers Adam, and opened in February 1777, contains in its tiny belfry the bell which for 100 years had hung in the belfry of the old church. It bears the inscription —' *Claudius Hamilton me fecit* 1677.' This Claud Hamilton, as Lockhart informs us, was the Episcopal Curate of Kirkoswald, and great-grandfather of Burns's staunch lawyer friend, Gavin Hamilton, at Mauchline."

In the churchyard are headstones marking the resting places of " Tam o' Shanter," " Souter Johnnie," Hugh Rodger, the schoolmaster, and Burns's mother's people, the Browns. On the 29th June, 1929, the Marchioness of Ailsa unveiled a bronze memorial tablet in the front of the building used at one time by Rodger for his school. This memorial was provided by the Rosebery Burns Club. On the tablet is recorded that " On this site stood the school kept by Hugh Rodger, which Robert Burns, the Ayrshire bard, attended in the summer of 1775."

KIRKOSWALD. SOUTER JOHNNIE'S HOUSE.

The old building, thanks to the efforts of the Rev. James Muir and a few other patriotic ladies and gentlemen, is now used as a Museum and contains many interesting and valuable relics. It is fast becoming a true Burns shrine. During 1929 nearly 1300 visitors paid their respects to the place. Various sums of money have been contributed by friends interested in the Museum scheme and further favours of funds, relics, books, etc., will be very acceptable at all times.

KILMARNOCK BURNS MONUMENT.

The good people of " Auld Killie " were somewhat tardy in erecting a memorial to the poet, but when in 1872 they finally decided to do so, they proceeded with the project in a whole-hearted and generous manner, as the result proves.

" It was long matter of surprise," says Mr. David Sneddon, compiler of the official Catalogue, "that no Monument existed in Kilmarnock to the memory of Burns, notwithstanding its intimate connection with the earlier period of his career, and the fact that from its provincial press was issued the first edition of his immortal poems. In the year 1872, the proposal to erect a statue in Glasgow by shilling subscriptions, gave an impetus all over the West of Scotland to the latent admiration for our National Poet, which required only the slightest touch to be called into unprecedented and enthusiastic activity. The credit of originating the movement in

Kilmarnock is due to Mr. James M'Kie, publisher . . . . The movement, however, was not brought before the public till the Burns Anniversary of 1877, when a public demonstration, presided over by Provost Sturrock, was held in the hall of George Hotel . . . The resolution to erect a statue of Burns in the town was unanimously adopted, and a committee appointed to carry out the proposal without delay. So liberal and hearty was the response, that in a few months the committee found themselves in possession of a fund far exceeding their most sanguine hopes, and which before the close of the year, had reached the handsome figure of £2055. It was then resolved to erect an ornamental building for the reception of the statue, the actual cost of which was over £1600. The memorial stone was laid by R. W. Cochran-Patrick of Woodside, M.P., on September 14th, 1878, in presence of thousands of spectators and representative deputations from the various orders and trades. The architect was Mr. R. S. Ingram, Kilmarnock. The design is Gothic, and the building consists of two storeys and a tower, the entire height being 75 feet. Premiums of £50 and £25 were then offered for the two best models of a statue, and public competition invited. Out of twenty-one models exhibited, that of Mr. W. G. Stevenson, sculptor, Edinburgh, was accepted by the committee. It was com-

pleted on August 2nd, 1879, and unveiled by
Colonel Alexander of Ballochmyle, M.P., on
Saturday, 9th August, 1879. . . . The statue
is of Sicilian marble, and is eight feet high.
As a likeness it follows the Nasmyth portrait,
the fidelity to which is most striking in the
profile. The figure is arrayed in the tight
fitting coat and knee breeches of the period.
The pose is dignified and graceful, and represents the Poet in the moment of inspiration
about to commit his melodious thoughts to
writing . . . .

The Museum contains the M'Kie Burnsiana
Library, one of the finest and most complete
collections of the kind in existence. It was
acquired for three hundred and fifty pounds—
minus a copy of the " Kilmarnock Edition "
which the Trustees of the Monument already
possessed through the generosity of Dr. A.
C. M'Laren, of London. The collection includes :—Burns Holograph Manuscripts—
Holograph Manuscripts other than Burns—
Editions of the Poet's Works chronologically
arranged—Editions of the Poet's Works,
without dates—Foreign Editions—Translations of the Works of Robert Burns—Im-
perfect Editions—Clarinda Correspondence—
Single Poems and Chapbooks—Burnsiana,
arranged chronologically—Burnsiana, without dates—Burnsiana Scraps—Pamphlets,
etc., bound in volumes—Scrap Books—Music
—Miscellaneous—Relics, etc.—Oil Paintings

—Etchings, Engravings, and Photographs. The collection of Scrap Books dates from 1854 and contains information of much value, bearing on the life and writings of the Poet.

The view from the Monument is almost unrivalled for extent and variety of pastoral beauty, and no one can contemplate the Monument and its surroundings without a feeling of veneration and pleasure.

KIRK'S ALARM, THE.   A Satire.

" M'Gill and Dalrymple, the two ministers of the town of Ayr, had long been suspected of entertaining heterodox opinions on several points, particularly the doctrine of original sin and even of the Trinity ; and the former at length published ' An Essay on the Death of Jesus Christ,' which was considered as demanding the notice of the Church-courts.   More than a year was spent in the discussions which arose out of this ; and at last, Dr. M'Gill was fain to acknowledge his errors, and promise that he would take an early opportunity of apologising for them to his congregation from the pulpit, which promise, however, he never performed.   The gentry of the country took, for the most part, the side of M'Gill, who was a man of cold, unpopular manners, but of unreproached moral character, and possessed of some talents.   The bulk of the lower orders espoused, with far

more fervid zeal, the cause of those who
conducted the prosecution against this erring
doctor. Gavin Hamilton, and all persons
of his stamp, were, of course, on the side of
M'Gill—Auld and the Mauchline elders with
his enemies. Mr. Robert Aiken, a writer in Ayr,
a man of remarkable talents, particularly
in public speaking, had the principal management of M'Gill's cause before the Presbytery,
and, I believe, also before the Synod. He
was an intimate friend of Hamilton, and
through him had about this time formed
an acquaintance which soon ripened into a
warm friendship with Burns. Burns, therefore, was, from the beginning, a zealous,
as in the end he was, perhaps, the most
effective, partisan of the side on which Aiken
had staked so much of his reputation."—
Lockhart.

KIRKTON or KIRKTOWN.

Any little village in Scotland where a
parish church had been established, was
generally called the Kirkton.

KNIGHTHOOD CONFERRED ON THE POET.
See under Bruce, Mrs. of Clackmannan.

L

LADIES' HOUSE, THE.

A place of refreshment at Kirkoswald, kept by Jean Kennedy, " Kirkton Jean," and her sister Ann. There was ever an air of respectability as well as quietness about the little inn and being conducted by the two sisters gradually became known even outside of Kirkoswald as " The Ladies' House."

LAND O' CAKES, THE.

Used by Burns in the opening line of his poem, "On the Late Captain Grose's Peregrinations Thro' Scotland : "

" Hear, Land o' Cakes, and brither Scots."

The expression, however, was not original with Burns. It was first applied to Scotland by Robert Fergusson in his poem. " The King's Birthday in Edinburgh : "

" Oh, soldiers ! for your ain dear sakes
For Scotland's, alias, Land o' Cakes."

LASS OF BALLOCHMYLE, THE. See Ballochmyle.

LATIN INSCRIPTION AND TRANSLATION.

When the Mausoleum was completed, a ponderous Latin inscription was composed with the view of informing visitors that

P

" Hoc Mausoleum " was built " in æternum honorem Roberti Burns, Poetarum Caledoniæ, sui ævi longe principis." By the rarest good fortune it was never put up although some of the Poet's biographers have quoted the whole inscription as " noted down from the original," and Allan Cunningham laments that " the merits of him who wrote Tam o' Shanter, and the Cottar's Saturday Night, are concealed in Latin ! "

In Aeternum Honorem
ROBERTI BURNS,
Poetarum Caledoniae sui aevi longe principis
Cujus carmina eximia, patrio sermone scripta,
Animi magis ardentis, ingenii que vi,
Quam arte vel cultu conspicua,
Facetiis, jucunditate, lepore, affluentia,
Omnibus litterarum cultoribus satis nota ;
Cives sui, necnon plerique omnes
Musarum amantissimi memoriamque viri
Arte poetica tam praeclari, foventes
HOC MAUSOLEUM,
Super reliquias poetae mortales,
extruendum curavere.
Primum hujus aedificii lapidem
Guliellmus Miller, Armiger,
Reipublicae architectonicae apud Scotos,
On regione australi, Curio Maximus provincialis,
Georgio Tertio regnante,
Georgio, Walliarum Principe,
Summam imperii pro patre tenente,
Josepho Gass, armigero, Dumfriesiae Praefecto,
Thoma F. Hunt, Londinensi, Architecto,
Posuit,
Nonis Juniis, Anno Lucis VMDCCCXV.
Salutis Humanae MDCCCXV.

Translation.

In perpetual honour of
ROBERT BURNS,
Incomparably the first Scottish Poet of his age,
whose exquisite verses, in the dialect of his country,
distinguished for the strength and fire of native genius,
more than for the acquired accomplishments
of polish and condition,
are admired by all men of letters
for their humour, pleasantry, elegance, and variety ;
his townsmen and others, who love polite literature,
and cherish the memory of so eminent a genius,
caused THIS MAUSOLEUM to be erected
over the mortal remains of the poet.
Of this edifice
the first stone was laid by
William Miller, Esq.,
Provincial Grand Master of the Southern District
of Free Masons in Scotland,
In the reign of King George III.,
During the regency of George, Prince of Wales,
Joseph Gass, Esq., being Provost of Dumfries,
Thomas F. Hunt, of London, being the architect,
On the 5th day of June, In the year of light 5815,
Of our Lord, 1815.

LEA RIG, THE.

The first song contributed by the poet to
Thomson's " Collection " A song with the
same title and sung to the same air was written
by Robert Fergusson, When sending the
song to Thomson, Burns wrote : " On reading
over ' The Lea Rig,' I immediately set about
trying my hand on it, and after all, I could
make nothing more of it than the following
which Heaven knows is poor enough."

Lea-Rig—An old pasture field, or land at one time ploughed but now in grass.

LEGLEN WOOD, THE.

Situated on the banks of the Ayr near the bend of the river, about three miles from Auchencruive. Blind Harry, the Minstrel, mentions it in his poem "Wallace" as a favourite hiding place of the Scottish hero. Among the books that fascinated Burns while a boy was the story of Wallace, abridged and in modern Scottish dialect by Hamilton of Gilbertfield. He tells us how in his boyhood's days he often stole out after the labours of the day, to spend an hour over the Tale of Scotia's ill-requited Chief. He was particularly impressed by the couplet :

Syne to the Leglen Wood, when it was late,
To make a silent and a safe retreat.

" I chose a fine summer Sunday," he wrote to Mrs. Dunlop (November, 1786), " the only day of the week in my power, and walked half a dozen of miles to pay my respects to the Leglen Wood, with as much devout enthusiasm as ever pilgrim did to Loretto ; and, as I explored every den and dell where I could suppose my heroic countrymen to have sheltered, I recollect (for ever then I was a rhymer) that my heart glowed with a wish to be able to make a song on him equal to his merits."

On the 14th September, 1929, a Memorial Cairn was unveiled here by the Marchioness of Ailsa.

The cairn stands on a mound in an arbour of trees overlooking the River Ayr, and is erected from a design submitted by Mr James Carrick, architect, Ayr, the material being Ailsa Craig granite boulders, kindly granted by the Most Noble the Marquis of Ailsa. The foundations and core of the cairn consist of reinforced concrete. The pillars at the entrance and the pathway and steps leading to the cairn are also of Ailsa Craig granite. The builders were Messrs J. & D. Meikle, Ayr. The inscribed panels, of " Duntrune " granite, were supplied by Messrs Scott & Rae, Glasgow. The cairn is meant to provide an enduring memorial of our two greatest national heroes.

The main panel bears the following inscription :—

WALLACE AND BURNS.

" O never, never
    Scotia's realm desert,
    But still the patriot
    And the patriot bard
    In bright succession raise,
    Her ornament and guard."

The inscription on the obverse panel is as follows :—

" Syne to the Leglen Wood when it was late,
    To make a silent and a safe retreat "

THIS MEMORIAL WAS ERECTED BY
THE BURNS FEDERATION,
Sept., 1929.

————

THE SITE WAS GIFTED BY
MR. JOHN M. HANNAH,
GIRVAN MAINS.

————

THE COST OF THE CAIRN WAS DEFRAYED BY
REV. J. G. HIGGINS, B.D.,
MINISTER OF TARBOLTON PARISH.

At the close of the unveiling ceremony Lady Ailsa placed two garlands on the cairn. One of them to Burns bore the following lines :—

" But still the burden of his song
    Is love of right, disdain of wrong ;
    Its master chords are Manhood, Freedom, Brother-
        hood—
    Its discords but an interlude between the words."

The other, " To Wallace, warrior, man of action," bore the following inscription :—

" The whole earth is the tomb of heroic men, and their story is not graven on stone only over their clay, but abides everywhere without visible symbol woven into the stuff of other men's lives."

On behalf of Ayr Burns Club, Miss Polly Hyslop, the secretary, placed a wreath of heather and thistle bearing the poet's lines on Independence :—

" Thou of an independent mind,
    With soul resolved, with soul resigned,
    Prepared power's proudest frown to brave,
    Who wilt nor be, nor have a slave,
    Virtue alone dost thou revere,
    Thy own reproach alone dost fear,
    Approach this shrine and worship here."

LAIGH KIRK, THE, Kilmarnock.

" Stands on the other side of the Cross in Bank Street, into which the tower and its basement project—the only part that remains of the ancient shrine of St. Marnock. From the conformation of the lower part of this structure it is evident that it originally abutted on the stream, and tradition avers that the ground floor was often used as a prison, probably before the erection of the Tolbooth, the site of which is preserved by the tablet in the causeway opposite the door of the Burns Tavern, to the memory of John Nisbet, a Covenanting hero, who was there hanged. In the poem of " The Ordination," Burns reviews the internal history of the Laigh Kirk from the time of the Rev. William Lindsay in 1764 to that of the Rev. James Mackinlay, who was his contemporary, and died in 1841, at the advanced age of 85. The " Old Light " satires of the Poet in connection with the divines of the Laigh Kirk are so well known that no details are here necessary. It must be considered a curious coincidence that the three individuals mentioned in the first verse of Tam Samson's elegy (to quote the words of Mr. M'Kay, the historian of Kilmarnock) ' are buried so near each other, that they all occupy one spot in the church-yard as they do one stanza in the poem—their dust being separated by only a few inches of ground.'   The spot is situated at the western angle of the north gable of the present modern erection."—David Sneddon.

LEITH STATUE.

Unveiled 15th October, 1898, by Mr. R. C. Munro-Ferguson, M.P.   The sculptor was Mr. D. W. Stevenson, R.S.A.   The statue is of bronze and is nine and a half feet high.   The panels represent—scenes from " The Cottar's Saturday Night," " Death and Doctor Horn-book," " Hallowe'en," etc.

LINCLUDEN ABBEY.

Now a mouldering ruin, situated at the junction of the rivers, the Clouden and the Nith, about a mile and a half northwest of Dumfries.   A favourite walk of the poet in the evening was along the banks of the Nith, then linger among the old ruins especially on moon-light nights.   Here he is said to have composed many of his poems and songs. He is understood to refer to the Abbey, in the poem, " As I stood by yon roofless tower," and in his version of " Ca' the Yowes to the Knowes," he refers to " Yonder Clouden's silent Towers." The Abbey was built about 1164 by Uchtred, Lord of Galloway, for a community of Benedict nuns. In the north end of the chancel is still shown the tomb of the Princess Margaret, daughter of King Robert III, and wife of Archibald, Earl of Douglas.

LINKUMDODDIE.

Used by Burns in his song of Willie Wastle, and in this connection it is supposed to be purely an imaginary locality.

LINLITHGOW.

An ancient and Royal Burgh sixteen miles distant from Edinburgh. Famous in history as the birthplace of James V. and Mary Queen of Scots. Burns visited the burgh while on his Highland Tour and made the following note regarding it in his Journal: The town " carries the appearance of rude, decayed idle grandeur—charmingly rural retired situation—the old royal palace a tolerably fine but melancholy ruin, sweetly situated on a small elevation by the brink of a Loch. Shown the room where the beautiful injured Mary Queen of Scots was born. A pretty good old Gothic church— the infamous stool of repentance, standing, in the old Romish way, on a lofty situation.

On the sixteenth of November, 1787, Burns was presented with the Freedom of the town.

LIVERPOOL—HIGHLAND MARY STATUE.

Unveiled 5th October, 1896, in the Palm House, Sefton Park, the gift of Mr. Henry Yates Thomson. The sculptor was Mr. Benjamin E. Spence, a Liverpool artist, who died in his forty-fourth year in Italy. The statue and its base form a very beautiful piece of workmanship and is an object of much interest to visitors to the park. On the front of the base is a verse from " Highland Mary," and on the left is the inscription " Robert Burns, Born at Alloway, 1759, Died at Dumfries, 1796," while the right side reads— " Benj. Evans Spence, Sculptor, Born at Liverpool, 1822, Died at Leghorn, 1886." A duplicate of the statue is in the New York Public Library on Fifth Avenue (q.v.).

LOCHLEA.

In 1777 the Burns family removed from Mount Oliphant to Lochlea, a farm consisting of a hundred and thirty acres in the parish of Tarbolton. This is described as " an upland undulating track of land on the north bank of the River Ayr, with a wide outlook, southward over the hills of Carrick, westward toward the Isle of Arran, Ailsa Craig, and down the Firth of Clyde, toward the Western Sea." It was within walking distance of Tarbolton (q.v.), only five miles from Kilmarnock, and about eight miles from Ayr. The Poet at this period had reached his eighteenth year and already had to his credit, his well-known Song to Handsome Nell, besides : " I dream'd I lay where flowers were springing," " Though fickle fortune has deceived me," " Winter— a Dirge," and one or two similar pieces, each embodying more or less a touch of the master poet of the future. But Robert's poetical leanings in these early days did not interest his brother Gilbert to any particular extent. Rather he admired him for his humour as well as for his general knowledge and his conversational powers. According to Robert Chambers, " Gilbert used to speak of his brother as at this period, to himself, a more admirable being than at any other. He recalled with delight the days when they had to go with one or two other companions to cut peats for winter fuel ; because Robert was sure to enliven their toil with a rattling fire of witty remarks on men and things, mingled with the expressions of a genial, glowing heart, and the whole perfectly free from the taint which he afterwards acquired from his contact with the World. Not even in those volumes which afterwards charmed his country from end to end, did Gilbert see his brother in so interesting a light as in these conversations in the bog, with only two or three noteless peasants for an audience."

The first years spent at Lochlea were thus passed in comparative comfort in contrast to the last years spent at Mount Oliphant, but later the family had various troubles to contend with. "My father took the farm of Lochlea," writes Gilbert, "in the parish of Tarbolton of Mr. Ferguson, a merchant in Ayr. He removed to this farm at Whitsunday, 1777, and possessed it only seven years. No writing had ever been made out of the conditions of the lease; a misunderstanding took place respecting them: the subjects in dispute were submitted to arbitration and the decision involved my father in ruin." "Four years," writes the Poet in his Autobiography, "we lived comfortably on the farm, but a difference between him and his landlord as to terms, after three years tossing and whirling in the vortex of litigation, my father was just saved from the horrors of a jail, by a consumption, which, after two years' promises, kindly stepped in, and carried him away to 'where the wicked cease from troubling and the weary are at rest.'" William Burness died at Lochlea, 13th February, 1784, and was buried at Kirk Alloway. Shortly afterwards the family took possession of the farm at Mossgiel (q.v.).

Speaking of his brother's early years, especially during the Lochlea period, Gilbert said: "Though when young he was bashful and awkward in his intercourse with women, yet when he approached manhood his attachment to their society became very strong and he was constantly the victim of some fair enslaver. The symptoms of his passion were often such as nearly to equal those of the celebrated Sappho. I never indeed knew that he ' fainted, sunk, and died away,' but the agitation of his mind and body exceeded anything of the kind I ever knew in real life. He had always a particular jealousy of people who were richer than himself, or who had more consequence in life. His love, therefore, rarely settled on persons of this description. When he selected any one out of the sovereignty of his good pleasure, to whom he should pay his particular attention, she was instantly invested with a sufficient stock of charms, out of the plentiful stores of his own imagination ; and there was often a great disparity between his fair captivator and her attributes."

There are many other incidents connected with the life of Burns during the Lochlea period that possess a special interest for his readers. For instance, it was during this time that he first ventured beyond the range of his father's control by going to a dancing school, to " give his manners a brush," as he termed it. Then we have the memorable summer spent from home at Kirkoswald (q.v.) ; the disastrous stay at Irvine (q.v.) ; the forming of the Bachelors' Club at Tarbolton (q.v.) ; the falling-in with the copy of Fergusson's Poems ; the beginning of his connection with the Masonic fraternity ; the songs and letters addressed to Elison Begbie, who after all refused to marry him. These, as well as other incidents which had a more or less direct bearing on his future career, are of deep interest to the lover of Burns and will amply repay a careful study of each in detail.

Among the Poems and Songs produced during the Lochlea period are : " O Tibbie I hae seen the day," " The Tarbolton Lasses," " The Ronalds of the Bennals," " The Lass of Cessnock Banks," " Mary Morrison," " My Nannie O," " Corn Rigs," " No churchman am I," " John Morison," " The Death and Dying Words of poor Mailie " and " Bonnie Peggy Alison."

LOCHMABEN.

An ancient royal burgh in the parish of Annandale, Dumfriesshire. It was one time the residence of King Robert the Bruce and has a statue to his memory, erected in 1875. The town lies about eight miles from Dumfries and has a pleasing appearance. It is referred to by Burns in his election ballad entitled " The Five Carlins."

LOCHRYAN MSS.

Consisting of letters and poems sent by Burns to Mrs. Dunlop who retained them until her death in 1815, when they passed along with the estate of Lochryan into the possession of her grand-son, General Sir John Wallace. Ultimately they became the property of Mr.

R. R. Adam, of Buffalo, N.Y., and in 1898, edited by Dr. William Wallace they were published in two volumes, under the title of " Robert Burns and Mrs. Dunlop."

LOGAN BRAES.

" Have you ever, my dear sir, felt your bosom ready to burst with indignation on reading how those mighty villains divide kingdom against kingdom, desolate provinces, and lay Nations waste, out of the wantonness of ambition, or often from still more ignoble passions ? " asks Burns in a letter to George Thomson. " In a mood of this kind to-day, I recollected the air of ' Logan Water,' and it occurred to me that its querulous melody probably had its origin from the plaintive indignation of some swelling, suffering heart, fired at the tyrannic strides of some Public Destroyer ; and overwhelmed with private distress, the consequence of a country's ruin. If I have done anything at all like justice to my feelings, the song following composed in three quarters of an hour's lucubrations in my elbow chair, ought to have some merit."

It is probable that the Logan here referred to is the stream of that name in Lanarkshire.

LORIMER, JEAN, MEMORIAL. See under " Chloris Memorial."

LOUNGER, THE.

An Edinburgh weekly publication which ran from the sixth of February, 1785, till the sixth of January, 1787. The editor was Henry Mackenzie, author of "The Man of Feeling," "Life of Dr. Blacklock," etc. In December ninth 1786 issue Mackenzie published the first lengthy appreciation that had appeared of the poems in the Kilmarnock edition. In this review he gave a generous extract from "The Vision," and quoted, "To a Mountain Daisy," in full, and his well-merited criticism did much to introduce the poet favourably to the Edinburgh literary public and others.

LOWRIE'S BURN.

A pseudonym for the St. Lawrence River. The line, "Down Lowrie's Burn he took a turn," occurs in the second stanza of the "Ballad on the American War." The ballad was first published in the "Edinburgh Edition" of the poems (1787).

LOYAL NATIVES' CLUB, THE DUMFRIES.

Was formed 18th January, 1793, for the purpose of "Supporting the Laws and Constitution of the Country." "At this period of our Poet's life," writes R. H. Cromek, "when political animosity was made the ground for private quarrel, some foolish verses were circulated containing an attack on Burns and his friends for their political opinions. They were written by some members of a club styling themselves the 'Loyal Natives,' of Dumfries, or rather by the united genius of that Club, which was more distinguished for drunken loyalty, than either for respectability or poetical talent.'' One of the verses handed to the poet while he sat at a convivial meeting contains the following lines :—

> '' Ye sons of Sedition, give ear to my song,
> Let Syme, Burns and Maxwell pervade every throng,
> With Craken, the attorney, and Mundell, the quack,
> Send Willie, the monger, to hell with a smack.

This brought forth the well-known reply :

> Ye true ' Loyal Natives ' attend to my song,
> In uproar and riot rejoice the night long !
> From envy and hatred your corps is exempt ;
> But where is your shield from the darts of contempt ?

And this is the last we hear of the '' Loyal Natives' Club.''

LUATH.

The name of a dog that belonged to the poet and which figures in '' The Twa Dogs.''

LUGAR.

A small stream in Ayrshire. It runs fifteen miles to the river Ayr near Barkskimming, as Burns sings, '' 'Mong moors and mosses many O ! '' It is associated with the beautiful song '' My Nanie O.''

> '' Beyond yon Hills where Lugar flows.''

Q

M

MACKENZIE'S HOUSE, DR. JOHN. Mauchline.

It stands on Castle Street adjoining the one in which Burns and Jean Armour began their married life,—now known as the Burns House, (q.v.)—and almost opposite the now famous "Nance Tinnock's" (q.v.). After Burns's time it was known locally as "the doctor's shop," from the fact that Dr. Dugald Stewart Hamilton had his drug shop there. but it is not certain that Dr. Mackenzie resided there—at least not for any length of time—although he possessed an interest in the property for many years. It was purchased in 1915 by the late Mr. Charles Rennie Cowie, J.P., who gifted it to the Glasgow and District Burns Association. After being thoroughly renovated under the supervision of the well-known Glasgow Architect, Mr. Ninian Macwhannell, F.R.I.B.A., it was divided into a number of small rooms and these are now occupied by aged and deserving persons, somewhat after the plan on which the "Cottage Homes" at the Tower is conducted. A granite slab built into the wall of the Burns and Mackenzie houses, contains the following inscription: "These Properties and 'Auld Nance Tinnock's,' opposite, were the gift of Mr. Charles Rennie Cowie, J.P., to The Glasgow and District Burns Association, 1915-1924." Surmounting the inscription is a medallion in bronze, the work of Mr. G. H. Paulin, A.R.S.A.   See also " Who's Who In Burns."

MACPHERSON, JAMES.

James Macpherson was a noted Highland free-booter of uncommon personal strength, and an excellent performer on the violin. After holding the counties of Aberdeen, Banff, and Moray in fear for some years, " he was seized by Duff of Braco, ancestor of the Duke of Fife, and tried before the sheriff of Banff (November 7, 1700).   In the prison, while he lay under sentence of death, he composed a song and an appropriate air, the former commencing thus :

> ' I've spent my time in rioting,
>   Debauch'd my health and strength ;
> I squander'd fast as pillage came,
>   And fell to shame at length.
>   But dantonly, and wantonly,
>   And rantingly I'll gae ;
>   I'll play a tune, and dance it roun'
>   Beneath the gallows-tree.'

When brought to the place of execution the cross of Banff (Nov. 16), he played the tune on his violin, and then asked if any friend was present who would accept the instrument as a gift at his hands.   No one coming forward, he snapped the fiddle across his knee, and threw away the fragments ; " after which he submitted to his fate."

The traditionary accounts of Macpherson's immense prowess are justified by his sword, which is still preserved in Duff House, at Banff, and is an implement of great length and weight—as well as by his bones, which were found a few years ago, and were allowed by all who saw them to be much stronger than the bones of ordinary men."

MAIDENKIRK.

An inversion of "Kirkmaiden" in Wigtonshire, the most southerly parish in Scotland. John o' Groat's House, on the other hand, was in the north extremity of the country, hence the line in "On Captain Grose's Peregrinations Thro' Scotland:"—
"Frae Maidenkirk to Johnie Groat's."

MAILIE.

The author's only pet yowe. See poem "Death and Dying Words of Poor Mailie."

MALT SHOVEL INN, THE.   See Carlisle.

MANUSCRIPTS, BURNS.   See under "Honresfield Collection."

MAN WAS MADE TO MOURN.   A Dirge.

"Several of the poems," says Gilbert Burns, "were produced for the purpose of bringing forward some favourite sentiment of the author's. He used to remark to me

that he could not well conceive a more morti-
fying picture of human life than a man seek-
ing work. In casting about in his mind how
this sentiment might be brought forward,
the elegy ' Man was Made to Mourn,' was
composed."

An old Scottish ballad had suggested the
form and spirit of this poem. " I had an old
grand-uncle," says the poet to Mrs. Dunlop,
"with whom my mother lived a while in her
girlish years. The good old man was long
blind ere he died, during which time his
highest enjoyment was to sit down and cry,
while my mother would sing the simple old
song of the ' Life and Age of Man.' "

MANSON'S TAVERN.

A small building in Tarbolton near the
end of the village and a short distance from
Willie's Mill. It is still standing on what is
now called Burns Street. Here St. David's
Lodge at one time held its meetings and here
on the 4th July, 1781, Burns it is claimed, was
initiated into the mysteries of the Craft.
James Manson was an enthusiastic Mason
and his place was much frequented by members of the fraternity and others for many
years.

MARY MORISON.

" Of all the productions of Burns," says
Hazlitt, " his pathetic and serious love-songs,

in the manner of the old ballads, are perhaps those which take the deepest and most lasting hold of the mind. Such are the lines to Mary Morison."

The true identity of Mary Morison has not been determined. As a love-song the piece ranks with any similar lyric in any language.

MASONRY. See under Freemasonry.

"MASSON'S ENGLISH COLLECTION."

A collection of English Prose and Verse, from several authors of established credit. By Arthur Masson, M.A., late Teacher of Languages in Edinburgh and Glasgow. Aberdeen, 1749.

This was one of the poet's school books and he makes mention of it in his autobiographic letter to Dr. Moore. The book was a popular one with teachers at the time and many editions of it were called for, the eleventh one being dated, Edinburgh, 1788.

MAUCHLINE.

This pleasantly situated little town is about one mile from Mossgiel and is commercially known to-day for its output of curling stones, fancy wood-work articles, and its manufacture of woollen goods. Spinning and weaving are also carried on, but only to a moderate extent. A quiet, industrious place at present, it must have been an enterprising and busy centre at one time, as it is credited with holding a number of fairs each year in addition to annual races. But apart from these features the town and its neighbourhood are reminiscent of Burns and his time. Here Jean Armour was born, and here as the poet's wife, she first " took up house." Here were " Poosie Nancie's " (q.v.), " Johnny Doo's," " Whitefoord Arms " (q.v.), " Nance Tinnock's " (q.v.) and other similar resorts. Here also were the Kirk and Kirkyard, the latter destined to become famous all over the world as the scene of " The Holy Fair " (q.v.). Here " Daddy Auld," "Holy Willie," John Richmond, Gavin Hamilton, James Smith, James Humphrey and many others whose names are familiar to us, could be seen daily as they traversed the streets of the Auld Toon. Nor must we forget the " six proper young belles," five of whom became more or less famous through the magic touch of the Poet's pen, the sixth, " the Jewel of them a'," was Jean Armour.

Much has been written from time to time, concerning Mauchline, past and present, its people, and its neighbourhood, and among those writers, Mr. J. Taylor Gibb, of Mauchline, is probably the best known. His articles on the subject, contributed on several occasions to the Burns Chronicle and other publications, have given general satisfaction, and being a native of the town and a life-long resident there his writings may be depended upon as being correct in all details. Mr. Gibb is also the author of a little book, "Mauchline Town and District," now very scarce and eagerly sought for by collectors and others.

A silent feature of the town—and one altogether apart from the Burns interests—is the Martyrs' Monument, or, as it is called, the Martyrs' Stone, which stands on the Loan Green. This is in the form of an obelisk and was erected in 1885. According to "Mauchline Town and District," the Monument is "in memory of five men who were hanged and buried here on the 6th of May, 1685, for their adherence to the covenanted work of Reformation. Their names, as recorded on the original stone, which is now inserted a few yards off in the wall facing the back of the monument, were Peter Gillies, John Bryce, Thomas Young, William Fiddison, and John Bruning. This original stone lettered, it is said, by ' Old Mortality,' bears this verse :—

> " Bloody Dumbarton, Douglass, and Dundee,
> Mov'd by the Devil and the Laird of Lee
> Dragg'd these five men to death with gun and sword,
> Not suffering them to pray nor read God's word ;
> The eighty-five was a Saint-killing time."

Mauchline has a very fine Burns Club which was instituted in 1923 and federated the same year (No. 310). The Membership is seventy and the Club meets in Poosie Nancie's Hall on the first Monday of each month from September to March. While the members are deeply concerned in all things relating to the poet, special attention is given to local Burns matters in particular.

MAUCHLINE. The Bleaching Green Incident.

" The mention of the Bleaching Green brings to mind the story, oft and many ways told, of the first meeting of Burns and Jean Armour. Some few days after Burns had been at a ball (penny reel) in Hugh Morton's ballroom at Mauchline on the race night, at which he had in the hearing of Miss Armour (Jean) expressed the wish that he ' had a lass wad lo'e him as weel as his dug ' (the dog tracking his master's footsteps ' through the lichtit ha'), he had occasion to pass through the Bleaching Green, when, as luck would have it, he foregathered with Miss Armour. She rallied him about his dog, which, as Robert Stevenson states in his ' Aspects of Burns,' ' was in its daffin staining with his four black paws the cloth she had laid out to whiten.' ' Ca' in your dog,' pertly she cried, most likely with many blushes, at the same time ' speerin' gin he had as yet gotten a lass to lo'e him as weel." So the story goes—a very fair beginning—the end being Miss Armour became Mrs. Robert Burns."—J. Taylor Gibb.

MAUCHLINE, BURNS'S HOUSE.

A two storey building standing on what was one time known as " Back Causeway," now named Castle Street. It was in a room on the second storey of this building that Burns and Jean Armour started house-keeping after their irregular marriage in 1788, and here Jean remained until Ellisland was ready to receive her. The building is at least two hundred years old and adjoins the one occupied by the poet's friend, Dr. John Mackenzie, almost opposite to that of the famous " Nance Tinnock's " (q.v.). It stood tenantless for many years and was fast degenerating into decay, when in 1915 it was purchased by the late Mr. Charles Rennie Cowie, J.P., who very generously deeded it over, free and clear of all encumbrances, to the Glasgow and District Burns Association. After being thoroughly renovated under the supervision of the well-known Architect, Mr. Ninian Macwhannell, F.R.I.B.A., Glasgow— who by the way rendered his services gratuitously—the rooms on the second storey were restored as far as possible to their original shape, while the ground floor was transformed into a number of smaller rooms and these are now occupied by a few aged and deserving persons free of rental, on a plan similar to that on which the " Cottage Homes " at the Tower is conducted. The building was formally opened 28th August, 1924. The room adjoining the one once occupied by Burns and Jean has been turned into a Museum and contains a collection of books, manuscripts, facsimiles, portraits and statues in addition to a few Burns and other choice relics. Contributions for this interesting room will be very much appreciated at all times.

A granite slab built into the wall of the two houses (Burns's and Mackenzie's) contains the following inscription : " These Properties and ' Auld Nance Tinnock's ' opposite, were the gift of Mr. Charles Rennie Cowie, J.P., to The Glasgow and District Burns Association 1915-1924." Surmounting the inscription is a medallion in bronze, the work of Mr. G. H. Paulin, A.R.S.A.

" MAUCHLINE CASTLE."

The name given to the residence of Govan Hamilton in Mauchline. Most probably it began to be called "Castle" after the Reformation when the building ceased to be Monastic.

MAUCHLINE KIRK AND KIRKYARD.

The latter, as every one knows, was the scene of " The Holy Fair." The Auld Kirk which dated from the 12th century was not a very imposing building, "but it had," to quote Rev. Dr. Edgar in ' Old Church Life in Scotland,' " a pedigree and a history. It was one of the pre-Reformation churches in

Scotland.   It was built in the time of Popery, and it witnessed all the stir of the Reformation.   It had been used for Catholic and Protestant services, both for Presbyterian and Prelatical forms of worship." The present church which occupies the site of the old one was erected in 1829, and has little or no interest to a stranger.   The churchyard, however, will ever remain a special point of more than ordinary interest to pilgrims from far and near, for here they may come at all times and linger beside the resting places of many whose names and deeds, in a number of instances, form a connecting link with the past, and for whose memories they cherish   deep respect.   To quote Mr. J. Taylor Gibb, "For more than 700 years 'the rude forefathers of the hamlet' have been carried to their last abode in the Auld Kirkyard.   Not many great, as the world calls great, yet withal a goodly company of those whose works do follow them.   One stone (erected in 1727 and re-erected in 1805) alone marks the grave of a Covenanter who was wounded by Captain Inglis and his dragoons at the Burn of Ann in Kyle, and thereafter died of his wounds in Mauchline prison for his adherence to the Word of God and Scotland's covenanted work of Reformation, A.D., 1684. How many more of covenanting stock lie here there is no record, yet Mauchline surely acted her part in the ' killing times.'

"No stone of very ancient date nor monumental structure 'rich and rare' can the Churchyard boast of, yet there are a few ornate in diction telling forth the virtues of those whose names they chronicle. Here a 'steady and sincere friend,' there 'an affectionate husband and parent,' while beyond repose the remains of one who was esteemed the

> ' Pearl of her sex and age,
>   Humble, sober, grave and sage.'

More than one student in the ' opening of activities,' and of soldiers (veterans) not a few —each bewailed in their day and generation.

One stone deserves a special notice. No name or record on its face, which may perhaps account for the numbers on its back, by whom composed we know not, but think that they were inspired :—

> ' How lov'd, how valued once avails thee not,
>   To whom related, or by whom begot ;
>   A heap of dust alone remains of thee,
>   'Tis all thou art, and all the proud shall be.'

> Life,   Eternity,
> How Short   How Long. "

MAUCHLINE, THE NATIONAL BURNS MEMORIAL AND COTTAGE HOMES.

Situated on a triangular piece of ground, within sight of Mossgiel, half a mile from

Mauchline, is one of the finest and most practical of all the Memorials erected to honour the memory of Robert Burns. The Tower is sixty feet high and behind it are the cottages consisting of one and two rooms each, these being occupied, rent free, by a number of old and deserving persons. The idea of the Memorial originated with the members of the Glasgow Mauchline Society. The designer was Mr. William Fraser, A.R.I.B.A. of Glasgow, and the builders Messrs W. Muir & Co., Kilmarnock. The Homes were ready for occupancy in November, 1897, and the Tower was officially opened 7th May, 1898, by Mr. J. G. A. Baird, of Wellwood, Muirkirk. He was M.P. for the Central Division of Glasgow.

The Tower is a square built turreted structure in the old Scottish baronial style of architecture and is divided into three floors. The whole of the interior is used as a Museum and contains numerous valuable Manuscripts and other relics of the Poet. From the flat roof on the top a magnificent view of the surrounding country is obtained.

Too much cannot be said in favour of the Cottage Homes part of the Memorial. These are simple and tasteful in design and pleasant to look upon. To quote from a circular recently issued by the directors, " The occupants get the houses free of rent and taxes, and also a few pounds per annum. The site

is an ideal one, right in the open country, and
each house has a garden of flowers and vege-
tables.

"There are no irksome restrictions. The
Cottagers bring their own furniture, have their
own key, and go in and out and have their
own friends visiting them as they please, without any paid official having the right to question them. This liberty they greatly appreciate, and never abuse. They have as near as
possible their 'ain fireside,' and during the
twenty-five years since the buildings were
erected, the Committee have never had to
question or censure a single one of the
Cottagers.

"The Cottagers are carefully chosen and
come from all quarters, there being no restrictions as to place of birth or residence. There
is no lack of suitable applicants, and once they
are admitted our aim is to let them live out
the remaining years of their lives in quiet
comfort. No wonder that many an old couple
have found that a home there, under these
sympathetic conditions, has made all the
difference between grinding poverty and comparative comfort. Many a time the old folks
have spoken with tears of joy in their eyes of
the change it has meant for them.

"The Cottage Homes give practical expression to the Poet's intense sympathy for those
suffering from old age and innocent misfortune. He taught us that 'The best o'

chiels are whiles in want,' and it is in such cases we are trying to help."

On Saturday, 28th June, 1930, a great grand-daughter of the poet, Mrs. Violet Burns Gowring, cut the first sod in connection with five additional houses. The erection of this group was made possible largely through the generosity of the late Mr. J. Bulloch, of Glasgow.

Additional funds to add to the number of Cottages or to assist in defraying the general expenses of the undertaking, are always acceptable and the officers will very much appreciate any help tended to them for either purpose. The names and addresses of these gentlemen may be ascertained by referring to the ' Directory of Burns Clubs and Scottish Societies ' in the latest issue of the " Burns Chronicle."

MAUSOLEUM, ST. MICHAEL'S CHURCHYARD, Dumfries.

Erected nineteen years after the Poet's death.

" The movement which brought about such a magnificent result," writes William M'Dowall in his ' Memorials of St. Michael's,' " had a very small beginning, and it was originated by the following circular, ' written by Mr. William Grierson, in company with Mr. John Syme : '

Sir,—It has long been a subject of regret and indeed a reflection against Scotland, that nothing yet has been done to perpetuate the memory, and do honour to the genius of its native bard, Robert Burns, by marking the spot where his ashes rest. There can be no doubt that, if a public subscription was opened, under the management of a respectable committee, a very liberal sum would soon be procured, in aid of that already promised from abroad, to erect a Monument at his grave, in St. Michael's Churchyard, Dumfries. A few of the friends and admirers of Burns having lately taken the affair into consideration, concluded that the most proper method would be to invite a meeting of such gentlemen as might be disposed to promote the measure, to take place in the George Inn, on Thursday, the 16th December, at two o'clock afternoon, in order to name a committee, and to adopt such resolutions as may appear best calculated to carry into effect so desirable an object. It is therefore hoped you will find it convenient to attend the meeting on the above mentioned day. Dumfries, 29th November, 1813.

To the appeal thus made only eighteen gentlemen responded literally by appearing at the meeting on the 16th of December, but it touched the chords of the national heart ; and those who made up the number were all influential persons, including John Syme, who fittingly presided as the attached friend of Burns ; William Miller of Dalswinton ; William Grierson ; Henry Duncan, the accomplished minister of Ruthwell ; Thomas Duncan, minister of the new Church (now Greyfriars') ; William M'Lellan of Keltonhead ;

R

Gabriel Richardson, ex-Provost, with whom the poet long lived on intimate terms ; and Adam Rankine, who had always a shoulder ready to put to the proverbial wheel when it required a push forward in the right direction. The Rev. H. (afterwards Dr.) Duncan and Mr. Grierson were appointed secretaries, the main burden of the business, however, devolving on the latter, who gave his services with unbounded enthusiasm. Soon money for the fund began to flow in liberally from all quarters—from abroad as well as from home, and from ' huts where poor men lie,' not less than from the palaces of nobles and kings. In due time several competent designs for the memorial edifice were received by the committee. The one which they selected was furnished by Mr. T. F. Hunt of London, who, emulating Burns's own unselfishness, refused to take a farthing for his work, considering that the honour of associating his name with the national bard in such a way was recompense enough. As originally drawn, the design bore four oblong, graceful sarcophagi placed over those parts of the entablature of the Mausoleum that touch each of the twin pillars by which the dome and its accompaniments are supported ; but these stone chests were omitted, and we think wisely, as they have a somewhat heavy aspect, and if they had been introduced they would have interfered with the noble simplicity of the structure.

Burns, in the dedication of his first volume, says : "The Poetic Genius of my country found me, as the prophetic bard Elijah did Elisha, at the plough ; and threw her inspiring mantle over me." It was rightly thought that a marble embodiment of the fine idea would form a fitting ornament for the interior ; and Signor Turnerelli, an Italian artist, was entrusted with the task. As he proceeded with the figures they were critically inspected by a committee including the poet's brother, Gilbert, who expressed himself satisfied with the appearance of the inspiring divinity and the airy lightness of her attire ; and guided by his correct eye and retentive memory, the sculptor (who had, we believe, never seen the poet) was enabled to render the principal figure wonderfully faithful. Though the statuary is not of the highest class, it gratifies all but fastidious hypercritics by the expressive way in which it tells its momentous tale to admiring eyes and sympathetic hearts. The foundation-stone of the Mausoleum was laid on the 5th of June, 1815, and the building was completed in the following September, the entire cost amounting to about £1500."

A Latin inscription (q.v.) was composed for the Mausoleum, but was never used.

Colonel William Nicol Burns, the poet's third son, left his father's Tomb in charge of the Dumfries Burns Club, and it is needless to point out how carefully and sacredly the charge has been attended to.

MAYBOLE.

A pleasantly situated little town about nine miles from Ayr, with a population of about five thousand. In ancient time it was the Capital of Carrick and it still possesses an old castle. The staple industry of the town is shoemaking.

Burns had many friends in Maybole and frequently passed through the town. On one occasion, August 28, 1786, while returning to Mossgiel from a southern journey on which he had been collecting money for subscriptions to the Kilmarnock edition of his poems, he prolonged his visit for a night and enjoyed the hospitalities provided by his friends. "I thank you with the most heartfelt sincerity for the worthy knot of lads you introduced me to," he writes his friend William Niven, of Maybole, two days later. "Never did I meet with as many congenial souls together, without one dissonant jar in the concert. To all and each of them make my friendly compliments." Niven and Burns even at this date were old friends, having known each other during their school days at Kirkoswald.

There is a note by Burns in "Johnson's Musical Museum" in regard to the old song "Johnny Faa, or The Gipsy Laddie." He says "The people in Ayrshire begin this song:

'The gypsies cam' to my Lord Cassilis' yett.'

They have a great many more stanzas in this song than I ever yet saw in any printed copy. —The castle is still remaining at Maybole, where his lordship shut up his wayward spouse and kept her for life."

Maybole has a flourishing Burns Club (Maybole St. Crispin Burns Club) of forty members. Instituted, 1927, No. 369 on Federation Roll.

MELBOURNE, VICTORIA STATUE.

Unveiled 23rd January, 1904, by His Excellency Sir John Madden, Lieutenant-Governor of Victoria, who also delivered an oration on the poet. The ceremony of unveiling was witnessed by over five thousand people. The statue, by George A. Lawson, R.S.A., is of bronze and stands on a granite pedestal. The name Burns is on the die in front. The other panel contains scenes from " The Cottar's Saturday Night," Burns at the Plough, and " Tam O' Shanter." On the base is a tablet with the inscription, " Erected under the auspices of the Caledonian Society of Melbourne, 1904." The statue occupies a prominent position on St. Kilda Road, Princes Bridge.

MELODIES, THE, attached to Burns's Songs. See under Dick, James C.

MERRY MUSES OF CALEDONIA, THE.

Burns occasionally noted down, and ultimately formed a Manuscript Collection of old fashioned and highly spiced Scottish Songs intended expressly for the use of the members of the Crochallan Club (q.v.). In Dumfries he kept the book under lock and key, but some years after his death it unfortunately fell into the hands of an unscrupulous person who caused it to be printed and stealthily published under the above title. This contemptible publication consists of 128 pages, and contains about ninety "Scots' songs, ancient and modern." About one third of them are said to be by Burns, in whole or in part, and of these the following are in nearly all editions of the poet, and were probably inserted to give an air of respectability to the affair : " Yestreen I had a pint o' wine," " We'll hide the cooper ahint the door," " Wha is that at my bower door ? " " Oh wha my babie-clouts will buy ? " " I am a bard of no regard," " Let me ryke up to dight that tear," and " I once was a Maid." The poet's name does not appear on the title page and the book is utterly useless for any purpose. The collection was never intended for publication as a whole, and never should have been printed, let alone published.

In his 1851 edition of Burns, Robert Chambers says that, " unluckily Burns's collection of the " facetiæ," including his own essays in the same walk, fell after his death into the hands of one of those publishers who would sacrifice the highest interests of humanity to put an additional penny into their own purse ; and to the lasting grief of all friends of our poet, they were allowed the honour of the press. The mean looking volume which resulted, should be a warning to all honourable men of letters against the slightest connection with clandestine literature, much more the degradation of contributing to it."

Persons further interested in the subject will find considerable information on it by consulting " The Burns Chronicle," volumes 3 and 20, or the following edition of the book :—

Merry Muses of Caledonia, The.

A collection of Favourite Scots Songs, Ancient and Modern, selected for use of the Crochallan Fencibles. A vindication of Robert Burns in connection with the above Publication and the Spurious Editions, which succeeded it. Edited by D. M'Naught, Kilmaurs, printed on hand-made paper, 8vo.

Printed and Published under the Auspices of the Burns Federation.

For Subscribers only, 1911.

MIERS, THE, SILHOUETTE OF BURNS. See under Portraits of Burns.

MONKLAND (or FRIARS' CARSE) FRIENDLY SOCIETY LIBRARY.

A parish library established at Friars' Carse by Burns and Captain Riddell. In a letter to Peter Hill, the Edinburgh bookseller, (Ellisland, 2nd March, 1790) Burns writes: "At a late meeting of the Monkland Friendly Society, it was resolved to augment the Library by the following books, which you are to send us as soon as possible :—" The Mirror," " The Lounger," " Man of Feeling," " Man of the World," (these, for my own sake I wish to have by the first carrier), "Knox's History of the Reformation," " Rae's History of the Rebellion, 1745," "A Display of the Secession Act and Testimony by Mr. Gibb," "Hervey's Meditations," "Beveridge's Thoughts," and another copy of " Watson's Body of Divinity."

The Library was established with the understanding that it was to run for three years and, at the expiration of this period, its affairs were to be wound up and the books sold to the individual members.

Captain Riddell, writing about the Library to Sir John Sinclair in connection with his " Statistical Account of Scotland," said : " Mr. Burns was so good as to take the whole charge of this small concern. He was treasurer, librarian, and censor to this little Society, who will long have a grateful sense of his public spirit and exertions for their improvement and information."

A full account of the Library and what it accomplished in the brief period of its existence, was afterwards written by the poet for Sir John Sinclair and was included in the latter's work already referred to.

MONTGOMERY CASTLE. See Coilsfield.

MONTREAL STATUE.

Unveiled Saturday, 18th October, 1930, by Mrs. Alexander Hutchinson, daughter of Mr. J. T. M'Call, a prominent member of the Board of Trustees of the Burns Memorial fund since its inception. The statue is nine feet high, a bronze replica of the one at Ayr. One of the four panels of the pedestal bears the words " Robert Burns, 1759-1796. The remaining three contain representative scenes from the Poet's works. Underneath the panel bearing the Poet's name are the last three lines of " A Man's a Man for a' that," and along the front of the base is the inscription " Erected by Admirers of Burns." The memorial stands in a prominent part of Dominion Square. On account of the inclemency of the weather, as soon as the unveiling ceremony was performed the party adjourned to the Windsor Hotel where the remaining exercises were held. These included addresses by the Hon. Rodolphe Lemieux, Mr John Williamson,

M.A., and an invocation by the Rev. Dr.
Malcolm Campbell of the First Presbyterian
Church.   Mr W. M. M'Broom presided and
the music was supplied by the Black Watch
Band and Pipers, R.H. of Canada, under the
leaderships of Captain H. G. Jones and Piper-
Major W. Johnston.   The completion of the
memorial was a great event for the Scottish
population of Montreal, and the day of unveiling will long be remembered.   Among these
prominent in promoting the erection of the
statue and not already mentioned were—
Mr John Shearer, Chief Justice Greenshields,
Mr John M'Donald, Captain V. A. Curmi, Mr
Archibald M'Allister, Mr J. Gordon M'Leod,
and Mr T. B. Macaulay.

MONTROSE STATUE.

Occupies a prominent position on the
Mid-Links of the burgh.   It was unveiled
on 7th August, 1912, by Mr Andrew Carnegie, who also delivered a brilliant oration
on the Poet, his life, works and time.   The
ceremony was witnessed by a vast assemblage of people from all parts of Great Britain,
the United States and Canada.   The statue
is of Binnie freestone and is nine feet high.
The poet is represented as wearing the knee
breeches, long vest and full skirted coat of
the period.   A sheaf of wheat and a portion
of a plough support the figure.   The pedestal
is twelve feet high, with panels on each of the

four sides and on which are representations in bas relief, symbolical of the Poet's sympathies with the labourer, the fair maiden, love of animal life, and an ideal figure suggesting Scotia's Muse. The sculptor was the eminent Mr W. Birnie Rhind, R.S.A., Edinburgh. Montrose is indebted to the members of their local Burns Club and especially to those constituting a part of the Burns Statue Committee, for the untiring efforts which resulted in the handsome memorial which now graces the city.

MONUMENTS AND MEMORIALS.

The World's Memorials of Robert Burns. Collected and described by Edward Goodwillie. The Waverley Publishing Company. Detroit, Michigan. (U.S.A. 1911). Portrait and illustrations.

" The various statues and memorials have been described in the chronological order of their unveiling or inauguration, and at the end have been given descriptions of the Memorials to some of Burns's more famous heroines. In addition there have been many appreciations of Burns by noted men and women of all countries, from the poet's time to the present."—Extract from Preface.

A very excellent book of its kind ; will remain the standard on the subject for many years.

MORHAM MAINS.

A farm in the parish of Morham, three miles from Haddington, which at one time belonged to Captain John Dunlop of Dunlop. He had built a house on the farm and occasionally lived there. After his death in 1785, Mrs. Dunlop, the poet's friend, continued to visit the farm.

Gilbert Burns was the factor on the farm from 1799 to 1803, at which date it changed ownership.

MOSSGIEL.

The farm of Mossgiel, consisting of one hundred and eighteen acres, is in the parish of Mauchline, about three miles from Lochlea. The Burns family entered into possession of it in March, 1784, the poet being then in his twenty-fifth year. Gilbert says: " When my father's affairs drew near a crisis, Robert and I took the farm of Mossgiel, at the rent of ninety pounds per annum, from Mr. Hamilton, as an asylum for the family in case of the worst. It was stocked by the property and individual savings of the whole family, and was a joint-concern among us. Every member of the family was allowed ordinary wages for the labour he performed on the farm. My brother's allowance and mine were seven pounds per annum each. The farm lies very high and mostly on a cold wet bottom."

Burns began life at Mossgiel with the best of resolutions. " I read farming books," he says, " I calculated crops ; I attended markets ; and in short, in spite of the devil, the world, and the flesh, I believe I should have been a wise man ; but the first year, from unfortunately buying in bad seed ; the second, from a late harvest we lost half of both our crops. This overset all my wisdom. . . . My brother wanted my hare-brained imagination, as well as my social and amorous madness ; but in good sense, and every sober qualification, he was far my superior." Later on he tells us : " I now began to be known in the neighbourhood as a maker of rhymes. The first of my poetic offspring that saw the light was a burlesque lamentation on a quarrel between two Reverend Calvinists, both of them *dramatis personæ* in my " Holy Fair." With a certain side of both clergy and laity, it met with a roar of applause." And it may be said that the applause accorded to this poem became louder and louder as other poems appeared and did not relax in any measure but became more universal with the publication of the now famous Kilmarnock edition of the poet.

The farm house at Mossgiel is still standing, although its walls have been raised and a slate roof has supplanted the thatched one of the poet's time. At the rear of the house

lies the field where he ploughed up the daisy
and in another field close by, is where he over-
turned the mouse's nest. The old house consisted of a one storey cottage with the usual
" but and ben," and a garret containing three
small rooms, the one in the centre being
occupied as a bedroom by the two brothers.
A table with a drawer stood in the room and
in this drawer the poet kept his papers. " To
this room," says Robert Chambers, " when he
had returned from his day's work, the poet
used to retire and seat himself at the table to
transcribe the verses which he had composed
in the fields. His favourite time for composition was at the plough. Long years after
this, his sister, Mrs. Begg, used to tell how,
when her brother had gone forth again to
field work, she would steal up to the garret
and search the drawer of the deal table for
the verses which Robert had newly trans-
scribed." And what a wonderful and exciting
experience this must have been for her !

Among the poems and songs composed
during the Mossgiel period were :—" The
Vision," " Address to the Unco Guid," the
two Epistles to Davie and three to Lapraik,
" Hallowe'en," " The Jolly Beggars," " The
Cottar's Saturday Night," " The Ordination,"
" The Author's Earnest Cry," " Address to
the Deil," " The Holy Fair," " Holy Willie's
Prayer," " Death and Doctor Hornbook,"
' Rantin' roarin' Robin," " Man was Made

to Mourn," "The Braes o' Ballochmyle," "The Twa Dogs," "Scotch Drink," and others—truly a galaxy of immortal writings.

To-day within sight of Mossgiel, stands one of the greatest and most practical of all the memorials erected to honour the genius of the poet, viz.—the National Burns Memorial and Cottage Homes, Mauchline (q.v.).

MOUNT OLIPHANT.

In 1766 the Burns family removed from the "Auld Clay Biggin," at Alloway, and settled on the farm of Mount Oliphant, some two miles distant, on the estate of Doonholm, about three miles from Ayr. William Burness took this step with the object of improving his worldy affairs and to keep his family about him as they grew older instead of sending them out to service. The farm of Mount Oliphant was upwards of seventy acres. The rental was forty pounds for the first six years, and afterwards forty-five pounds. For the purpose of stocking the farm William Burness endeavoured to dispose of his leasehold property at Alloway, but being unsuccessful in this, his new landlord, Provost Ferguson of Ayr, came to his assistance and lent him one hundred pounds.

Previous to their removal to Mount Oliphant Robert and Gilbert had received the benefit of a little education, first from Wm. Campbell, of Alloway, and later from William

Murdoch, of Ayr, the latter a name which figures very largely and very favourably in the early days of the Burns family. " In the month of May, 1765,"writes Mr. Murdoch, " I was engaged by Mr. Burness and four of his neighbours to teach the little School at Alloway. My pupil, ROBERT BURNS, was then between six and seven years of age, his preceptor about eighteen. Robert and his younger brother Gilbert, had been grounded a little in English before they were put under my care. They both made a rapid progress in reading, and a tolerable progress in writing . . . and were generally at the upper end of the class, even when ranged with boys far their seniors. . . . . Robert's countenance was generally grave, and expressive of a serious, contemplative mind. Gilbert's face said ' Mirth with thee I mean to live ; ' and certainly, if any person who knew the two boys had been asked which of them was the most likely to court the Muses, he would surely never have guessed that Robert had a propensity of that kind . . . . . . In the year of (1767) Mr. Burness quitted his mud edifice, and took a farm of his own improving. This farm being at a considerable distance from the school, the boys could not attend regularly, and some changes taking place among the other supporters of the school, I left it, having continued to conduct it for nearly two years and a half."

Writing of Mount Oliphant Gilbert said the soil was almost the poorest that he ever knew of in a state of cultivation, and, in consequence of this, his father soon fell into difficulties which were increased by the loss of several of his cattle by accident and disease. The family lived very sparingly and for several years butcher's meat was a stranger in the house, while all the members exerted themselves to the utmost of their strength and rather beyond it in the labours of the farm. "My brother," he says, "at the age of thirteen assisted in threshing the crop of corn, and at fifteen was the principal labourer on the farm—for we had no hired servants. I doubt not, but that the hard labour and sorrow of this period of his life was, in a great measure, the cause of that depression of spirits with which Robert was so often afflicted through his whole life afterwards." To add to the troubles of the family Mr. Ferguson, the landlord, died and the estate, including the farm of Mount Oliphant, passed under the control of a factor. "My generous master died," wrote Burns in his autobiography, "the farm proved a ruinous bargain; and to clench the curse we fell into the hands of a factor, who sat for the picture I have drawn of one in my tale of "Twa Dogs."... There was a freedom in his lease in two years more, and to weather these, we re-trenched expenses. We lived

S

very poorly. . . . A novel-writer might per-haps have viewed these scenes with some satisfaction ; but so did not I. My indig-nation yet boils at the recollection of the scoundrel factor's insolent, threatening letters which used to set us all in tears."

The life at Mount Oliphant, however, was a memorable time for the poet, as it was during it that he first fell in love and wrote his first song, " O' once I loved a bonnie lass," besides a number of other compositions.

" You know our country custom of coupling a man and a woman together as partners in the labours of harvest. In my fifteenth autumn," the poet writes, " my part-ner was a bewitching creature, who just counted an autumn less. My scarcity of English denies me the power of doing her justice in that language, but you know the Scotch idiom—she was a ' bonnie, sweet, sonsie lass.' In short, she, altogether unwittingly to herself, initiated me into a certain delicious passion which, in spite of acid disappointment, gin-horse prudence, and book-worm philosophy, I hold to be the first of human joys, our chiefest blessing here below ! How she caught the contagion I can't say ; you medical folks talk much of infection by breathing the same air, the touch, etc. ; but I never expressly told her that I loved her. Indeed, I did not well know myself why I liked so much to loiter

behind with her, when returning in the evening from our labours ; why the tones of her
voice made my heart strings thrill like an
Æolian harp ; and particularly why my pulse
beat such a furious rantann, when I looked and
fingered over her hand to pick out the nettle-
stings and thistles. Among her other love-
inspiring qualifications, she sung sweetly ;
and 'twas her favourite Scotch reel that I
attempted to give an embodied vehicle to
in rhyme. I was not so presumptive as to
imagine that I could make verses like printed
ones, composed by men who had Greek and
Latin ; but my girl sung a song which was said
to be composed by a small country laird's
son, on one of his father's maids with whom he
was in love ; and I saw no reason why I might
not rhyme as well as he ; for, excepting
smearing sheep and casting peats (his father
living in the moors), he had no more scholar-
craft than I had.

Thus with me began love and poesy,
which at times have been my only, and, till
within the last twelve months, have been
my highest enjoyment. My father struggled
on till he reached a freedom in his lease,
when he entered on a larger farm, about ten
miles farther in the country. The nature of
the bargain was such as to throw a little
ready money in his hand at the commencement, otherwise the affair would have been
impracticable "

The farm to which the poet refers was that of Lochlea (q.v.) which the family took possession of in 1777.

MURISON COLLECTION. See under Dunfermline.

N

" NANCE TINNOCK'S."

Immortalized by Burns as " Auld Nance Tinnock's," although the place had long been known as " The Sma' Inn " and was even well known after his day by that name. It stands in Castle Street (formerly named the Back Causeway), almost opposite the house occupied by the poet's friend, Dr. John Mac-Kenzie, adjoining the one known as " The Burns House," and dates back, we are told, to 1712. It overlooks the Parish Church, and in former days had a stairway leading down to the Churchyard, the latter now celebrated far and wide as the scene of " The Holy Fair " (q.v.). On Communion occasions, which were usually attended by large crowds, Nancie's Changehouse was the centre of attraction for such worshippers as required material refreshments between and after the services. It was at such time that

" Now, butt an' ben the Change-house fills
    Wi' yill-caup commentators ;
Here's crying out for bakes an' gills,
    An' there the pint-stoup clatters ;
While thick an' thrang, an' loud and lang,
    Wi' logic an' wi' Scripture,
They raise a din, that, in the end,
    Is like to breed a rupture
    O' wrath that day."

The building is now the property of the Glasgow and District Association, having been gifted to it by the late Mr. Charles Rennie Cowie, J.P., the donor of the MacKenzie house and the one adjoining it, now styled " The Burns House." After being renovated under the supervision of the well-known Architect, Mr. Ninian Macwhannell, F.R.I.B.A., Glasgow,—who rendered his services gratuitously— it was divided into small rooms and these are occupied by a number of aged and deserving persons, free of rent, on a plan similar to that which prevails at the Tower in connection with the " Cottage Homes." A granite slab built into the front of the Burns and Mac-Kenzie Houses contains the following inscription : " These Properties and ' Auld Nance Tinnock's ' opposite, were the gift of Mr. Charles Rennie Cowie, J.P., To the Glasgow and District Burns Association, 1915-24." The inscription is surmounted by a medallion in brass, the work of G. H. Paulin, A.R.S.A. See also " Who's Who In Burns."

NANCY STAIR.

A novel, by Elinor Macartney Lane, author of " Mills of God," D. Appleton and Company. MCMIV.

This is purely a work of fiction in which Robert Burns is made to appear as one of the central figures. From the foot-notes embodied in the book many persons are led to believe that the story was taken from real life, or that it was founded on facts and that the heroine's poems had been published in book form. No such volume, however, has ever been published, and Nancy Stair herself is nothing but a myth, or, in other words, a clever creation of Mrs. Lane's imagination.

NASMYTH, THE, PORTRAIT OF BURNS. See under Portraits of Burns.

NETHERTON.

A part of Kilmarnock in which carpet weaving at one time was the main industry. The place is referred to in " The Ordination."

> " Or, to the Netherton repair
> And turn a carpet weaver."

NEW LICHTS, THE. See under Auld Lichts, The.

NEW YORK CITY HIGHLAND MARY STATUE.

Stands in the New York Public Library on Fifth Avenue. It is pure white marble, the work of Benjamin E. Spence, a Liverpool artist, who died at an early age in Italy. The figure clasps a Bible in the right hand, while a Scottish plaid falls gracefully from the head and shoulders. The statue is a dupli-cate—life size—of the one in Sefton Park, Liverpool, England (q.v.). " It was indeed a happy thought," says George Savage, " to

thus perpetuate in enduring stone the sculptor's admirable conception of the beloved
one whose name will always be associated
with that of him who sang of her." It was
thought to place this duplicate in a noble
temple in one of the greatest cities of the
world, where all may observe with delight
that amid the many treasures of genius
gathered within its walls, is a silent but eloquent memorial of Scottish purity, love and
poetry.

NEW YORK CITY STATUE OF BURNS.

On the 15th August, 1881, the foundation
stone was laid of a Statue to Sir Walter Scott,
in the Central Park, New York, presented to
the City by the resident Scotsmen. The
suggestion was then made that he should
not remain solitary on his pedestal, but that
he ought to have the genial society of Scotland's great Poet, Robert Burns. A commission was given to the same sculptor, Sir
John Steell, R.S.A., for a bronze Statue at a
cost of two thousand guineas. It is erected
opposite the Scott Statue. On the front of
the pedestal in golden letters is inscribed—
Robert Burns, on the reverse side—Presented
to the City of New York, by admirers of
Scotia's Peasant Bard, on the 121st anniversary of his birth.

The ceremony of unveiling the Statue took place on Saturday, 2nd October, 1880. Mr. John Paton, chairman of the Burns Monument Committee, made the formal presentation of the Statue to the City. The Mayor accepted the Statue on behalf of the City amid loud cheering, the Bands playing, " There was a lad was born in Kyle." The oration was given by George William Curtis, and was an impassioned, enthusiastic address. The ceremony concluded by the vast multitude singing, " Auld Lang Syne."

NITH, THE RIVER.

Rises some seven miles south west of New Cumnock, and flows to the Solway Firth. The banks of the Nith, like those of the Ayr, were favourite grounds on which the poet loved to linger, and references to them are frequently made in his writings. There is a little song of his entitled, " The Banks of Nith," which is said to depict the feelings of an inhabitant of Nithsdale, then residing in London, reflecting upon the innocent scenes of his youthful days on the banks of the Nith. " The poet's familiarity with the River Nith was probably not very great," says ' The Ordnance Gazetteer,' "until he removed from Ayrshire to Dumfriesshire (in 1788), where, for the first few years, he lived at his farm of Ellisland, afterwards removing (in 1791) to the County Town of Dumfries, where he died. Great parts of

its course, present many pleasing and picturesque features—exquisitely rich in many
varieties of landscape, now exhibiting a
narrow acclivitous pass, diversified with wood,
escarpment, and rocks, now bursting into an
expanse of valley, blooming as a garden, and
screened with warm-coloured and finely out-
lined mountain-heights, and now presenting
such rapid alternations of shape, undulation,
haugh, and hill, as charm and surprise the
eye by the mingled wealth and number of the
transitions. . . . . Nowhere is the magnifi-
cence of the famous Solway ' bore ' displayed
with finer effect than in the estuary of the
Nith."

NUBILIA, IN SEARCH OF A HUSBAND.

London, 1809.

The name of a novel, published anonymously in which the author severely criticised
George Thomson, for his failure to properly
remunerate Burns for his work in connection
with the "Select Collection of Original
Scottish Airs." Mr. Thomson made a lengthy
reply to the accusation and satisfied the public that the author's insinuations were both
unjustifiable and inexcusable.

The author of the novel was William
Mudford.

O

OCHTERTYRE HOUSE.

In Perthshire. Occupied in Burns's time by Sir William Murray. Accompanied by Dr. James M. Adair, Burns on invitation visited Sir William in October, 1787, and was very much flattered by the reception accorded to himself and his friend. It was here he composed the verses—" On Scaring some Water-Fowl in Loch Turit," and the song—" Blythe was she."

O, MY LUVE IS LIKE A RED, RED ROSE.

Mr. Stenhouse says of the charming lyric : " This song was written out by Burns and sent to Johnson for the Museum. The original MS. is now before me ; Burns's MS. does not prove the song his, however. Various versions of what have been called the original song, have from time to time been laid before the public notice by such collectors as Peter Buchan, Allan Cunningham, William Motherwell, and last but not least, Robert Chambers."

OH, WERT THOU IN THE CAULD BLAST.

This fine song is another tribute of the poet's Muse to his ministering angel, Jessy Lewars. According to Jessy's own state- ment, the poet having called upon her one morning, said, if she would play him any favourite air for which she might wish new words, he would endeavour to produce something that should please her. She accordingly sat down to the piano, and played once or twice the air of an old ditty beginning with the words :—

> " The Robin cam' to the wren's nest,
>   And keekit in, and keekit in ;
>   Oh, weel's me on your auld pow,
>   Wad ye be in, wad ye be in, . ."

After a few minutes' abstraction, the poet produced the beautiful song as we know it. It is not now usually sung to the air of " The Wren " but to music of exquisite tenderness composed for it by Felix Mendelssohn.

OLD ROME FOREST.

In the neighbourhood of Kilmarnock. Burns had an aunt (on his mother's side) named Allan who resided there and to whom he occasionally paid a visit. At the time of the trouble with the Armour family, and to avoid certain disagreeable legal complications with them, he took up his residence in his aunt's house, until the boat that was to take him to the West Indies, was ready to sail. It is also surmised that he took this step so as to be within hailing distance of John Wilson, who was then engaged in getting the Kilmarnock edition of the poems ready. Nothing

remains, as far as is known, of old Rome
Forest to-day, unless it be the location, and
even that is doubtful.

ORDINATION, THE.

"The Ordination" was written on the
occasion of the admission of the Rev. James
Mackinlay as one of the ministers of the Laigh
or parochial kirk of Kilmarnock. Mackinlay
was a member of the "Auld Licht" or ortho-
dox school, to which the poet was opposed.
The following by Mr. Chambers will show how
small a hold the moderate or liberal party
had on the sympathies of the bulk of
the people:—"This note by Burns is far
from sufficient to explain his allusion to a
modern reader. Rev. William Lindsay, or-
dained to the Laigh Kirk in 1764, was the first
moderate clergyman known in the place.
He was supposed to have obtained the appointment through the interest of his wife, whose
maiden name was Margaret Lauder, who had
been housekeeper to the Earl of Glencairn,
patron of the kirk—hence the scoffing ballad
to which the poet refers. The general meaning of the stanza is, that Common Sense, in
other words, Arminian doctrine, was introduced into the church of Kilmarnock by Mr.
Lindsay; that Oliphant and Russell, two
zealous Calvinists, had often attacked her;
but that now Mr. Mackinlay, the new entrant,
was likely to effect her complete extrusion.

We obtain a notion of the general feeling of Kilmarnock respecting the moderate doctrine, from the fact that Mr. Lindsay's induction had to be effected by the use of force, and that his friends of the Presbytery were on that occasion so pelted as to be obliged to fly from the town."—Gunnyon.

P

PAINTINGS BY CHARLES MARTIN HARDIE, A.R.S.A. Number 1, " Burns In Edinburgh, 1787."

The subject of this celebrated painting is taken from an incident in the life of Burns while at the height of his popularity in the Scottish Capital. It represents a meeting of the " literati " and other notables assembled in the drawing room of the Edinburgh residence of Her Grace the Duchess of Gordon. The Poet is seen, attired in the prevailing costume of the time—blue coat with brass buttons, yellow striped vest, buckskin breeches and top boots—standing before the group in the act of reciting his poem " A Winter Night." " Attitude and expression have both been excellently seized," says a recent writer, and the whole is no unworthy rendering of the man whom Scotland has taken more closely than any other man to her heart. Manifestly great care and much thought and research work have been expended upon the work. Opposite Burns, and fronting him, is his hostess, the Duchess of Gordon, seated resplendent in rose-coloured drapery and gown of rich brocade, posed somewhat as she appears in Reynolds' half-length, her cheek propped by her hand, intently listening. Over the back of her chair appears the eager out-stretched face of the fair Peggy Chalmers, and the raven-locked Miss Burnett leans upon a harp beside her ; while on the right side is the seated figure of the pallid and snow-haired poet, Dr. Black-lock, and on the other, the erect, slim, soldierly shape of the Earl of Glencairn. Nearer the Poet, seated at the dark old fashioned table which occupies the centre of the room, is the portly form of William Fraser Tytler, the defender of Mary Queen of Scots, and beside him, nursing his attenuated knee, the alert little figure of Lord Monboddo, the eccentric author of the " Origin and Progress of Language," his grotesque face given much as it was drawn by his friend John Brown, the excellent portraitist of the time, of whose art our own Society of Antiquaries possesses so many fine examples. A little more remote, a little less engrossed, is the critic and rhetorician, Dr. Hugh Blair, in wig and clerical bands ; and near him Henry Mackenzie, " The Man of Feeling ; " Creech, the publisher ; and Alexander Nasmyth, the portrait painter ; while to the left, behind the poet, are seated Dr. Adam Ferguson ; the placid, grey-haired Dowager-Countess of Glencairn ; and the meditative Dugald Stewart. The extreme left corner is occupied by a card table, over which the young keen-faced Harry Erskine bends, directing the attention of the players to the marvellous recital ; and this group is balanced on the right by a pair of servants in the Gordon liveries of white and red, set in the soft light of a curtained window, stopping their punch-brewing to listen to the poet ; while in the centre of the room the eye is led away through an half-open door, thronged with the heads of eager domestics, into a remote passage, with a vista of staircase window and a gleam of sharp clear daylight." In 1887, W. Cuthbertson, Picardy Place, Edinburgh, issued a booklet in reference to the Painting which contains considerable valuable information. The title is " Robert Burns In Edinburgh, 1786-87, Containing a poem by Alexander Anderson and sixteen Biographical Sketches of Notable Scottish Characters, By Margaret Farquharson Dott."

Number 2. Another celebrated painting by the same artist commemorates the meeting between Sir Walter Scott and the poet when the former was in his fifteenth year. The scene is in the house of Professor Adam Ferguson, Edinburgh, and the painting, like the one already described, is a masterly work of art. A brief description of the meeting will be found under Scott, Sir Walter.

PAISLEY STATUE.

Unveiled 26th September, 1896, by Lord Rosebery. The sculptor was Mr. F. W. Pomeroy. The statue is of bronze, and the pedestal of grey granite. One panel in front

T

represents a scene from " Tam O' Shanter," and below there is an inscription, " Burns, 1759-1796."

PEG NICHOLSON.

The name of a mare belonging to William Nicol, the poet's friend. The mare was named after Margaret Nicholson, a mad woman who made an unsuccessful attempt on the life of George III. in 1786.

PICKERING MSS.

This consisted of about two hundred letters and poems collected by William Pickering, the publisher, for use and comparison in connection with the second edition of his famous Aldine Burns. This edition was published in 1839 in three volumes, edited with Memoir and Notes by Sir Nicholas Harris Nicholas. The first edition, also edited by Sir Harris Nicholas, was in two volumes, published in 1830.

Most of the manuscripts are now in the British Museum.

PISTOLS, BURNS'S.

In a letter to Mr. David Blair, Gun Maker, St. Paul's Square, London (Ellisland, 23rd January, 1789), in referring to the pistols which he had received, Burns says : " The defensive tools do more than half mankind do; they do honour to their maker, but I trust that with me they shall have the fate of a miser's gold—to be often admired, but never used."

" The pistols which form the subject of the above letter," says Scott Douglas, " were presented by Burns before he died to Dr. William Maxwell, his principal medical attendant. They came, through the hands of Dr. Maxwell's daughter, into the possession of the Roman Catholic Bishop Gillis, of Edinburgh, by whom they were presented to the Society of Antiquaries of Scotland on 24th January, 1859. Dr. Maxwell removed his residence from Dumfries to Edinburgh in 1834, and at a sale of his effects in May of that year, several pistols and swords were disposed of, but he had too much veneration for the memory of Burns, to part with his dying gift in that manner. Allan Cunningham acquired a pair of pistols and an old Highland broadsword, which had been bought at that sale, in the belief that they had formerly been the property of Burns, and hugged himself on possessing such precious relics. In the first edition of his biography of Burns, he refers to that brace of pistols, as having been " bought " by the poet from Johnson, the gunsmith, and having tried them he wrote ' I have proved the pistols, and can say of them what I would not do for the bulk of mankind—they are an honour to their maker.' " It thus appears that Allan had heard some floating rumour about the letter in the text ; but his misquotation, as well as blunder in the maker's name, proves he had never seen it. Dr. Maxwell died at Edinburgh in October, 1834, and Miss Maxwell who, constituted Bishop Gillis her heir, died in September, 1858. The Bishop, in an elaborate paper which he read to the Society of Antiquaries on the subject of Burns's pistols, observed that Dr. Maxwell ' incurred heavy responsibilities with Blair of Birmingham for the manufacture of firearms,' in his enthusiastic efforts to help on the Revolution in France. It is known as a fact that Maxwell in one capacity or another was present on the scaffold when King Louis XVI. was beheaded on 21st January, 1793 ; and it is said that he preserved a handkerchief which, on that occasion, he had dipped in the royal blood.

PITTSBURGH (Pa. U.S.A.) STATUE.

Occupies a prominent position in Schenley Park. The unveiling took place on the 27th October, 1914, by Dr. Andrew Carnegie, who also gave the dedicatory oration. Mayor Armstrong in a brief but appropriate address accepted the statue on behalf of the City of Pittsburgh. The donors of the statue were— Mrs. E. E. Pitcairn, Thomas Morrison, Alexander H. Peacock, James Scott, James H. Lockhart, George Lauder, Alexander Demster, David M. Kirk, and Dr. Andrew Carnegie. The sculptor was Mr J. Massey Rhind of New York City. The subject represented in the statue is typical of Burns addressing the daisy. The Poet is standing at the plough, his left hand resting on it. He has just upturned a daisy and is holding it in his right hand. The statue is nearly nineteen feet in height and rests on a large granite base. On account of the inclemency of the weather, the unveiling ceremonies had to be curtailed and the other exercises commemoratory of the event were transferred to the Carnegie Music Hall. According to a writer in *The Caledonian* the memorial is considered one of the finest ever erected to the memory of the Poet, as well as a masterpiece of the eminent sculptor who designed it." Brief as the services at the unveiling were, they were nevertheless particularly impressive and were witnessed by many thousands of Scots and others from Pittsburgh and adjoining cities.

POET LAUREATE OF LODGE CANONGATE KILWINNING (?).

There is absolutely nothing in Masonic history to substantiate the claim that Burns held this title. It is asserted that the distinguished honour was conferred on him at a meeting held in St. John's Chapel, on the 1st of March, 1787, and that he held the title from that date until his death in 1796. As a matter of fact, however, until 1835, there was no such office in Canongate Kilwinning as that of Poet Laureate, and further, it was not until 1815, that the claim was put forth of the poet having been inaugurated to that office. The most conclusive evidence of all, however, is the minute of the meeting held on the 1st of March, 1787. It makes no mention of such inauguration ceremony, and no one will believe that such an important affair took place and the Secretary failed to mention it in the evening's minutes.

The claim was made wholly on tradition, backed up by the painting of the alleged event, by Stewart Watson, one of the members of the Lodge.

Writing to the " Scotsman " under date of August 18th, 1891, D. Murray Lyon, then Grand Secretary of the Grand Lodge of Scotland, said :

" The Poet's connection with Canongate Kilwinning lay in his having been ' assumed a member ' while on his visit to Edinburgh in 1787. His admission is thus referred to in the minute of the Lodge, dated 1st February, 1787, and is attested by the Master, Alexander Fergusson ; the Depute Master, Charles Moir ; and the Junior Warden, John Millar ; . . . The Right Worshipful Master having observed that Brother Burns was at present in the Lodge, who is well known as a great poetic writer, and for a late publication of his works, which have been universally commended, and submitted that he should be assumed a member of this Lodge, which was unanimously agreed to, and he was assumed accordingly."

Beyond this Burns had no connection with Canongate Kilwinning. The beautiful story of his inauguration appears to have been concocted in 1845-46 to supply Mr. Stewart Watson (a well-known Edinburgh artist), a member of the Lodge, with a subject for a beautiful picture. Mr. Stewart Watson also, it may be here remarked, executed two other similar paintings—that of the Knight Templars and Supreme Royal Arch Chapter of Scotland in conclave, both of which, except as regards the features of the members portrayed, are purely imaginative.

In a notice in the " Freemasons' Quarterly Review " of 31st December, 1845, the artist is reported as being engaged on a ' painting of the Poet Burns in the act of being received into membership with the Canongate Kilwinning Lodge.' When the picture was finished it was reviewed in the columns of " The Scotsman " on the 25th March, 1846, and the reviewer then seems to have been imposed upon by interested parties, for under the heading ' The Inauguration of Burns,' he described the occurrence as ' one of the few occasions on which, during his lifetime, his poetical genius was publicly acknowledged and proclaimed.' . . .

Attached to the original painting presented

by the family of the late Chevalier James
Burnes to the Grand Lodge of Scotland in
1863, is the inscription :—' The Inauguration
of Robert Burns as Poet-Laureate of Lodge
Canongate Kilwinning, 1st March, 1787.'
This date is accepted by the Lodge as correct.

In all statements and discussions, in support of the story of the inauguration, the
minute of the meeting at which the event is
alleged to have happened has been studiously
kept out of sight.   It had better be published,
and here it is :—

> ' St. John's Chapel, 1 March, 1787.
> ' The Lodge being duly constituted, it was
> reported that since last meeting R. Dalrymple,
> Esq., F. T. Hammond, Esq., R. A. Maitland, Esq.,
> were entered apprentices ; and the following
> brethren passed and raised :—R. Sinclair, Esq.,
> A. M'Donald, Esq., C. B. Clive, Esq., Captain
> Dalrymple, R. A. Maitland, Esq., F. T. Hammond,
> Esq., Mr. Clavering, Mr. M'Donald, Mr. Millar,
> Mr. Sime, and Mr. Gray, who all paid their dues to
> the Treasurer.
> ' No other business being before the meeting,
> the Lodge adjourned.

Entries	...	...	£3	13	6
P. & R.	...	...	6	6	6
Collected	...	...	1	1	0
			£11	1	0

> Alexander Ferguson, M.
> Chas. More, D.
> Jo. Millar, J.W.'

The concluding sentence of the foregoing

minute proves beyond question that no such event as the inauguration of Burns as Poet-Laureate of Canongate Kilwinning took place at the meeting of 1st March, 1787. Hogg, the Ettrick Shepherd, was the first of its Poets-Laureate, and he was made so in 1835.

D. Murray Lyon,
Grand Secretary, Grand Lodge of Scotland.

POOSIE NANCIE'S, MAUCHLINE.

This famous old time beggar's howff is still to the fore, but is now a well established hostelry, enjoying a reputation for respect- ability and cleanliness which it sadly lacked in Burns's time. Within its walls, as every reader of the poet's works knows, was staged one of the best of his immortal creations. "The Jolly Beggars" (q.v.). The building stands in one of the oldest parts of the town in a street known as the "Cowgate," only a few steps from the Kirk and the Kirkyard, the latter famous all over the world as the scene of another immortal poem "The Holy Fair" (q.v.). In the poet's early days the howff was tenanted by Mr. and Mrs. George Gibson, and the latter's "sobriquet" of "Poosie Nancy," or Nancy, was no doubt familiar to all the beggars in the surrounding neighbour- hood. Mr. Scott Douglas says she used the building " as a licensed ale-shop and lodging house for all and sundry pedlars, cadgers and other vagrants," but Mr. J. Taylor Gibb is more correct when he states " the house was not a public house in the sense of the word, but a ' foregathering ' place, a howff, or lodging house for ' gangrel bodies '—not an ale house for general refreshments, and therefore cannot possibly answer to the many fancy sketches that have been scribbled about it."

The interior of the building has no doubt undergone some changes during the years, but outwardly it remains practically the same as it was more than a hundred and fifty years ago.   See also " Who's Who In Burns."

POOR ROBIN'S ALMANAC, REFERENCE TO.

" For my own affairs, I am in a fair way of becoming as eminent as Thomas a Kempis or John Bunyan; and you may expect henceforth to see my birthday inserted among the wonderful events, in the Poor Robin's and Aberdeen Almanacs, along with the Black Monday, and the Battle of Bothwell Bridge " —Letter to Gavin Hamilton, 7th December, 1786.

POLYHYMNIA, THE.

A collection of poetry, original and selected by a society of gentlemen.

Glasgow, John Murdoch, N.D.(1799).

Issued and compiled in twenty numbers of eight pages each. Number eighteen contains " The Lass o' Ballochmyle," in which a few of the words differ from those of the version generally included in the poet's works.

PORTRAITS OF BURNS.

Alexander Nasmyth. The most popular of all the portraits. Shows the head and bust on a canvas 15x12. Said to have been painted at the suggestion of William Creech, the publisher, with the view of having an engraving made from it, as a frontispiece for the first Edinburgh edition of the poems. Burns gave many sittings to Nasmyth. The portrait was gifted to the National Gallery of Scotland, Edinburgh, by William Nicol Burns. A replica of it is in the National Portrait Gallery, London. The best large engraving of the Nasmyth portrait was made by William Walker, of London, in 1830. The plate ultimately became the property of Colonel Joseph Laing, of New York, who is said to have struck off thousands of copies of the engraving and distributed them all over the United States and Canada.

John Beugo.—Small engraving of Nasmyth's portrait, done as a frontispiece for the first Edinburgh edition of the poems. Burns also gave one or two sittings to Beugo while engaged in the work. Plate is now in the Scottish National Portrait Gallery, Edinburgh.

Alexander Nasmyth.—Full length portrait. Now in the National Gallery of Scotland.

The portrait was not painted from sittings, but from a pencil sketch taken by the artist while in the company of the poet. Mr. Lockhart says : " Mr. Nasmyth also prepared, for ' Constable's Miscellany,' a sketch of the poet at full-length, as he appeared in Edinburgh in the first hie-day of his reputation ; dressed in light jockey boots, and very tight buckskin breeches, according to the fashion of the day, and in what was considered as the Fox-livery, viz., a blue coat and buff waistcoat, with broad blue stripes. The surviving friends of Burns who have seen this vignette, are unanimous in pronouncing it to furnish a very lively representation of the bard as he first attracted public notice on the streets of Edinburgh. The scenery of the background is very nearly that of Burns's native spot—the Kirk of Alloway, and the Bridge of Doon."

Archibald Skirving.—Bust portrait. Done in crayon on greyish toned paper. There is no positive evidence that Burns gave sittings to Skirving, the general opinion being that the portrait was painted from the recollections of the artist and a study of the Nasmyth portrait. It is known, however, that Burns and Skirving were frequently seen together. The portrait is very popular with some persons. It is now in the Scottish National Portrait Gallery.

Peter Taylor. Portrait.—Now in the Scottish National Portrait Gallery. Burns is supposed to have given sittings to Taylor, and while the features resemble those of the poet, still the likeness is disappointing. Mrs. M'Lehose, however, in 1828 said : " In my opinion it is the most striking likeness of the poet I have ever seen; and I say this with much confidence, having a perfect recollection of his appearance," and Sir Walter Scott said : " But Burns was so remarkable a man, that his features remain impressed on my mind as if I had seen him only yesterday ; and I could not hesitate to recognise this portrait as a striking resemblance of the Poet, though it had been presented to me amid a whole exhibition."

Alexander Reid.—Miniature portrait on ivory. Painted at Dumfries in 1795. Now in the Scottish National Portrait Gallery. There has always existed a doubt as to this being the miniature that Reid painted. Mr. E. Barrington Nash, founder of the Burns Portrait Society, at one time asserted that it was not the work of Reid, and claimed he had traced the genuine miniature to the home of a gentleman in Yorkshire.

A miniature engraving entitled, the " Kerry Miniature," with the initials " R. B., 1796" underneath, is reproduced by the Rev. O. Hately Waddell, in his " Life of Burns." The claim is made that the miniature is the work of Alexander Reid, but the portrait and the claim have been ignored by persons interested in the portraiture of the poet.

John Miers.—Silhouette. Now in the Scottish National Portrait Gallery. Declared by Mr. D. W. Stevenson to be in perfect harmony with the Nasmyth Portrait.

William Allan.—Full length portrait. " Several people think that Allan's likeness of me is more striking than Nasmyth's."—Burns to George Thomson, May, 1795.—An engraving was made from Allan's Portrait in 1838 by John Burnet.

James Tassie.—Miniature medallion. Now in the Scottish National Portrait Gallery. Evidently based on the Nasmyth portrait. It has been claimed that Sir Henry Raeburn did the principal work on this Medallion. It has inscribed on it " H. Raeburn, 1792."

J. C. Ibbetson.—Portrait painted in 1790, but it is very doubtful if the artist ever met the poet. This portrait until July, 1922, was in Burdett Coutts' Collection. It was then sold to an English firm. Copies of it from a small photo, were reproduced in the " Weekly Scotsman " of February 16th, 1922. It is entirely different in its delineation of the poet's features from all other portraits.

Sir Henry Raeburn is said to have painted a portrait of Burns, but no one has ever been able to locate it. Mr. Barrington Nash, the well-known authority on Burns portraiture, at one time claimed that he had found the portrait through some spiritualistic means, but the Burns cult has never taken Mr. Nash seriously in the matter. An original portrait of Burns by Raeburn——if one was painted—has yet to be found. This must not be confused, however, with the fact that this artist made a copy of Nasmyth's Portrait for Cadell and Davis, the London publishers. " I have finished a copy of Burns, the Poet, from the original painted by Mr. Nasmyth," Sir Henry wrote in 1803. " I have shown it to Mr. Cunningham, who thinks it very like him." To-day no one seems to know even where this portrait is.

" PRESBYTERY RELIEF." See under Buchan- ites, The.

Q

QUEEN O' THE LOTHIANS CAM CRUISIN' TO FIFE, THE.

This song or ballad appeared in the sixth volume of the "Scots Musical Museum," published in 1804, and was not credited to Burns. The original manuscript, however, in the poet's hand-writing is in the Honresfield Collection of Manuscripts belonging to Sir Alfred J. Law. Refer also to the "Burns Chronicle," 1926, p. 67.

R

RAEBURN, PORTRAIT OF BURNS, THE. See under "Portraits of Burns."

RAMAGE'S INN.

A place of refreshment in the village of Wanlockhead occasionally frequented by the poet while on excise duty. It was here he wrote the verses to John Taylor, beginning "With Pegasus upon a day."

REID, MINIATURE PORTRAIT OF BURNS, THE. See under "Portraits of Burns."

REVIEWS.

Early Critical Reviews on Robert Burns. By John D. Ross, LL.D., Glasgow, 1900.

Ten Reviews selected chiefly from leading Scottish periodicals comprising :—

Henry Mackenzie ; from "The Lounger," December, 1786.

"The Monthly Review," December, 1786.

Dr. James Currie ; from "The Works of Robert Burns," 1800.

David Irving, LL.D., 1804.

Lord Jeffrey ; from "The Edinburgh Review," 1809.

Sir Walter Scott ; from "The Quarterly Review," 1809.

Josiah Walker, 1811.

Alexander Peterkin, 1813.

Professor John Wilson ; from "Blackwood's Magazine," 1829.

Thomas Carlyle ; from "The Edinburgh Review," 1829.

" The papers are of great interest, not only in themselves, but in the evidence they afford of the change and growth in the reputation and standing of the poet in the eyes of the critics and of the world, and lovers of Burns will count it a boon to be able to consult them in so accessible a form."—" Scotsman."

RHYMER, THE. By Allan M'Aulay.

Charles Scribners, Sons, New York, 1900.

A work of fiction featuring Burns and Clarinda.

RIDING THE STANG.

A form of mob law in bygone times, against obnoxious persons, and consisted of carrying them through the village astride a rantle-tree. Burns has reference to the old custom when he says in " Adam Armour's Prayer,"—

" Because we stang'd her through the place."

RELIGION.

In a letter to Clarinda (8th January, 1788) Burns explicitly affirms his belief in a Supreme Being and an eternal hereafter.

"He who is our Author and Preserver, and will one day be our Judge, must be—not for His sake in the way of duty, but from the native impulse of our hearts—the object of our reverential awe and grateful adoration.

" He is almighty and all-bounteous ; we

are weak and dependent ; hence prayer and every other sort of devotion. He is not willing that any should perish, but that all should come to everlasting life ; consequently, it must be in everyone's power to embrace this offer of 'everlasting life ; ' otherwise He could not in justice condemn those who did not. A mind pervaded, actuated, and governed by purity, truth and charity, though it does not *merit* Heaven, yet is an absolutely necessary requisite, without which Heaven can neither be obtained nor enjoyed ; and, by Divine promise, such a mind shall never fail of attaining 'everlasting life : ' hence the impure, the deceiving, the uncharitable, exclude themselves from eternal bliss by their unfitness for enjoying it.

" The Supreme Being has put the immediate administration of all this—for wise and good ends known to Himself—into the hands of Jesus Christ, a great Personage, whose relation to Him we cannot comprehend, but whose relation to us is a Guide and Saviour, and who, except for our own obstinacy and misconduct, will bring us all, through various ways, and by various means, to bliss at last.

" These are my tenets, my lovely friend, and which I think cannot be well disputed. My creed is pretty nearly expressed in the last clause of Jamie Dean's grace, an honest weaver in Ayrshire—' Lord, grant that we

may lead a gude life, for a gude life makes a
gude end—at least it helps weel.' "

ROB M'QUECHAN'S ELSHIM.

The name of a drama which the Poet
had intended to write.

ROBERT BURNS MEMORIAL ASSOCIATION, THE.

New York City, U.S.A. Founded in
1927 by Robert C. M. Auld.   The membership
is drawn from Scottish and kindred associations throughout the City and State.
Ceremonies befitting the occasion are held
on a Saturday afternoon, either in June or
July, at the Burns Monument in Central
Park.   Prominent speakers address the
audience, while vocal, bagpipe and other
music combine to make the services both
solemn and interesting. Previous to the
meeting, a parade to the park starts from the
headquarters of the Caledonian Club and in
this thousands of persons of various nation-
alities take part.   At the close of the services
held in 1930, nearly a hundred floral pieces
contributed by associations and admirers of
the Poet in the States and Canada, were
banked around the base of the statue. Colonel
Walter Scott, New York City, is Honorary
President of the Association.

ROCKING.

"On Fasten-e'en (Shrovetide) we had a rocking." "The term," says Gilbert Burns, "is derived from primitive times when the country-women employed their spare hours in spinning on a rock or distaff. This simple instrument is a very portable one, and well fitted to the social inclination of meeting in a neighbour's house; hence the phrase of "going a-rocking," or with "the rock." As the connection the phrase had with the implement was forgotten when the rock gave place to the spinning-wheel, the phrase came to be used by both sexes on social occasions and men talked of going with their rocks as well as women." It was at one of these "rockings" held at Mossgiel, that Burns first heard Lapraik's song, "When I upon thy bosom lean," and which was the means of the two poets becoming acquainted with each other.

ROWTIN' BURN, THE.   See Kelly Burn (The).

ROYAL ARCHERS OF SCOTLAND.

Now known as the "King's bodyguard in Scotland." This organization dates from 1686, but is supposed to have been in existence during the reign of King James I. Burns was granted a diploma of membership in the Company on 10th April, 1792. The diploma which is now preserved in the Municipal Museum in Edinburgh reads: "The

Council of the Royal Company of Archers
after trial taken by the judges of the Company
and their report, has admitted and received
and hereby admit and receive you, Robert
Burns, Esq., to be one of His Majesty's Royal
Company of Archers, giving and granting you
all the privileges and immunities that are or
may be competent to any of the said Company. In witness thereof those presents are
sealed with the common seal and signed by
the Secretary, day and place aforesaid.
James Gray, Sy., R.C.A.''

At the time of the poet's enrolment the
majority of the membership were noblemen,
the Dukes of Buccleuch, Hamilton, Gordon,
Athol, Montrose and others, being of the number. The dress or uniform consisted of '' a
green frock lapelled yellow, with gilt metal
buttons ; white cloth waist-coat and breeches,
with small metal buttons to match those on
the coat, and white silk stockings. Black
feathers were worn on the cap. A few of the
poet's personal friends were members of the
Company. These included the Earl of Glencairn, Lord Daer, Partick Heron, Dr. James
Adair and others.

S

SAN FRANCISCO, CALIFORNIA, STATUE.

Unveiled 22nd February, 1908, by Miss Lois C. Calder. Mr. James C. Fyfe, president of the St. Andrew's Society, delivered the oration, and Mayor Taylor accepted the statue in the name of the City, at the same time paying a high tribute of respect to the poet and his works. The statue is of bronze, the work of Mr. Earl Cummings, and stands eleven feet high, while the pedestal measures nine feet in height. The name " Burns," in bold letters is displayed on the front of the latter. The statue stands in a prominent position at the Eighth Avenue entrance to Golden Gate Park. Much of the credit for the erection of the statue is due to Mr. John D. M'Gilvray, a well-known San Francisco Scot.

SANQUHAR.

A prosperous town in upper Nithdale, Dumfriesshire, about twenty-six miles from Dumfries. Burns while temporarily residing at the Isle (q.v.) had to pass through the town, when riding to and from Mauchline, and usually lodged with Bailie Edward Wigham, who " kept the only tolerable inn in the place." It was here that the funeral of Mrs. Oswald of Auchincruive arrived one evening, in consequence of which Burns was compelled to ride for accommodation, for himself and his horse, twelve miles farther to the next inn, which was at New Cumnock. See his "Ode sacred to the Memory of Mrs. Richard Oswald of Auchincruive."

SCOTCH DRINK.

This poem, written after the manner of Fergusson's "Caller Water," is not to be taken as evidence of the poet's feelings and practices. It was suggested by the withdrawal of an Act of Parliament empowering Duncan Forbes of Culloden to distil whisky on his barony of Ferintosh, free of duty, in return for services rendered to the Government. This privilege was a source of great revenue to the family; and as Ferintosh whisky was cheaper than that produced elsewhere, it became very popular, and the name Ferintosh thus became something like a synonym for whisky over the country. Compensation for the loss of privilege, to the tune of £21,580, was awarded to the Forbes family by a jury. Attention was further drawn to "the national beverage" at this time by the vexatious and oppressive way in which the Excise laws were enforced at the Scotch distilleries. Many distillers abandoned the business; and as barley was beginning to fall in price in consequence, the county gentlemen supported the distillers, and an Act was passed relieving the trade from the obnoxious supervision.

These circumstances gave the poet his cue ; and the subject was one calculated to evoke his wildest humour. Writing to Robert Muir, Kilmarnock, he says, " I here enclose you my ' Scotch Drink,' and may the—— follow with a blessing for your edification. I hope some time before we hear the gowk, [cuckoo], to have the pleasure of seeing you at Kilmarnock, when I intend we shall have a gill between us in a mutchkin stoup which will be a great comfort and consolation to your humble servant, R. B."—Gunnyon.

Preceding the poem, and under the title, Burns quotes the lines :—

> " Gie him strong drink, until he wink,
>   That's sinking in despair ;
> And liquor guid to fire his bluid,
>   That's prest wi' grief and care ;
> There let him bowse, and deep carouse,
>   Wi' bumpers flowing o'er.
> Till he forgets his loves or debts,
>   And minds his griefs no more."
>
> —Solomon's Proverbs xxxi. 6, 7.

SCOTT, SIR WALTER.

In one of his letters, Sir Walter makes mention of how, when a boy of fifteen, he saw Burns. He says : " I was a lad of fifteen in 1786-7, when he came first to Edinburgh, but had sense and feeling enough to be much interested in his poetry, and would have given the world to know him ; but I had very little acquaintance with any literary people, and still less with the gentry of the west country, the two sets that he most frequented. Mr. Thomas Grierson was at that time a clerk of my father's. He knew Burns, and promised to ask him to his lodgings to dinner, but had no opportunity to keep his word ; otherwise I might have seen more of this distinguished man. As it was, I saw him one day at the late venerable Professor Ferguson's, where there were several gentlemen of literary repu- tation, among whom I remember the cele- brated Mr. Dugald Stewart. Of course we youngsters sat silent, looked, and listened. The only thing I remember which was remark- able in Burns's manner, was the effect pro- duced upon him by a print of Burnbury's, representing a soldier lying dead on the snow, his dog sitting in misery on one side,—on the other, his widow, with a child in her arms. These lines were written beneath :—

> ' Cold on Canadian hills, or Minden's plain,
> Perhaps that parent wept her soldier slain—
> Bent o'er her babe, her eye dissolved in dew,
> The big drops, mingling with the milk he drew,
> Gave the sad presage of his future years,
> The child of misery baptised in tears.'

Burns seemed much affected by the print, or rather the ideas which it suggested to his mind. He actually shed tears. He asked whose the lines were, and it chanced that nobody but myself remembered that they occur in a half-forgotten poem of Langhorne's, called by the unpromising title of " The Jus-

tice of Peace." I whispered my information
to a friend present, who mentioned it to Burns,
who rewarded me with a look and a word,
which, though of mere civility, I then received,
and still recollect, with very great pleasure . ."

The house of Professor Adam Ferguson
is still in existence. At the time to which
Sir Walter refers, it was called Sciennes Hill
House, but is now No. 7 Braid Place. On the
12th of March, 1927, through the efforts of the
Edinburgh Sir Walter Scott Club, in conjunc-
tion with the Edinburgh District Burns Clubs'
Association, a tablet was placed on the
original front of the house, bearing the inscription: "This Tablet Commemorates The Meeting of Robert Burns and Sir Walter Scott
Which Took Place Here In The Winter Of
1786-87."

There is also a painting by the celebrated
artist, Mr. Charles Martin Hardie, A.R.S.A.,
portraying the meeting of Sir Walter and the
poet. (See under Paintings by Hardie, Mr.
Chas. M.).

SCOTS MUSICAL MUSEUM.

What must always be esteemed as the
most valuable collection of the early songs and
music of Scotland, Johnson's " Scots Musical
Museum," was begun at Edinburgh in 1786.
James Johnson was a music-seller and
engraver in Edinburgh, and was the first who
used pewter plates for engraving music. The

work seems to have been projected by William Tytler, of Woodhouselee, the celebrated antiquary (whose " Dissertation on Scottish Song and Music " was long the standard authority on the subject, though now but of little use), Dr. Blacklock, and Samuel Clark who appears to have acted as musical editor. From the note addressed " To the True Lovers of Caledonian Music and Song," prefixed to the first volume, we find that the work originated from " A just and general complaint, that among all the music books of Scots songs which have been hitherto offered to the public, not even altogether can be said to have merited the name of what may be called a complete collection ; having been published in detached pieces and parcels ; amounting, however, on the whole to more than twice the price of this publication ; attended, moreover, with this further disadvantage, that they have been printed in such large unportable sizes that they could by no means answer the purpose of being pocket-companions, which is no small encumbrance, especially to the admirers of social music." Each volume was to contain one hundred songs with music, etc.   In the second volume, the author's names so far as known were given, and several of the old pieces marked as such. The work would probably not have reached a third volume had not Robert Burns entered into the scheme.   Burns had been introduced

to Johnson in Edinburgh, and contributed
two original songs to the first volume. To the
second volume he contributed largely, and
continued to furnish the publisher with songs
original, or collected, or half of each. He
informed a friend that he had "collected,
begged, borrowed, and stolen gnats," all the
songs he had met with, and this enthusiasm
continued to the last. Without his aid in
rousing contributors, finding material, old
or new, the Scots Musical Museum would have
been on a level with Thomson's Orpheus
Caledonius, instead of occupying the important position it now enjoys in the literature
of our song. The work finished with the sixth
volume. One thing was wanted, as Johnson
left it, to make it complete, and that was,
a series of good and trustworthy notes. This
was undertaken by William Stenhouse, an
accountant in Edinburgh who died in 1827,
leaving his task unfinished. Mr. David Laing
next took up the work, and with the assistance of Mr. Charles Kirkpatrick Sharpe,
gave a series of additional notes illustrative
and corrective of those of Stenhouse, added
prefaces and indexes, and in 1853 gave all
lovers of Scottish Song an edition of Johnson,
the value of which is immeasurable. To it
we gratefully acknowledge our obligations for
much and valuable information.—Peter Ross,
LL. D. in "The Songs of Scotland" chronologically arranged.

SCOTS COLLEGE AT ROME.

Founded in 1600. The first students from Scotland for the College arrived in 1602.

Through the influence of Bishop John Geddes, who entered the College in 1750, a number of subscriptions were received for the first Edinburgh edition of the poems. The Colleges at Paris, Vallodolid and Douai also recorded a number of subscriptions credited to the same source.

Bishop Geddes and Burns were introduced to each other in Edinburgh in 1787, and became very great friends. The Bishop died at Aberdeen, 1799. See also, Geddes's Burns, The.

SCOTS WHA HAE WI' WALLACE BLED. See Bruce's Address to his Army at Bannockburn.

SCOTTISH BARD.

" The appellation of a Scottish bard is by far my highest pride ; to continue to deserve it, is my most exalted ambition. Scottish scenes, and Scottish story, are the themes I could wish to sing. I have no dearer aim than to have it in my power, unplagued with the routine of business, for which Heaven knows, I am unfit enough, to make leisurely pilgrimages through Caledonia ; to sit on the fields of her battles, to wander on the romantic banks of her rivers, and to muse by the stately towers or venerable ruins, once the honoured abodes of her heroes. But these are Utopian views.''—Letter to Mrs. Dunlop, Edinburgh, 22nd March, 1787.

See also under " Caledonia's Bard.''

SEAL, BURNS'S.

The familiar seal designed by the poet, was carefully cut in Edinburgh, and was used by him until his death. In a letter to Alexander Cunningham dated Dumfries, 3rd March, 1794, the matter of the seal is very carefully gone into.—" There is one commission that I must trouble you with. I lately lost a valuable seal, a present from a departed friend, which vexes me much. I have gotten one of your Highland pebbles, which I fancy would make a very decent one ; and I want to cut my armorial bearing on it ; will you be so obliging as inquire what will be the expense of such a business ? I do not know that my name is matriculated, as the heralds call it, at all ; but I have invented arms of myself, so you know I shall be chief of the name ; and, by courtesy of Scotland, will likewise be entitled to supporters. These, however, I do not intend having on my seal. I am a bit of a herald, and shall give you, *secundum artem*, my arms. On a field, azure, a holly-bush, seeded, proper, in base ; a shepherd's pipe and crook, saltier-wise, also proper, in chief. On a wreath of the colours, a wood-lark perching on a sprig of bay-tree, proper, for crest. Two mottoes ; round the top of the crest, " Wood-notes wild ; " at the bottom of the shield, in the usual place, " Better a wee bush than nae beild." By the shepherd's pipe and crook I do not mean the nonsense of painters in Arcadia, but a " Stock " and " Horn," and a " Club," such as you see at the head of Allan Ramsay, in Allan's quarto edition of the " Gentle Shepherd."

SELECT MELODIES OF SCOTLAND. See under Thomson, George.

SELKIRK GRACE, THE.

Although accepted by many persons as the work of Burns it is known to those familiar with his writings that he was not the author of it. " The Grace," writes Dr. George F. Black, in a note on this subject to the " Weekly Scotsman," 17th November, 1928, " first appeared in Allan Cunningham's edition of Burns (London, 1834, v. 3, p. 311), with the note :—' On a visit to St. Mary's Isle, the Earl of Selkirk asked Burns to say grace at dinner. These were the words he uttered—they were applauded then, and have since been known in Galloway by the name of ' The Selkirk Grace.' ' No such grace was said by Burns. Nine years previous to the appearance of Cunningham's edition of the Poet's works a version of the grace appeared anonymously in a Belfast weekly literary paper, " The Rushlight " (v. 1, No. 41, September 9th, 1825), which reads as follows :—

GRACE BEFORE MEAT.

' There's fowk hae meat
　　That downa eat ;
There's fowk could eat—that want it ;
　　But we hae meat
　　An' we can eat—
And sae—the Lord be thankit.'

Cunningham ' lifted ' these lines, dressed them in the garb they now wear, and palmed them off on Burns, a trick of which he was guilty on more than one occasion."

A similar form of Grace, however, was in existence long before Burns's time. In the MSS. of Dr. Plume of Maldon, Essex, in a handwriting of about 1650, we have :—

" Some have meat but cannot eat;
　Some could eat but have no meat.
　We have meat and all can eat;
　Blest, therefore, be God for our meat."

SHANTER FARM.　See Tam o' Shanter's Farm.

SHERIFFMUIR.　See Battle of Sheriffmuir.

X

SILVER TASSIE, THE.

There is a legend to the effect that this song was composed by the poet after witnessing a young military officer parting from his sweetheart on the pier of Leith. The first four lines are part of an old song.

"SIMPSON'S."

A noted tavern at the Auld Brig end. Burns.

SIR WILLIE'S NOTES.

Bank notes of the banking house of Sir William Forbes of Edinburgh.

SKIRVING, PORTRAIT OF BURNS, THE. See under "Portraits of Burns."

SKULL, BURNS'S, MEASUREMENTS.

According to Robert Chambers, a cast from the skull having been transmitted to the Phrenological Society of Edinburgh, the following view of the cerebral development of Burns was drawn up by Mr. George Combe and published in connection with four views of the cranium by W. & A. K. Johnston, Edinburgh.

Dimensions of the Skull.	Inches.
Greatest circumference	22¼
From Occipital Spine to Individuality, over the top of the head	14
do. Ear to ear vertically over the top of the head	13
do. Philoprogenitiveness to Individuality (greatest length) ...	8
do. Concentrativeness to Comparison ...	7⅛
do. Ear to Philoprogenitiveness ...	4⅞
do. do. Individuality	4¾
do. do. Benevolence	5½
do. do. Firmness	5½
do. Destructiveness to Destructiveness...	5¾
do. Secretiveness to Secretiveness ...	5⅞
do. Cautiousness to Cautiousness ...	5½
do. Ideality to Ideality	4⅝
do. Constructiveness to Constructiveness	4½
do. Mastoid Process to Mastoid Process	4¾

The cast of a skull does not show the temperament of the individual, but the portraits of Burns indicate the bilious and nervous temperaments, the sources of strength, activity and susceptibility ; and the description given by his contemporaries of his beaming and energetic eye, and the rapidity and impetuosity of his manifestations establish the inference that his brain was active and susceptible. An interesting account of the circumstances attending the taking of the cast of the skull will be found in " A Little Book of Burns Lore " (Stirling, Eneas Mackay, 1926).

SMA ' INN, THE. See Nance Tinnock's.

SMITH, ALEXANDER HOWLAND.

"Antique Smith." Convicted at Edinburgh, 27th June, 1893, of forging and selling as genuine, Burns and other manuscripts. The sentence was one year's imprisonment.

SNOW FALLS.

"Or like the snow falls in the river." This is the wording of Burns's own manuscript of "Tam o' Shanter." Wrong renderings are "snow-falls" and "snow-fall."

SOUTER JOHNNIE'S HOUSE.

See under Kirkoswald.

SPITTLESIDE.

A farm in the neighbourhood of Tarbolton. In Burns's time it was the house of David Siller, the inspirer of the "Epistles to Davie, a Brother Poet."

STAIR.

A small village on the Ayr, about five miles distant from Mauchline. Stair House, or Lodge, was occupied by Major-General Stewart, M.P., when Burns was just beginning to realize his power as a poet, and one of his songs accidently falling into the hands of Mrs Stewart, resulted in a friendship being formed with the family that lasted through life. See also under the "Stair" and "Afton" Manuscripts.

STAIR.   Burns and Stair.

By John M'Vie, Hon. Secretary, Edinburgh Ayrshire Association.   Kilmarnock,
1927.

An interesting and useful book. Contains papers on Stair Kirk, The Dalrymples
of Stair, David Sillar, Mrs. Stewart of Stair,
The Stair Manuscripts, etc., along with four
appropriate illustrations.

STAIR MSS.

This consisted of a parcel of manuscripts
presented by Burns to Mrs. Alexander Stewart,
of Stair.   On the death of Mrs. Stewart the
manuscripts became the property of her
grandson, and were sold by him to Mr. Dick,
bookseller, Ayr.   On his death they were disposed of in the Auction Room.   Among the
manuscripts were copies of " The Lass of
Ballochmyle," " The Gloomy Night is Gathering Fast," " My Nannie, O." " Handsome
Nell," " Song in the Character of a Ruined
Farmer," " Tho' Cruel Fate should bid us
part," " The Vision," and " Misgivings of
Despondency on the Approach of the Gloomy
Monarch of the Grave."

STATUES OF TAM O' SHANTER AND SOUTER JOHNNIE BY JAMES THOM.   See under Thom, James.

STENCHER.

"Stencher" instead of "Lugar" was used in all the author's editions of "My Nannie, O," including that of 1794, but George Thompson says, "B. sanctioned the change to Lugar in 1792."

STEUART, JOHN A., THE IMMORTAL LOVER. A Burns Romance. London, 1930.

This is a well written work of fiction on an ever-fascinating theme. Boldly, broadly, and skilfully Mr Steuart presents Burns the poet and Burns the man. Ignoring the usual cumbersome methods of conventional biography, he has written "The Immortal Lover" with feeling and imagination as a biographical novel. The book opens with the parting of Burns with his lovely "Highland Mary," and follows the course of his life and loves. Although an ardent admirer of Burns, the author has made no attempt to whitewash his shortcomings, obeying rather the Poet's own injunction :

> " But still the preaching cant forbear,
> And ev'n the rigid feature."

STEWART KYLE.

That part of the central district of Ayrshire which lies between the rivers Irvine and Ayr.

STINCHER.

A small stream in the vicinity of Ballantrae, Ayrshire. It is now associated with the poet's

beautiful song. " My Nannie, O," having
been used by him in the first line, " Behind
yon Hills where Stincher flows." Afterwards
he concluded that the word "Stincher" was too
harsh and prosaic, and changed it to the more
agreeable " Lugar."

STIRLING.

This royal and prosperous burgh stands
on the right bank of the river Forth, and is
about thirty-six miles distant from Edinburgh. Its origin is lost even in tradition.
The principal attraction in the burgh is the
Castle, thus described in " Williams's
Gazetteer :—" The Castle crowns the summit
of the hill, and forms a bold feature in an
extensive landscape ; is separated from the
town's head by an esplanade, used as a parade
ground ; retains massive features of great
military strength, but serves now only as a
barrack garrison; and has, around two courts, a
quondam parliament hall, erected by James
III ; a quondam royal palace, erected by
James V., and an edifice of 1856 on site of the
apartment in which James II. slew the Earl
of Douglas."

Burns while on his Highland Tour made
several stops at Stirling. In his letter to
Robert Muir, 26th August, 1787, he says :
" And just now from Stirling Castle I have
seen by the setting sun, the glorious prospect of the windings of the Forth through the

rich Carse of Stirling." And he also makes
reference to the town in a letter to his friend,
Gavin Hamilton, 28th August, 1787. It was
while staying at an inn here that he inscribed
the lines beginning, " Here Stuarts once in
glory reign'd," on one of the window panes,
and for which he was so bitterly criticised by
his friends, that on his return to the town, it is
said, he destroyed the pane—which failed,
however, to destroy the sentiment inscribed
on it, and which had already been copied and
circulated throughout the neighbourhood.

STIRLING.

A large bust of Burns, from the studio of
Mr. D. W. Stevenson, Edinburgh, is in the
" Hall of Heroes," in the National Wallace
Monument. The unveiling took place with
imposing ceremonies, by Dean of Guild
Mercer, 4th September, 1886, the oration
being delivered by the Rev. Dr. Rogers. The
bust is of white marble and was the gift of
Mr. Andrew Carnegie.

STIRLING STATUE.

Unveiled 23rd September, 1914, by Miss
Christina Bayne, daughter of the donor, Provost David Bayne. After a brief address by
the Provost, Bailie Thomson, the Senior Magis-
trate of the town, accepted the gift on behalf
of the community. They lived, he said, in
troublesome times, and living as many of them

did within cry of Bannockburn, the battle
ground upon which the forefathers gained
their liberty, it was fitting, he thought, that
they should recall that in these latter days
they had also experienced agonies—agonies
for the men who had gone under on the plains
of Europe in the cause of Liberty against
Despotism. It was appropriate, therefore,
that they should be receiving at the hands of
their worthy Provost such a gift, a gift com-
memorating the man who stood, if ever man
stood, for the coming of the time when " Man
to Man the World o'er shall Brithers Be."

The statue is bronze, the work of Mr Albert
H. Hodge, the eminent Glasgow sculptor, and
stands on a triangular plot of ground between
the Corn Exchange and Dumbarton Roads.
The pedestal is of Aberdeen granite and is
twenty-one feet, six inches in height and weighs
about eighteen tons—altogether a very imposing memorial. On the top base appears
the name " Robert Burns " and the middle
base is richly carved showing Scotch thistles
in bold relief. The four bronze panels have
representations of " Burns at the Plough,"
" Tam o' Shanter," " The Cottar's Saturday
Night," and " The Guiding Star," while the
frieze on the top of the die has in raised letters
the words, " Then gently scan your brother
man, still gentler sister woman." The cost
of the statue was in the neighbourhood of two
thousand pounds. After the unveiling cere-

monies the company adjourned to the Golden
Lion Hotel, where tea was served and where
Principal R. S. Rait in response to the toast,
" The Immortal Memory of Robert Burns,"
delivered a glowing and memorable oration
on the Poet and his writings.

STIRLINGSHIRE.   Robert Burns in Stirlingshire.

By William Harvey.   Editor " The Harp
of   Stirlingshire,"   etc.   Stirling,   Eneas
Mackay, 1899.

Deals with the places he visited, the
persons with whom he associated, and the
songs and poems of local interest. The
correspondence between Burns and Dr. John
Moore is given in full.   Has frontispiece bust
of Burns in the National Wallace Monument.

ST. LOUIS, MO., U.S.A., STATUE.

Unveiled 2nd June, 1928, by Miss Betty
MacIvor, daughter of the Rev. John MacIvor,
pastor of the Second Presbyterian Church.
The statue which is of heroic size occupies a
prominent position on the Campus of the
Washington University and represents the
Poet as he appeared a century and a half ago.
He is standing with a long sickle and a cloak
under one arm.   Behind him is a sheaf of
rye.   The monument is intended to be emble-
matic of the Bard's close association with the
people.   The statue was erected under the
auspices of the Burns Club of St. Louis.

W. K. Bixby was chairman of the statue committee. Members of the executive committee were George S. Johns, John Hill, Robert Johnston, James D. Grant, and Craig M'Quaid, treasurer. David L. Gray was chairman of the finance committee. Robert Guthrie was assistant treasurer. The erection of the monument was supervised by J. P. Jamieson. George S. John was chairman at the unveiling ceremony. After an invocation by Rev. D. M. Skilling, pastor of the Webster Groves Presbyterian Church, the monument was accepted on behalf of Washington University by George R. Throop, acting chancellor. A tribute to the Poet was given by W. R. MacKenzie, professor of English at the University. The address was given by Rev. Mr. MacIvor. Burns was an opponent of the "holier than thou spirit that still prevails," he declared. His poetry is an inspiration to all those who are fighting for liberty, politically, economically or socially. The poetry of Burns was responsible for the realization that exclusive ecclesiasticism must give away to religion with life in it. Burns's songs are songs that will ring down through all time, he said. He wore the garb of Scotland, but he was the Singer of the World. Democracy's debt to Burns should never be forgotten. He was the Bard of the Beating Heart.

STOOL, BURNS'S.

Alexander Smellie, the Edinburgh printer, used to relate the following anecdote : " There was a particular stool in the office which Burns uniformly occupied while correcting his proof-sheets ; as he would not sit on any other, it always bore the name of Burns's Stool. In 1844 it was still in the office, and in the same situation where it was when Burns sat on it. At this time Sir John Dalrymple was printing in Mr. Smellie's office an ' Essay on the Properties of Coal Tar.' One day it happened that Sir John occupied the stool when Burns came into the correcting-room looking for his favourite seat. It was known that what Burns wanted was the stool; but before saying anything to Sir John on the subject, Burns was requested to walk into the composing-room. The opportunity was taken in his absence to request of Sir John to indulge the bard with his favourite seat, but without mentioning his name. Sir John said : ' I will not give up my seat to yon impudent staring fellow.' Upon which it was replied : ' Do you know that that staring fellow, as you call him, is Burns, the poet ? ' Sir John instantly left the stool, exclaiming : ' Good gracious ! Give him all the seats in your house ! ' Burns was then called in, took possession of his stool, and commenced the reading of his proofs."

SWORD CANE STORY, THE.

Inquiry is sometimes made by readers as to the real facts in connection with the amusing story originally circulated by John Syme. So we turn to Robert Chambers and quote his version of the circumstances: "Syme possessed vivid talents, which Dr. Currie regarded with such respect, that he pressed him to undertake the editing of the poet's life and writings. That he was also a man of probity and honour, a long respectable life fully testifies. Yet it is also true that Mr. Syme, like many other men of lively temperament, could not boast of an historical accuracy of narration. He most undoubtedly was carried away by his imagination in his statement regarding the composition of Bruce's Address to his troops. So also he appears to have been in a story, of which several versions have been given to the public. It relates to a conversation on some particulars of Burns's personal conduct, which took place in one of their social evenings at Ryedale. 'I might have spoken daggers,' says Mr. Syme, ' but I did not mean them.' Burns shook to the inmost fibre of his frame, and drew his sword-cane when I exclaimed: ' What! Wilt thou thus, and in mine own house? The poor fellow was so stung with remorse that he dashed himself down on the floor.' This anecdote having been unluckily communicated to the public in an article of the " Quarterly Review " by Sir Walter Scott, an undue importance has come to be attached to it.   When the matter was rigidly investigated, nothing more could be substantiated than that Syme and Burns had one evening become foolishly serious in the midst of their merry-making and that some allusion by the one to the sins or irregularities of the other, led to a piece of mock-heroic very suitable to the occasion.   Burns touching the head of his sword-cane, as implying that his honour might be avenged for any indignity, and Syme making a corresponding tragic start, with the words : " What ! in mine own house ? " It was very natural for Mr Syme to retain but an obscure recollection of the incident ; but he cannot be acquitted of culpable incautiousness in allowing it to come before the world with a shade of seriousness attached to what never was more than a piece of rodomontade.

SYDNEY, N.S.W., AUSTRALIA, STATUE.

Unveiled 30th January, 1905, by His Excellency, Admiral Sir Harry Rawson, K.C.B., Governor of New South Wales.   The oration was delivered by the Hon. G. H. Reid, M.H.R., Prime Minister of the Commonwealth of Australia.   The statue is of bronze. the sculptor being Mr. F. W. Pomeroy, of London.   On the front of the granite pedestal is the inscription, " Robert Burns, 1759-1796."

T

TAIT, ALEXANDER ("SAUNDERS") RHYMES.
See under "Burns's Passionate Pilgrim."

TAM O' SHANTER.   A Tale.

Captain Grose, in the introduction to his "Antiquities of Scotland," says, "To my *ingenious* friend, Mr. Robert Burns, I have been seriously obligated; he was not only at the pains of making out what was most worthy of notice in Ayrshire, the country honoured by his birth, but he also wrote, expressly for this work, the pretty tale annexed to Alloway Church." In a letter to Captain Grose, Burns gives the legend which formed the groundwork of the poem :—" On a market day in the town of Ayr, a farmer from Carrick, and consequently whose way lay by the very gate of Alloway kirkyard, in order to cross the river Doon at the old bridge, which is about two or three hundred yards farther on than the said gate, had been detained by his business, till by the time he reached Alloway it was the wizard hour, between night and morning.   Though he was terrified with a blaze streaming from the kirk, yet it is a well-known fact that to turn back on these occasions is running by far the greatest risk of mischief,—he prudently advanced on his road.   When he had reached

the gate of the kirkyard, he was surprised
and entertained, through the ribs and arches
of an old Gothic window, which still faces the
highway, to see a dance of white witches
merrily footing it round their old sooty
blackguard master, who was keeping them all
alive with the power of his bagpipe. The
farmer, stopping his horse to observe them a
little, could plainly descry the faces of many
old women of his acquaintance and neighbourhood. How the gentleman was dressed
tradition does not say, but that the ladies
were all in smocks ; and one of them happen-
ing unluckily to have a smock which was
considerably too short to answer all the purpose of that piece of dress, our farmer was so
tickled that he involuntarily burst out, with a
loud laugh, ' Weel luppen, Maggie wi' the
short sark ! ' and, recollecting himself, instantly spurred his horse to the top of his
speed. I need not mention the universally-
known fact that no diabolical power can
pursue you beyond the middle of a running
stream. Lucky it was for the poor farmer
that the river Doon was so near, for notwithstanding the speed of his horse, which was a
good one, against he reached the middle
of the arch of the bridge, and consequently
the middle of the stream, the pursuing, venge-
ful hags, were so close at his heels that one of
them actually sprang to seize him ; but it
was too late, nothing was on her side of the

stream but the horse's tail, which immediately gave way at her infernal grip, as if
blasted by a stroke of lightning ; but the
farmer was beyond her reach. However,
the unsightly, tailless condition of the vigorous
steed was, to the last hour of the noble
creature's life, an awful warning to the Carrick farmers not to stay too late in Ayr markets."

Douglas Graham of Shanter Farm was the
hero of the poem, and John Davidson, a shoe-
maker of Kirkoswald is said to have been his
companion during the evening, before he took
the memorable ride.

According to Mrs. Burns the poem was
composed in one day. She informed Cromek
" that the poet had lingered longer by the
river side than his wont, and that, taking the
children with her, she went out to join him,
but perceiving that her presence was an
interruption to him, she lingered behind him ;
her attention was attracted by his wild
gesticulations and ungovernable mirth, while
he was reciting the passages of the poem as
they arose in his mind."

Burns speaks of " Tam o' Shanter," as
his first attempt at a tale in verse—unfortunately it was also his last. He himself regarded
it as his masterpiece of all his poems, and
posterity has not, says Principal Shairp,
reversed the judgment. Lockhart wrote :
" In the inimitable tale of Tam o' Shanter,

Y

Burns has left us sufficient evidence of his abilities to combine the ludicrous with the awful and even the horrible. No poet, with exception of Shakespeare, ever possessed the power of exciting the most varied and discordant emotions with such rapid transitions. His humorous description of death in the poem on Dr. Hornbook, borders on the terrific ; and the witches' dance in the Kirk of Alloway is at once ludicrous and horrible."

TAM O' SHANTER FARM, THE.

This now famous homestead, which was possessed for many years by the immortal " Tam "—Douglas Graham—is situated about fourteen miles from Ayr on the Carrick shore and nearly three miles from Kirkoswald, where the hero is buried.

TAM O' SHANTER INN, THE.   High Street, Ayr.

If you are visiting the Auld Toon, "You will know it from its ancient appearance," says the " Official Guide to Ayr," as it is the same building which was there in Burns's time, and which he has immortalised in the poem of " Tam o' Shanter." You will the more readily know it from its thatched roof and the large picture over the door, representing Tam o' Shanter setting forth on the eventful ride, of which all the civilised world has heard. He is on the back of his grey mare " Meg," as his drouthy cronie—

Souter Johnny—and the landlady are seeing him off, while the landlord stands at the door, lantern in hand, with a semi-intelligent look on his face. Within the howff are a few relics of Burns's time, but the great bulk of what used to be there has been removed to the Cottage at Alloway."

Sale of Tam o' Shanter Inn.—The Tam o' Shanter Inn, situated in High Street, Ayr, and known all over the word as the rendezvous of Tam o' Shanter and Souter Johnny, his ancient trusty, drouthy cronie, was exposed for sale by public roup in the King's Arms Hotel, on November 2nd, 1892. The property belonged to the Weavers' Incorporation, but on that body becoming extinct it fell to the Crown. Application was made by the Town Council to the Crown asking it as a gift. This application, however, was refused, and the Crown authorities determined to sell it. There was a large attendance, and bidding was brisk, the upset price—£2,500—being surpassed to the extent of £610. The property fell to the bid of Councillor Fraser, Ayr, at £3,190.

In connection with this sale the " Glasgow Herald " said :—

" Did not the good teetotal folk of Ayr miss a great chance in connection with the sale of Tam o' Shanter Inn ? This inn is well-known to those who visit the famous town for the purpose of seeing and making themselves acquainted with everything connected with the name and fame of Burns, whether real or mythical. It has been supposed that this inn was the howff in which the two cronies Douglas Graham and John Davidson, whom the poet took as models for Tam o' Shanter and Souter Johnny, were in the habit of meeting on market days and ' bousing at the nappy.' Burns is also believed to have had many a delectable sederunt in the same place. Whether these things are true or the reverse, they form the basis of a tradition suitable enough for an inn, where the special attractions are a chair in which Burns used to sit, and a quaich from which he used to drink.

Pious visitors to the house have the privilege of sitting in the hallowed chair for nothing, and drinking from the sacred cup on payment for the tipple, which is generally whisky. Many a fool has sat in the chair and been none the wiser ; and many a wise man has drained the cup until he became a fool—all to the glory of Burns, who probably never saw either chair or quaich. On the Weavers' Incorporation, to which the property belonged, becoming extinct, it fell to the Crown, who, declining to give it as a gift to the Town Council, determined to sell it to the highest bidder. This is so like the Crown, which has no respect for Scottish rights or sympathy with Scottish wrongs. But what was the chance missed by the Ayr teetotallers ? Why, the chance of purchasing the Tam o' Shanter Inn, and converting it into a temperance hotel, where the chair could be let at so much a ' sit ' and the quaich sent round at so much a ' sip,' the tipple being, of course, of the temperance order."

TANTALLAN.

A fortress in East Lothian.

TARBOLTON.

A small unpretentious village in the time of Burns, situated about a mile from the farm of Lochlea (q.v.) to which place the Burns family had removed in 1775. From that date until 1784 the village figures very largely in the life and writings of the Poet, and it is difficult to write about Tarbolton without directly associating it with the farm at Lochlea.

Weaving was still carried on to a small extent, but farming was the principal occupation of the surrounding district. In many respects Tarbolton at that date had remained in an almost primitive state and the villagers did not have a physician or even a druggist to call upon in an hour of need.

It was while returning home one evening from a Masonic meeting held in the village, that the Poet conceived the idea of his famous poem " Death and Doctor Hornbook " (q.v.), and it was here that he and his brother Gilbert formed the Bachelors' Club (q.v.). Tarbolton Mill (" Willie's Mill " q.v.) owned by the Poet's friend, William Muir, was in the neighbourhood, and it was with the miller's wife and at the mill that Jean Armour took refuge when she was denied the shelter of her parents' house. But the Tarbolton of to-day is a very different place to the Tarbolton of the past. Now it can boast of churches and schools, post office and rail-

way stations, in addition to a number of well
kept inns and hotels.

TARBOLTON MILL.   See Willie's Mill.

**TASSIE, JAMES.   Miniature Medallion of Burns.
See under Portraits of Burns.**

**TAYLOR, PORTRAIT OF BURNS, THE.   See
under Portraits of Burns.**

TEA TABLE MISCELLANY.

The first of our collections of songs is the
Tea Table Miscellany of Allan Ramsay, the
first volume of which appeared in 1724.
Scottish music had become fashionable about
that time, and Allan Ramsay, the bookseller,
considered a collection of the songs of his
country would answer as a publishing speculation, while his own talents as a poet and
those of his friends, would assist him in making
a respectable-sized volume. The work has
been a perfect mine to all future collectors
and editors of song, and its extent may be
learned from the fact that it gives us upwards
of twenty presumably old songs, upwards of a
dozen old songs altered, and about one hundred by Allan himself, Crawford, Hamilton,
and others ; we also have a great number of
names of old airs to which the new songs were
directed to be sung, and a host of the popular
English songs of the day. As an editor,

Ramsay has been much blamed by antiquaries for preferring to give his own songs rather than the old versions on which he based some of his pieces, but surely these gentlemen do not reflect sufficiently on the character of a great majority of these old songs. When Ramsay set about collecting, he had a task before him at once delicate and dangerous. He required to prune the old songs of indelicacies before submitting to the taste of

> " Ilka lovely British lass,
>   Frae ladies Charlotte, Ann, and Jean,
>   Down to ilk bonnie singing lass,
>   Wha dances barefoot on the green."

He dared not present any thing which would be flouted as immoral at the rigidly righteous tea-meetings which then abounded, and as a poet he exerted his skill in covering over these blemishes, in providing new verses to fill up obvious gaps, and to furnish totally new songs in place of old ones at once worthless and wicked. A trenchant editor, certainly, for the antiquary ; but no lover of poetry can regret the cause which drew so many fine songs from the best Scotch poets of the time. Hamilton, Crawford, and Ramsay himself gave not a bad exchange, for songs in all likelihood trashy and licentious, and we have sufficient confidence in Ramsay's judgment to believe, that no piece at all worthy of preservation which came under his notice in its entirety was not duly preserved.—Peter Ross, LL.D., in " The Songs of Scotland," chronologically arranged.

TERRAUGHTIE HOUSE.

In Kirkcudbrightshire, in the neighbourhood of Dumfries. The estate was repurchased by John Maxwell, whose family had at one time possessed it, and Burns, who was well acquainted with the new owner, welcomed him home on his birthday, in an epistle beginning, " Health to the Maxwell's Vet'ran Chief ! "

THAMES EMBANKMENT STATUE.

Unveiled by Lord Rosebery, 26th July, 1884. Sir John Steele, R.S.A., Sculptor. The Statue was the gift of Mr John Gordon Crawford, a native of Glasgow. On the front of the pedestal and underneath the name Robert Burns, and the figures 1759-1796, is a quotation from the preface to the first Edinburgh edition of the poems. The Statue is of bronze and is practically a replica of those in Dundee and New York.

THOM, JAMES.

The sculptor of the " Tam o' Shanter," and " Souter Johnnie" statues stationed in the Statue House on the grounds of the Burns Monument at Alloway. He was born at Skeoch, in the parish of Tarbolton, 17th

April, 1802, but the family shortly afterwards removed to Meadowbank in the parish of Stair, and here he attended the village school for a comparatively short period. At an early age he was apprenticed as a mason to the firm of Howie & Brown, builders, Kilmarnock. From the first he evinced a decided taste for carving in stone, and this having attracted the attention of Mr David Auld, of Ayr, he commissioned Thom to undertake work on a statue of "Tam o' Shanter" and later, on a companion piece, that of "Souter Johnnie." On completion of the work Mr. Auld was so elated with the statues that he took the two pieces on an exhibition tour, making extended stops with them at Glasgow, Edinburgh, London and other large cities, and it is said that he realised the sum of thirty-five hundred pounds from this source, before he returned with the group to Ayr. About 1832 the statues were taken by Mr. Auld into the grounds of the Monument and the present house was built for them. Here they have remained ever since, and here under the care of the Monument Trustees they are likely to remain indefinitely.

About 1836 Thom sailed for America in pursuit of an agent who had absconded with some of his funds, and having been successful in recovering a large portion of the same, he settled for a time at Newark, New Jersey, continuing to work with more or less success at his profession. At a later period we find he purchased a farm near Ramapo, also in New Jersey, and here he lived in comfortable circumstances for some years. He died in New York City, 17th April, 1850.

In alluding to the statues the writer in the guide to the Burns Monument says :—

> " Thom's counterfeits of the two drouthy cronies of Burns's masterpiece form one of the chief attractions pertaining to the Monument. They are formed from blocks of rough-grained sandstone, which lends itself admirably to the delineation of such rustic ideals. No such realistic contributions of Scottish life and character had been produced before, nor have been produced since. To any one who enters the Statue House, the figures present themselves as startingly lifelike, and no matter how often one encounters them, they always present the same aspect of unexpectedness. . . . . . The statues are Thom's masterpiece, and though he executed a number of replicas of them, and many other groups and figures came from his chisel, he never surpassed, if indeed, he ever equalled, his prentice effort."

THOMSON, GEORGE.

A select collection of original Scottish Airs for the voice with introductory and concluding symphonies for the pianoforte, violin, and violoncello. Six vols. 1793-1841.

Thomson's " Select Melodies of Scotland," as it is called, has been characterised as ' a sort of drawing-room edition ' of the ' Scots Musical Museum.' Its publication was begun in 1793 by Mr George Thomson, Clerk to the

Board of Trustees, Edinburgh. Mr Thomson's idea was to give the favourite airs accompanied where possible by the words. When from their character, these were unfitted for the perusal of ladies he proposed to print original verses. He also gave symphonies and accompaniments to the airs by the best composers of his time, as Haydn, Beethoven, and Pleyel; and greatest of all, he secured for the literary portion the services of Robert Burns, who entered into the spirit of the work with the greatest enthusiasm and enriched it with a great number of original songs (about one hundred and twenty), many of them being the best that came from his pen, and given to Thomson without fee or reward. Sir Walter Scott, Sir Alexander Boswell, Johanna Bailie, Thomas Campbell, and many others contributed to the work, and as it also contained a selection of the best of the old songs, with the music carefully given, the work was altogether a noble undertaking, well planned and carried out.—Peter Ross, LL.D.

A further reference to George Thomson and his work will be found in " Who's Who In Burns."

TIMARU, NEW ZEALAND, STATUE.

Unveiled May 22, 1913, by Miss Craigie, daughter of the donor. The oration was delivered by Sir Robert Stout, and excellent addresses were also made by Mr W. B.

M'Ewan, past-President of the Dunedin Burns Club, Mr James Craigie and Mr David Stuart. The pedestal on which the statue stands contains the words " Robert Burns, Born 1759, Died 1796," and underneath this :—

> " The largest soul of all the British lands."— Carlyle. " The rank is but the guinea's stamp, the man's the gowd for a' that."

Timaru is a seaport of Geraldine County, New Zealand. The population in 1927 was 15,635. The unveiling of the statue will always remain a red letter day in the annals of far-off Timaru.

TO A MOUNTAIN DAISY, On turning one down with the plough in April, 1786.

" The ' Mountain Daisy ' was composed at the plough. The field where he crushed the ' Wee, modest, crimson-tippéd flower ' lies next to that in which he turned up the nest of the mouse, and both are on the farm of Moss-giel, and still shown to anxious inquirers by the neighbouring peasantry."—Chambers.

TODDY KETTLE.

Presented to the Dumfries Burns Club in 1923 by Colonel Walter Scott of New York City. Accompanying the gift was the following explanation as to how the kettle had travelled to America.

" The story of this article was told in our public press throughout the country in the year 1915, when an estate was to be disposed of here in New York. Friends furnished me with newspaper clippings regarding the sale, which I attended, purchasing the kettle. It has been viewed by thousands since it came into my possession, not to speak of the many more who previously had the opportunity. The history is engraved on the outside, and since the acceptance of the relic by the Dumfries Burns Club I have added the closing line. The freshly engraved portion is, of course, much brighter than the preceding lines, but it will become as dark as the rest of the engraving in a short time. It is as follows —

" ' ROBERT BURNS' TODDY KETTLE.

" ' Most prized of the Burns Relics. Copper kettle used by Burns at his home in Dumfries. After his death it became the property of the Globe Tavern. Sold to John Allan of New York ; then owned by J. V. L. Pruyn of Albany, who presented it to his daughter. At sale of her effects (about 1875,) it was purchased by Mr George P. Philes, who held and treasured it until his death. Bought at Public Sale of the Philes Collection in February 1915.

" ' By Walter Scott of New York.
Past Royal Chief of the Order of Scottish Clans, and presented by him to Dumfries Burns Club, January 25, 1923.'

" I am very happy in the thought that this kettle will henceforth be the property of the Dumfries Burns Club. In a way I am sorry to part with it, because it has occupied a conspicuous place in my office ever since its purchase, always creating an atmosphere of tenderness in the hearts of those who have seen it, and serving as a con·stant reminder to me of the author of the ' World's

Doxology.' However, I believe it should go back
to Dumfries—the last earthly home of our beloved
Poet—and find a final resting-place among other
articles used by him.

—Walter Scott."

TO MARY IN HEAVEN.

Composed on the anniversary of the death
of Mary Campbell. When Jean Armour's
father had ordered her to relinquish all claims
on the poet, his thoughts naturally turned to
Mary Campbell. It was arranged that Mary
should give up her place with the view of
making preparations for their union ; but
before she went home they met in a
sequestered spot on the banks of the Ayr.
Standing on either side of a purling brook
(see under Fail), and holding a Bible between
them, they exchanged vows of eternal
fidelity. Mary presented him with her
Bible, the poet giving his own in exchange.
This Bible has been preserved, and on a blank
leaf in the poet's handwriting, is inscribed,
" And ye shall not swear by My name falsely;
I am the Lord " (Lev. xix. 12). On the
second volume, " Thou shalt not forswear
thyself, but shalt perform unto the Lord thine
oath " (Matt. v. 33). And on another blank
leaf his name and mark as a Royal Arch
Mason. The lovers never met again, Mary
Campbell having died suddenly at Greenock.
On the third anniversary of her death Mrs.
Burns noticed that the poet, towards evening,

grew sad about something, went to the barn-yard, where he strode restlessly up and down for some time, although repeatedly asked to come in. Immediately on entering the house he sat down and wrote " To Mary in Heaven " which Lockhart characterises " as the noblest of all his ballads."

See also Campbell, Mary, in " Who's Who In Burns."

TORONTO, CANADA, STATUE.

Unveiled 21st July, 1902, by Mrs David Walker, wife of the president of the Burns Monument Committee. The oration was delivered by the Rev. Professor Clark. The statue is of bronze, a replica of the one at Leith, by D. W. Stevenson, R.S.A., and stands in a prominent position in Allan Gardens. The base contains in large letters the name " Burns," while on each side of the pedestal are bronze panels containing scenes from " Tam o' Shanter," " John Anderson, My Jo, John," " The Cottar's Saturday Night " and the poet upturning the daisy.

TOURS.

Border or Southern Tour, 5th May to 9th June, 1787. Accompanied by Robert Ainslie. Visited Duns, Kelso, Jedburgh, Berwick, Dunbar, etc.

Short Tour in the Western Highlands. No definite particulars.

Highland Tour, 5th August to 16th September, 1787. Accompanied by William Nicol. Visited Crieff, Linlithgow, Falkirk, Dunfermline, Stirling, Dunkeld, Inverness, etc.

Short Tour in the Highlands, during October, 1787. Accompanied by Dr J. M'K. Adair. Visited Stirling, Ochtertyre, Harviestoun, etc.

TRANSLATIONS. By William Jacks, LL.D.

Robert Burns in Other Tongues, being a critical account of translations in foreign languages, with the foreign texts. Glasgow, MacLehose, 1896.

The author has taken the same songs and poems throughout, in order to offer a means of comparing the powers of different languages in expressing the sense of the works.

Examples are given of one or more of the poems and songs in German, Danish, Swedish, Bohemian, Hungarian, Russian, French, Italian, Gaelic, Latin, and Welsh.

TOUN.

A hamlet, a farm, and sometimes even a farm-house, in olden times was called a toun. Burns makes frequent use of the term in his writings. The word originally meant something fenced in.

TUNES, attached to Burns's Songs, THE. See under Dick, James C.

TWA DOGS, THE. A Tale.

Gilbert Burns says—" The tale of 'The Twa Dogs' was composed after the resolution of publishing was nearly taken. Robert had a dog, which he called Luath, that was a great favourite. The dog had been killed by the wanton cruelty of some person, the night before my father's death. Robert said to me that he should like to confer such immortality as he could bestow on his old friend Luath, and that he had a great mind to introduce something into the book under the title of ' Stanzas to the Memory of a Quadruped Friend ; ' but this plan was given up for the poem as it now stands. Cæsar was merely the creature of the poet's imagination, created for the purpose of holding chat with his favourite Luath." The factor who stood for his portrait here was the same of whom he writes to Dr. Moore, in 1787 :—" My indignation yet boils at the scoundrel factor's insolent threatening letters, which used to set us all in tears."

TWA HERDS, THE, or the HOLY TUILZIE, meaning the two Shepherds or the holy brawl.

" The Twa Herds " were the Rev. John Russell, assistant minister of Kilmarnock,

Z

and afterwards minister at Stirling, and the
Rev. Alexander Moodie, parish minister of
Riccarton, two zealous " Auld Licht " men,
members of the clerical party to whom Burns
was opposed on all occasions. " They had
quarrelled," says Allan Cunningham, " over
some question of parish boundaries ; and in
the presbytery, where the question had come
up for settlement, they fell foul of each other
after the manner of the wicked and ungodly."
Mr Lockhart says : " There, in the open court,
to which the announcement of the discussion
had drawn a multitude of the country-people,
and Burns among the rest, the reverend
divines, hitherto sworn friends and associates,
lost all command of temper, and abused each
other *coram populo*, with a fiery virulence
of personal invective such as has long been
banished from all popular assemblies wherein
the laws of courtesy are enforced by those
of a certain unwritten code." Burns seized the
opportunity, and in " The Twa Herds " gave
his version of the affair. For some reason
he did not include this poem in any of the
editions of his works published during his life
time.

V

VANCOUVER, B.C., BURNS FELLOWSHIP AND MONUMENT.

The Fellowship was organised in 1924, federated the same year and is number 325 on the Federation Roll. The membership is now (1929) nearly three hundred. The Fellowship was organised, " To encourage amongst its members the study of the life and works of Robert Burns; and to encourage the study of the poems of Burns in the Public Schools by offering prizes for essays on the subject, also to inaugurate a movement amongst the Scottish Societies and the public generally, with a view to erecting a statue of Burns in Stanley Park." This latter object was successfully accomplished in a comparatively short time, and in the presence of twelve thousand people gathered to witness the ceremonies, the statue was unveiled and presented to the city on the 25th August, 1928. The Hon. Ramsay MacDonald at the time delivered an oration on the life and genius of Burns, which was said to be one of the finest orations ever delivered on a similar occasion.

The statue is a replica of the one in Ayr, by Mr. George Lawson, F.R.S.A. The pedestal is of native granite. Accompanying the pedestal are large panels, three of them depicting scenes from the poet's writings, while the fourth contains the inscription " Robert Burns, 1759-1796."

A profusely illustrated little volume entitled "Vancouver's Tribute to Burns," and containing a history of the Fellowship, the principal addresses at both the unveiling and the banquet, photographs of the Officers, etc., was issued by the Federation shortly after the great event had become a part of the history of Vancouver.

VISION, THE.

This beautiful poem depicts, in the highest strain of poetical eloquence, a struggle which was constantly going on in the poet's mind between the meanness and poverty of his position and his higher aspirations and hopes of independence, which he found it impossible ever to realise. It must have been evident to his mind that poetry alone was not to elevate him above the reach of worldly cares; yet in his poem, as in many others, he accepts the poetical calling as its own sweet and sufficient reward. In the appearance of the Muse of Coila, the matter is settled after a fashion as beautiful as poetical. In the Kilmarnock edition of his poems, the allusion to his Jean in his description of the Muse's appearance—

> " Down flow'd her robe, a tartan sheen,
> Till half a leg was scrimply seen,
> And such a leg ! my bonny Jean,
>   Could only peer it ;
> Sae straught, sae taper, tight, and clean,
>   Nane else cam near it—"

was replaced by the name of another charmer, in consequence, it is presumed, of his quarrel with her father. When the Edinburgh edition appeared, his old affections had again asserted their sway, and her name was restored.— Gunnion.

VOLUNTEERS, DUMFRIES.

In the spring of 1795, a volunteer corps was raised in Dumfries, to defend the country, while the regular army was engaged abroad, in war with France. Burns offered himself, and was received into the corps. If he could not handle his musket deftly, he could do what none else in that or any other corps could, he could sing a patriotic stave which thrilled the hearts not only of his comrades, but every Briton from Land's-End to Johnie Groat's. This song (" Does haughty Gaul ") flew throughout the land, hit the taste of the country people everywhere, and is said to have done much to change the feelings of those who were disaffected.

A little book deserving of much praise on the subject of the Volunteers, was published by Mr. William Will, in 1919. The title page reads—" Robert Burns as a Volunteer. Some fresh facts which further help to confound the poet's critics."

Mr. Will was for many years President of the London Robert Burns Club.

WABSTER'S GRACE, THE,

> " Some say we're thieves, and e'en sae are we !
> Some say we lie, and e'en sae do we !
> Gude forgie us, and I hope sae will He !
> Up and to your looms, lads."

This is quoted by Burns at the end of a letter addressed to Miss Margaret Chalmers, November, 18 1787.

WALKER, ENGRAVING OF BURNS, THE. See under "Portraits of Burns."

WESTMINSTER ABBEY.

Bust of the poet, unveiled by Lord Rosebery, 7th March, 1885. Sculptor, Sir John Steele, R.S.A. The Westminster Abbey Guide contains the following reference to the Memorial.

> " This Memorial, erected eighty-nine years after his death, the work of a Scottish artist, and paid for in shilling subscriptions, contributed by all classes from the highest to the lowest, attests the Ayrshire poet's hold over the hearts of his countrymen."

WHISTLE CONTEST, THE.

Burns says, " As the authentic prose history of the ' Whistle ' is curious, I shall here

give it :—In the train of Anne of Denmark,
when she came to Scotland with our James
the Sixth, there came over also a Danish
gentleman of gigantic stature and great
prowess, and a matchless champion of Bacchus.
He had a little ebony whistle, which at the
commencement of the orgies he laid on the
table, and whoever was the last able to blow
it, everybody else being disabled by the
potency of the bottle, was to carry off the
whistle as a trophy of victory. The Dane
produced credentials of his victories, without
a single defeat at the courts of Copenhagen,
Stockholm, Moscow, Warsaw, and several of
the petty courts in Germany ; and challenged
the Scots Bacchanalians to the alternative
of trying his prowess, or else of acknowledging
their inferiority. After many overthrows
on the part of the Scots, the Dane was en-
countered by Sir Robert Lawrie of Maxwelton,
ancestor of the present worthy baronet of
that name, who, after three days' and three
nights' hard contest, left the Scandinavian
under the table,—

" And blew on the whistle his requiem shrill."

Sir Walter, son of Sir Robert before mentioned,
afterwards lost the whistle to Walter Riddel
of Glenriddel, who had married a sister of Sir
Walter's.—On Friday, the 16th of October,
1789, at Friars' Carse, the whistle was once
more contended for, as related in the ballad,

by the present Sir Robert Lawrie of Maxwelton ; Robert Riddel, Esq., of Glenriddel, lineal descendant and representative of Walter Riddel, who won the whistle, and in whose family it had continued ; and Alexander Ferguson, Esq., of Craigdarroch, likewise descended from the great Sir Robert, which last gentleman carried off the hard-won honours of the field."

A good deal of doubt was at one time felt as to whether Burns was present at the contest for the whistle—Professor Wilson having contended that he was not present, citing as evidence a letter to Captain Riddel, which will be found in the General Correspondence. These doubts have long been set at rest. Captain Riddel, in replying to the letter mentioned, invited the poet to be present. He answered as follows :—

" The king's poor blackguard slave am I,
    And scarce dow spare a minute
But I'll be with you by and by,
    Or else the devil's in it ! "—B.

Mr Chambers places the matter still further beyond doubt by quoting the testimony of William Hunter, then a servant at Friars' Carse, who was living in 1851, and who distinctly remembered that Burns was there, and, what was better still, that Burns was remarkably temperate during the whole evening, and took no part in the debauch.

See also, " Riddell, Captain Robert," in " Who's Who In Burns."

WHITEFOORD ARMS, THE, MAUCHLINE.

This well-known inn was situated on the Cowgate (now Castle Street) opposite the Parish Church, and almost adjoining the home of the Armour family.   In Burns's time, the landlord was John Dove, familiarly known to his patrons as " Johnny Doo," or Dow, while to those still more intimate with him, he was jokingly alluded to as " Johnnie Pigeon."   It was for many years a howff or rendezvous of the "Wits" of the town and was the meeting place of the members of " The Court of Equity," and one or two other similar associations. The old house was demolished many years ago and a new one was erected on its site.   On the front wall of the present edifice are the lines :—

> " This is the house, though built anew
> Where Burns cam' weary frae the plough
> To hae a crack wi' Johnnie Doo
>   On nights at e'eu
>   And whiles to taste the Mountain Dew
>   Wi' bonnie Jean."

WILLIE BREW'D A PECK O' MAUT.

" The air is Allan Masterton's, the song is mine. The occasion of it was this— Mr. William Nicol of the High School, Edinburgh, being at Moffat during the autumn vacation, honest Allan—who was at that time on a visit to Dalswinton—and I went to pay Nicol a visit. We had such a joyous meeting that Masterton and I agreed, each in our own way, that we should celebrate the business," —Burns.

WILLIE'S MILL.

This old mill, which has become famous the world over through the poet's reference to it in " Death and Doctor Hornbook," stood at the end of Tarbolton Village on the road to Mossgiel, and a short distance from the Masonic Lodge of which the poet was a member. It was owned by William Muir, an early friend and neighbour of the family. It was with Mrs. Muir that Jean Armour took refuge when she was expelled from her father's house. At that time the Mill was known as Tarbolton Mill. Muir's name appears among subscribers for the Edinburgh edition of the poems ; doubtless he already possessed the Kilmarnock one.

WINTER ; A DIRGE.

" As I am what the men of the world, if they knew such a man, would call a whimsical mortal, I have various sources of pleasure and enjoyment which are in a manner peculiar to myself, or some here and there such out-of-the-way person. Such is the peculiar pleasure I take in the season of Winter more than the rest of the year. This, I believe, may be partly owing to my misfortunes giving my mind a melancholy cast ; but there is something even in the

' Mighty tempest, and the heavy waste,
  Abrupt, and deep, stretch'd o'er the buried earth'.

which raises the mind to a serious sublimity favourable to everything great and noble. There is scarcely any earthly object gives me more—I do not know if I should call it pleasure—but something which exalts me— something which enraptures me—than to walk in the sheltered side of a wood, or high plantation, in a cloudy winter-day, and hear the stormy wind howling among the trees and raving over the plain. It is my best season for devotion ; my mind is wrapt up in a kind of enthusiasm to Him, Who, in the pompous language of the Hebrew bard, ' walks on the wings of the wind."—Burns, Common Place Book, April, 1784.

WOODLEY PARK.

The residence of Mr. and Mrs. Walter Riddell. So named by Walter Riddell in honour of his wife's family name—Woodley. In ancient times the place had been called the Holm of Dalscairth, and previous to its becoming the property of the Riddells, was known as Goldielea. It is beautifully located, about four miles south-west from Dumfries. It was here that Burns one evening after dining with the family, and while under the influence of the wine with which he had been liberally supplied, unfortunately so far forgot himself as to seriously offend his hostess by an act of discourtesy towards her. This caused an estrangement between him and the family which lasted for many years.

A well-written and sympathetic article on the poet and his writings, from the pen of Mrs. Riddell, appeared shortly after his death and still holds its place with the public, as one of the finest of the early tributes paid to the memory of the poet.

WYOMING, U.S.A., STATUE AT CHEYENNE.

Unveiled by Mrs. Mary Gilchrist, December, 1929, in the presence of the Governor of Wyoming and a large, enthusiastic gathering of people from all parts of the State, assembled in Gilchrist Park to witness the ceremonies. The statue was cast in Paris from a model supplied by the late Mr. H. S. Gamley, R.S.A., Edinburgh, and stands on a granite pedestal twelve feet high. The donor was Mrs. Mary Gilchrist, a native of Glasgow, and long prominent as one of the pioneers of the Rocky Mountain State.

Y

YE BANKS AND BRAES O' BONNIE DOON. See under " Banks o' Doon, The."

Z

ZELUCO.

A novel by Dr. John Moore. 2 vols. London, 1789.

The Poet's own copy of this book was presented by him " To my much esteemed friend Mrs. Dunlop of Dunlop."

" I desired Mr. Cadell to write to Mr. Creech to send you a copy of Zeluco. This performance has had great success here, but I shall be glad to have your opinion of it, because I value your opinion and because I know you are above saying what you do not think." Dr. Moore to Burns, 10th June, 1789.

" I have been busy with Zeluco . . . . . Zeluco is a most sterling performance."— Burns to Mrs Dunlop, 6th September, 1789.

INDEX

2 A

A SELECTED LIST OF BOOKS PRINCIPALLY RELATING TO

SCOTLAND

ENEAS MACKAY .·. **CRAIGS, STIRLING**

BY MOUNTAIN, MOOR AND LOCH : TO THE DREAM ISLES OF THE WEST. By Thomas Nicol. With Introduction by Professor A. D. Peacock. Fifty illustrations. 7/6 net. (post, 6d.)

SMILES AND SIGHS IN SUBURBIA. By Jeffrey Gunion. A delightful book of whimsical humour. 2/6 net. (post, 3d.)

THE WOLFE OF BADENOCH. By Sir Thomas Dick Lauder. New Edition. 7/6 net. (post, 6d.) A stirring romance of Scotland in the Fourteenth Century. With Foreword by R. B. Cunninghame Graham.

HUMAN VOICES. A collection of verse by G. R. Malloch. A notable addition to our Scottish verse. 2/6 net. (post, 2d.)

THE GRENADIER. A play in one act. By George Reston Malloch. 2/6 net. (post, 2d).

STIRLING : TWENTY-ONE DRAWINGS. By G. Elmslie Owen. Notes by David B. Morris. 3/6 net. (post, 4d.) Charming Woodcut effects.

SCOTTISH DIARIES AND MEMOIRS 1550-1746. Edited by J. G. Fyfe, M.A., with an Introduction by Principal R. S. Rait, C.B.E., LL.D., Historiographer Royal for Scotland. Fully Illustrated. 5/- net. (post, 6d.)

THE ELUSIVE GAEL. By Dugald Coghill, with Introduction by the Duke of Sutherland. Cr. 8vo. 5/- net. (post, 4d.) Timely in its censure of many current misconceptions.

A HIGHLAND CHAPBOOK. By Isabel Cameron, the author of " The Doctor." Stories of Highland Superstition and Folklore. Cr. 8vo. 3/6 net. (post, 4d.)

SMUGGLING IN THE HIGHLANDS. An account of Highland Whisky Smuggling Stories and Detections. By Ian MacDonald, I.S.O. With Illustrations of Smuggling Bothies, Distilling Utensils, etc. Post 8vo. 3/- net. (post, 4d.)

BURNS IN STIRLINGSHIRE. By William Harvey. Demy 8vo., boards, 1/6 net ; cloth, 2/6 net. (post, 4d.)

WHO'S WHO IN BURNS. By J. D. Ross, LL.D. Containing over 600 references and cross references, and specially designed map. 7/6 net. (post, 6d.)

A LITTLE BOOK OF BURNS LORE. By J. D. Ross, LL.D. With a Preface by James D. Law, author of " Dreams o' Hame." Crown 8vo. 3/6 net. (post, 4d.)

ROBERT BURNS.—An appreciation by Lord Rosebery. Crown 4to. Fully Illustrated. 1/- net. (post, 3d.)

ROBERT BURNS AND HIS RHYMING FRIENDS. By J. D. Ross. With Notes by Geo. F. Black. Demy 8vo. 3/6 net. (post, 6d.)

HENLEY AND BURNS OR THE CRITIC CEN-SURED. Edited by John D. Ross, LL.D. Crown 8vo. 1/6 net. (post, 3d.)

THE POEMS OF CLARINDA. With a Biographical sketch of the Heroine. By John D. Ross, LL.D. Demy 8vo. 2/6 net. (post, 3d.)

STRANGE TALES OF THE WESTERN ISLES. By Halbert J. Boyd. 7/6 net. (post, 6d). Nine weird and exciting tales.

FEUDS OF THE CLANS. By the Rev. Alexander MacGregor, M.A. Together with the History of the Feuds and Conflicts among the Clans in the Northern parts of Scotland and in the Western Isles. Crown 8vo. 3/6 net. (post, 4d.)

PLACE NAMES OF THE HIGHLANDS AND ISLANDS OF SCOTLAND. By Alexander Mac-Bain, M.A., LL.D. With Notes and Foreword by William Watson, M.A., LL.D. Demy 8vo. 21/- (post, 6d.)

THE LEGEND OF LANGUORETH AND VARIOUS VERSES. By George Eyre-Todd. 3/6 net. (post, 3d.)

CULLODEN MOOR, AND THE STORY OF THE BATTLE. With Description of the Stone Circles and Cairns at Clava. By the late Peter Anderson, of Inverness. Post 8vo. 5/- net. (post, 4d.)

THE MASSACRE OF GLENCOE. By G. Gilfillan Campbell and Professor Blackie. Demy 8vo. 2/- net. (post, 3d.)

HIGHLAND SUPERSTITIONS. By Alexander MacGregor, F.S.A. New Edition, with Introductory Chapter upon Superstitions, and their Origin by Isabel Cameron. Demy 8vo. Gilt top. 3/6 net. (post, 3d.)

CELTIC MYTHOLOGY AND RELIGION. By Alexander MacBain. With Chapter upon Druid Circles and Celtic Burial, with Introductory Chapter and Notes by Professor W. J. Watson. Demy 8vo. 7/6 net. (post, 6d.)

A GAELIC-SCOTS VOCABULARY. By R. L. Cassie. Cr. 8vo. 3/6 net. (post, 3d.)

GAELIC PROVERBS AND PROVERBIAL SAYINGS, WITH ENGLISH TRANSLATIONS. By T. MacDonald. Crown 8vo. 5/- net. (post, 6d.)

SCOTLAND: PICTURESQUE AND TRADITIONAL By George Eyre-Todd. Fifty-seven illustrations from photographs. Fourth edition. 5/- net. (post, 6d). The author of this book is an eminent authority on Scottish History and has a fine gift of description.

SONGS OF THE GAEL (Gaelic and English). A collection in Sol-fa and Staff Notations. Paper edition, 1/-.

THE ROMANCE OF POACHING IN THE HIGHLANDS OF SCOTLAND. As illustrated in the Lives of John Farquharson and Alexander Davidson, the last of the Free Foresters. By W. M'Combie Smith. Crown 8vo. 3/6 net. (post, 4d.)

ANTIQUARIAN NOTES : A SERIES OF PAPERS REGARDING FAMILIES AND PLACES IN THE HIGHLANDS. By Charles Fraser-Mac-Kintosh of Drummond, F.S.A., Scot. 2nd Edition with the Life of the Author by Kenneth MacDonald. 21/- net. (post, 2d.)

THE PROPHECIES OF BRAHAN SEER. By Alexander Mackenzie, F.S.A. Scot. With Introductory Chapter by Andrew Lang. Demy 8vo. 3/6 net. (post, 4d.)

THE MISTY ISLE OF SKYE : ITS SCENERY, ITS PEOPLE, ITS STORY. By J. A. MacCulloch. New and Revised Edition. With Introduction by MacLeod of MacLeod, C.M.G. Crown 8vo., 336 pp., 24 Halftone Plates, and specially designed Map. 5/- net. (post, 6d.)

THE PRIORY OF INCHMAHOME : THE PLAY-GROUND OF MARY QUEEN OF SCOTS. By A. A. Fitz-Allan. Fully Illustrated. 1/6 net.

THE LITERATURE OF THE HIGHLANDERS. By Nigel MacNeill. New Edition. Edited and revised by J. MacMaster Campbell. A history of the literature of the Scots-Gaelic race from the earliest times down to the present day. The most complete account yet published. 7/6 net. (post, 6d.)

ROBERT LOUIS STEVENSON AND THE SCOTTISH HIGHLANDERS. By David B. Morris. Interesting stories connected with the Jacobite Families of the Highland borders. Cr. 8vo., 5/- net. (post. 6d.)

44 CRAIGS, STIRLING

FOLLOW THE RAINBOW HAME. By Thomas Wylie. A collection of Verse. 2/6 net. (post, 3d.)

STIRLING CASTLE : ITS PLACE IN SCOTTISH HISTORY. By Eric Stair-Kerr. Introduction by The Earl of Mar and Kellie, and a Chapter on the Recent Excavations by J. S. Richardson. Fully Illustrated. 3/6 net. (post, 6d.)

THE CALLING OF BRIDE. By Isobel Hutchison. Decorations by Helen Rolland. Cr. 8vo. 3/6 net, (post, 3d.)

THE ROMANTIC STORY OF HIGHLAND GARB AND THE TARTAN. By J. G. MacKay. With an Appendix by Lieut.-Colonel Norman MacLeod, C.M.G., D.S.O., dealing with the Kilt in the Great War. Illustrated in Colour and Black and White. 42/- net. (post, 9d.).

THE HISTORY OF THE 7th BATTALION QUEEN'S OWN CAMERON HIGHLANDERS. By Colonel J. W. Sandilands and Lieut.-Colonel Norman Macleod. With War Diary and Illustrations. 4/6 net. (post, 4d)

PIPING FOR BOYS. By J. Perry Sturrock. To enable young men and boys to teach themselves to play the bagpipes. Cloth, 3/6 net; boards, 2/6 net. (post, 4d.)

THE LAKE OF MENTEITH, Its Islands and Vicinity, with Historical Accounts of the Priory of Inchmahome and Earldom of Menteith. By A. H. Hutchison. Fully Illustrated. 15/- net. (post, 9d).

THE LIFE OF FLORA MACDONALD. By Alexander MacGregor, M.A., with which is included *FLORA MACDONALD IN UIST.* By William Jolly, F.R.S.E., F.G.S. 3/6 net. (post, 4d).